LW46

9

The Snake & The Tiger

Memoirs of an Adventurous and Travel Filled Life

Ana Lydia Armstrong

authorHOUSE®

AuthorHouse™ UK Ltd.
500 Avebury Boulevard
Central Milton Keynes, MK9 2BE
www.authorhouse.co.uk
Phone: 08001974150

First published by AuthorHouse 10/6/2009

ISBN: 978-1-4490-3115-2 (sc)

This book is printed on acid-free paper.

To all the important men in my life:
My Dad without whom I would not be here
My husband with whom I have shared so much love and laughter
My two grandsons Anthony and Adrian for their love and
mischievousness that keeps me from 'getting old'
And especially to my daughter Lyana for her love and friendship.

My heartfelt thanks go to my brother-in-law editor Jon Searle for his expert advice and editing of this book. Thanks also to my husband who has helped me so much and was the first to read my manuscript, to my daughter Lyana, who has with Adrian worked so hard every time I lost my manuscript in the computer, and to Al for his help and comments.

Last, but not least, to my young friend George Bottino for 'pushing' me into writing this book.

Contents

Part Four
Tropicana 1961 - 1967

Part Five
Land Of The Incas 1967 - 1970

Part Six
New Horizons 1970 - 1980

Chapter 1

ROOTS – AN INTRODUCTION

The Gallego Family

The Gallego Ibanez family, hailed from Southern Spain. Ramón Gallego Pérez from Vélez Málaga and Pilar Ibáñez Dona-Gálvez from Nerja. An illustrious family they had regrettably lost all their fortune and by the late 1800's were living in a very poor condition.

They had two sons. The eldest was Rafael, an engineer already in his late twenties and Emilio, only ten years of age who although very bright had been unable to attend school due to the scarce family resources. Upon hearing that in the frontier town of La Linea de La Concepcion, Cadiz Province, the authorities were allocating plots of land at token prices to families willing to work and settle down there, they packed up and came to try and solve their problems and start a new life

The family found themselves the proud owners of a magnificent plot of land and immediately built a wooden house consisting of two bedrooms, and big kitchen. They planted vines and many fruit trees, tilled the soil and grew vegetables and flowers. As the eldest son Rafael found work across the border in Gibraltar they were able to live in vastly improved conditions and were soon able to invest in chickens and other small farm animals.

Rafael, seeing his parent's improved finances, eventually decided to return to Velez Malaga where he had left his sweetheart. They married and emigrated from Spain to Buenos Aires, Argentina where he was offered a good position with the Railways. His brother the teenager Emilio found a job with a prominent Gibraltarian family settled in Tangiers, Morocco as a help to the other servants.

This Gibraltarian family had a beautiful school aged daughter called Clemencia, she loved studying and when she found that Emilio did not know how to read or write was keen to teach him. She taught him the alphabet and how the letters sounded. She made him copy the letters as he read them out. An ambitious, bright young boy, he was soon able to read and write and often share the text books available to his young friend. Emilio worked hard and became a trustworthy employee who was promoted to assistant manager of the estate.

The estate was beautifully kept. The mansion was adorned with works of art. There were beautiful gardens with mosaic patios, fountains and waterfalls. Emilio loved the splendour of his surroundings and made notes of all he saw and loved.

The Luz Family

The Luz family were Gibraltarian born descendants of Austrian, German, Portuguese and Spanish settlers. It was said that an Austrian priest named Von Keppel assigned to Spain and falling in love with the beautiful Spanish lady hung up his cassock and became a married man. Eventually their family came to live in Gibraltar as it had become a British Garrison. One of these descendants, Carlota Luz Von Kepple, married Rafael Nuza, a much older man, a building contractor, who had settled down in Gibraltar where he gained a very good reputation and was most successful.

They had two children Rafael and Elena who were brought up with loving care and given a good education. The family were very good friends of the family living in Tangiers and they often visited as Elena was Clemencia's friend. It was inevitable. Elena met and fell madly in love with Emilio who was not welcomed into the family due to his lower, social position. In 1886 the parents finally agreed to let their daughter marry. It was not considered correct for Elena to settle in Tangiers and so after the wedding the young couple set up home in La Linea with Emilio getting work in the Gibraltar Dockyard and augmenting his finances by helping his parents with their vegetable business. They had three children but all died very young until finally Clemencia named after Elena's friend, was born in 1910 and Carlota two years later.

When the children were aged three and one their Spanish grandparents passed away and the land, business and house was left for the two sons Rafael and Emilio. When Rafael was told of his inheritance he left it all to his younger brother. This was because of his good financial position, owning his house in Buenos Aires, Argentina and with two grown up daughters one of whom was already married to an Argentinean. They had no intentions of returning to their native Spain to live.

Emilio was now the sole owner of his parents' estate and he started to build his own brick and mortar house with his wife Elena. Young Clemencia, then only three years of age, 'helped' her parents by carrying water and earth. Once the house was completed he decorated all the façade with pieces of broken china and named the place Villa Mosaico. The family moved to their house and eventually they started a restaurant business and bowling green. The restaurant was called La Media Luna (The Half Moon).

Both the business and the two young daughters were well known in the town of La Linea as the girls from the Half Moon. Clemencia was a beautiful brunette who took after her good looking father, and Carlota was a gorgeous blonde with green eyes just like her mother. Unfortunately Elena and Emilio were often at loggerheads because they were too different and tempers often flared.

The Danino Family

The Danino family originated in Genoa, Italy. They were merchants who called at Gibraltar looking for business. Eventually when Gibraltar became a British garrison they came to settle permanently here where they bought properties, as well as in neighbouring Spain. The family were in the meat business, so had a farm where they kept cattle for slaughtering and which they brought into Gibraltar.

As was the custom they intermarried with other Italian families. One of their descendants, Abelardo, married Magdalena Achinelli in 1871, a family also from Genoa. They had several children. Son James broke away from tradition and in 1900 married Ana Baro from Farajan near Ronda in Spain. One of their sons, Manuel, eventually became a bullfighter and in Peru where he was known as 'Barito, el Leon de Gibraltar, he married his manager's daughter. He never returned to his home. Then there was James, Abelardo and Domingo, who from a tender age helped on the grandparents' farm looking after their livestock as well as maintaining and driving the Gharries (horse drawn carriages) they owned both in Gibraltar and La Linea. Other children were Alfredo, who was a scholar, Maria who remained at home and the youngest Julio who was only 18 years old when he was killed fighting in the Spanish Civil War.

Domingo was a handsome young man. He loved sports. He played football as well as boxing but his favourite pastime was amateur bullfighting. By 1926 he was self employed and a well established business man and at 21 years of age met the lovely brunette Clemencia who was 17 and fell madly in love. They married within a year and a year later their first child Ana Lydia was born. That was in 1929. At this time Elena and Emilio, Clemencia's parents, were going through a crisis that they were not able to overcome and separation became inevitable. Elena and her other daughter Carlota came to Gibraltar from where they departed for the United Kingdom.

Clemencia and Domingo, popularly known as Dani, came to live in the southern part of Gibraltar where most of the military people lived. They chose the Scud Hill district very close to the huge barracks. Dani's meat business was usually situated under their home or very near by. The young couple was delighted to hear that a child was on the way and as it was the custom and aspiration of most young men they dearly hoped that their first child would be a boy who would carry the family name and continue with the meat business.

Part One

The Early Years 1929 -1949

Chapter 2

BIRTH

On the 12th May 1929, I, their first child, a daughter was born. In spite of the first disappointment Dani completely adored this child. For two and half years I grew up with all their love and attention and then an addition to the family, another little girl came home.

Dani, my Dad, was the most gorgeous person I was ever to meet. He was tall and with kind beautiful eyes that always wrinkled at the corners. His smile was open and frank and if he enjoyed any of the mischievous pranks played on him he would blush and close his eyes as he cried out laughing. It was a happy home and I loved my dad.

Mummy was beautiful, just like a film star; she loved dressing up and wearing flowers whenever she could. A year and half later a third child, another girl was born, and later there was one more girl. Each time Daddy expected a boy yet each time he fell for all his little girls, but by then I made a discovery which I did not like very much. I was the eldest and therefore had to set an example to my sisters and behave. I hated this situation even at this tender age; on the other hand I had become closer than ever to my dad who spent much time with me. In particular he taught me to make little piles of money like those he made as an example and like this I was kept amused and he was able to add up his day's takings much quicker. "Chamaca," he would say "if only you had been born a boy I would have been the richest man in the world" (I was to be dad's Chamaca, his little girl, for ever more.)

At this time I also learned that if I wanted to have an enjoyable time dancing around mum's room where the mirrors surrounded practically her whole bedroom and where I could see myself as I danced and sang to the Holy picture of the Good Shepherd , when I heard her approach I had to hide away out of her sight.

Mama Carlota Imossi (having been widowed young she had remarried) lived close by with her husband Papa Rosendo. Mama Carlota was my mother's granny. She was small, closer to my height than any one else in the house. She wore long skirts usually in sombre colours and black tops. She made up for the lack of colour by wearing bright house coats while doing the housework. She had a lovely round face that was always smiling and she fascinated me by the way she only had lots of teeth when she went out but not while at home. She had very thick hair which she piled up on the top of her head and held in place with huge ornamental hair clips.

Papa Rosendo was very tall and elegant with lots of white hair and a huge moustache which he curled at the end. He was always dressed as if going to a party and he loved to look at his gold watch and heavy gold chain which hung from his waistcoat to a trouser pocket.

Papa Rosendo loved telling us stories so almost every day he would visit home with Mama Carlota, had tea with us and then when we were put to bed he would sit by the side of our beds and proceed with his made up stories. Papa had one fault, so I heard Mum say. He would not stop telling a story even if we had all fallen asleep and no one was listening. When admonished he replied "I have to proceed to the end as otherwise how will I know the end of the story?"

I loved spending time with Mama Carlota. She always made me feel very grown up in a nice kind of way. If she knew I was going to visit her she would leave a few things so that I could wash them up. Every time this happened she would put one of her pinafores on me which covered me down to my toes, place me on top of a chair and then prepare the washing up basin. I remember so well how she would put the warm water in an earthenware basin and with what appeared to be dry grass rub a piece of blue and white soap until the water gained lots of bubbles and there was a fine lather. She would then place the cups and saucers or whatever other things she had dirty, roll up my sleeves and allow me to wash up. I loved it and made the job last as long as I could.

As soon as the kitchen was tidied up we would go to the cosy sitting room from where we would look out of the window waiting for one of the street vendors to come selling their speciality. They would come crying out their wares. "Cositas buenas, cositas buenas" And my goodness, they were good things, delicious things to eat, sometimes there were all sorts of dried fruit, peanuts, dried cooked chick peas, almonds, walnuts and hazelnuts. Mama would call the vendor and then throw a little shopping basket to which she had attached a long rope and the man would put the goodies in the basket which she would pull up. What a feast! Because she had no teeth, (far fewer than me), she would put all these goodies inside a mortar and with a pestle she would grind all the nuts together. After which she would share with me on a small piece of paper or in a saucer with spoon but I preferred the paper which I would lick clean to savour every morsel... Other times the vendor would call out "Calentita, Calentita, ay! que buena esta la calentita" and then she would call and ask him to wait as we would hasten down the steps to the front gate and then have the separate sections of this polenta-style Gibraltarian delicacy in pieces of paper. A visit to her was always extremely pleasurable.

Sometime the neighbours' daughters would ask my mother's permission to take me for a walk and since I was a very energetic child full of spirit I would never tire. Mummy saw their offer as a blessing and allowed them to take me up the Rock. I loved this walk and particularly when I could gather wild flowers which had a very sweet strong smell and which made mummy very happy.

I was born with practically no hair and mummy never forgot the embarrassment I caused her as she had sewn some curls of hair in a bonnet which covered my bald head and when people were admiring me I took it off. My second sister, Clementina was a beautiful child and when two and a half, she had lots of curly hair and a sweet face. Lottie, my third sister, was like a doll, round rosy face and more curls. My sister Lena was the baby. I made up by spirit and independence even at that age. I dared to do so many things that I was nicknamed 'rabo del diablo' (the devil's tail) and because of this I was even more daring.

We now lived at Carlton House, a lovely big place which looked just like a bullring. The house belonged to a Mr. Bertuchi who lived upstairs while we had the bottom section of the house. We entered through a tall doorway over two very wide stone steps into a broad corridor leading to what then seemed a tremendous patio. .It was full of flower pots and in two large bins a tall palm tree and a mature fruit- bearing tree something like loquats called 'nísperos'. Papa Rosendo loved birds and although dad would not allow any birds inside the house he did agree for dozens of bird cages to hang along the entrance corridor and all around the patio making way only for the water pump.

This house was more superior to the previous ones we had lived in, where there were only salt water faucets and all fresh water for washing and cleaning had to be bought from the Council and gathered from the water fountain at the top of Scud Hill. People would go with pails and pay in accordance with the quantity taken. Drinking water in demy-johns was brought in from Spain. We now had both running waters, fresh City Council water as well as the salt water which ran in the kitchen taps. The drinking water was pumped out from the water cistern under the house and placed in a huge earthenware container placed just by the front kitchen door. This huge pot like a barrel had a wooden cover and on top of it a mug with a big handle which was used to get the water out into glasses or any other receptacle. The water tasted very good and was always lovely and cool.

The toilet was outside by the patio but the room was long and spacious and we were often bathed in a huge zinc bath in there. We all loved this house and enjoyed the happy goings on. Just by the kitchen door there was another room, the laundry room and Adela was in charge of keeping all our clothes washed and ironed. Adela was a huge fat lady with lots of thick curly hair gathered up in a big bun on top of her head. She always carried plenty of pins inside her mouth and while she hung the washing on the clothes line placed nearby the water pump and under cover if raining or upstairs in another big patio called 'sotea' she would take out the pins and like this secure the clothing. Ironing was also fascinating, The thick heavy iron was placed on top of an open fire to make it hot so she would frequently spit on it to see how hot it had become, clean it with a piece of cloth and then proceed to iron. Adela worked at home every day of the week as she was responsible for all the clothing at home as well as the men's uniforms and aprons from the shop. To do the housework and kitchen there were two daily women who came from neighbouring La Linea. Mum was a perfectionist who could always do everything very well and when the servants fell short of her standard they would be asked to look elsewhere for work. It seemed that only Adela matched Mummy's standards.

During the warm summer months my Dad would have his men put up a tarpaulin to cover the patio and then a big table and chairs would be placed there so that we could enjoy open air eating in a cool place. We loved meal times which were always taken together en famille. News was shared every day and there was usually a lot of laughter. Summertime we enjoyed a lot of fruit particularly melon, water melon and cherries. Daddy would make earrings out of the cherries that were attached and we would clap and laugh particularly if he decided to wear a pair too.

I had a close playmate, the youngest daughter of my parents' friends Andre and Odilia. I was often allowed to go to her home to play. One day when I arrived to play I found Yolanda was going out with her big sister to a huge hall where there were many children to play with. I went with them and decided to stay with her and play. I had thus started going to kindergarten without my family being aware. My parents only found out when the Mother Superior in charge of St. Joseph's school sent them a letter. Dad thought it rather clever of me while my Mum was rather annoyed as she had planned for me to go to the Loreto Convent. I remained at St. Joseph's school until my sister Clementina was old enough to go to school and then both of us attended the Loreto Convent at its old site near the Governor's residence downtown.

Many times when Dad imported cattle for slaughtering any pregnant animal would be spared until after giving birth and each little animal, be it piglet, goat, or calf would be brought home. How we loved having them. One of my favourites was the tiniest of piglets... We insisted on grooming him and no sooner had we made him beautiful even to tying a ribbon round his tail, he would run into any mess he could find amongst the flower pots. The animals were well fed and loved by all the children with friends coming to enjoy them but unfortunately once they had grown to a reasonable size they mysteriously disappeared - probably on to someone's table. Never on ours as even the parents considered them as pets. It was a happy home.

When I was five and half my youngest sister Lena made her appearance and with her came dear Clara who was only fourteen years old to look after the two small sisters and play with us all. Clara was to become our most loved person and it was she who defended me from my mother's rage for I had a way of upsetting her all the time. Those outsiders who dared say I was the ugly duckling of the family were dealt with by Clara, as she thought me as beautiful as any of my sisters. She made me feel good from the day she arrived.

A couple of years before the Spanish Civil War, Mama Carlota was sick and we were all told that she had gone to heaven. Too young to understand the full meaning of this word we all thought that perhaps she was travelling like Granny Elena. Papa Rosendo then became very sad and after a while he too had gone to join Mama Carlota. At this time I was nearly seven and I missed having him around very much, often he used to get his cages and show us all the little birds inside. He had names for every one of them and took great care and pride in them. The birds seemed to know when he was around as they would chirp and sing and Papa would start whistling to them. We often used to go to Rosia Parade where we would pick some yellow flowers with which he loved to feed the birds. Now with him gone the patio was silent as dad never being fond of the birds had given them all away.

It was around this time too that one day I discovered I had two granddads. In our family relatives appeared not all at one time, but sprang out when least expected. We had got accustomed to granny Elena's comings and goings, different uncles visiting and bringing presents, so we never questioned and accepted everyone happily. One day while out with Clara she became very nervous on seeing some working men coming down the street, "Quickly, quickly, come here let's hide" she said. Surprised, I asked her why. "It's your Granddad from Spain. Oh my God, don't tell your mother I have told you so!" Being like I am I had to know and although too scared to say anything more when I went home I asked my Dad. Looking at me and holding my hand Dad said "Chamaca, he is your mother's father from Spain and since he and Granny Elena are not together and Granny lives with us we have nothing to do with him, he now belongs to another family" At this age his reply was acceptable.

Grandad Danino was a lovely tall man. He looked like my Dad but of course older version. He came home with a lovely big black dog which we all loved. He wore striped black grey trousers and always a huge wide leather belt, his shirts were white and crisp and I don't remember him ever wearing coat or jacket. On his head he wore a tall wide brim Spanish hat. I loved him dearly and often went for walks with him and Blackie the dog.

The house upstairs was much bigger than ours. I often managed to go visiting upstairs as the owners were rarely there. The person who kept house was a young woman who had once been a nun. I heard comments from visitors and friends why she had left the convent. Apparently she had been brought up by the nuns as she was an orphan. Not knowing any other life she had taken the vows. Later she discovered she did not have sufficient vocation to be a nun so left the convent – but there was no one to confirm whether or not this was true. In 1936 when war started in Spain the whole flat upstairs was filled with refugees escaping from the neighbouring towns. We had been forbidden to go upstairs but as usual I was fascinated by all the comings and goings and the amount of people there. With the noise they made the moment I could I went to visit. I shall always remember the sad scenes I saw. The whole house which had been elegant and luxurious had been turned into a refugee camp; partitions with curtains divided the area so that many families could live in some kind of privacy. The people did not remain long as they either found better homes or left for other countries. I heard my parents commenting amongst themselves and close friends on the fate of these poor refugees. One family had run away from Spain when they heard that their eighteen year old son had been killed by Franco's Nationalists. Discovering his identity they had gone to look for the boy's family who feared that they also would be killed. Others who had not been involved in the fighting had to flee because some extended family member had joined the wrong political party. People were taken away and disappeared.

Chapter 3

ADOLESCENCE

Soon after this Mr. Bertuchi put the whole building up for sale and Dad bought it. The upstairs house was refitted and painted and beautiful furniture was brought from France. When we moved upstairs it was like a celebration. To enter there was a lovely front door with a   coloured glass section. By the front door there was another one which led to a little open office space and a huge walk in cupboard. The first flight of stairs which led to the shower room and toilet was fully carpeted as was the second flight leading to a lovely long corridor also carpeted. Mum had placed a sofa and two arm chairs with a coffee table at one end of the corridor by the window. . On the left side were two doors one leading to a small room where my baby sister and Clara slept, the other to a lovely big room, our parents bedroom. I was delighted to see that my parents had actually brought up their bedroom furniture and Holy picture of The Good Shepherd which always stood above the bed. There were many mirrors once again and I could still dance around the bed and make up songs to the Good Shepherd. The next door was opposite three long windows where Mum had put a table and chairs with flower pots. This door led to a huge sitting room with a fireplace. How we clapped and danced at all the beautiful things with which Mum had adorned this room. From the sitting room a panelled glass door opened into a smaller but again exciting room which was our dining room leading to the kitchen which could also be entered from the corridor.

This time there was no need for the earthenware water pot as the house had the city council water plus the collected rain water for all our use. There was no need to heat up water for dish washing as there was a boiler which gave all the hot water needed. Returning to the other end of the house and facing the South Barracks was a great big bedroom housing two double twin beds, a huge wall-to-wall wardrobe giving each of us a section, and a heavy big cupboard with four deep drawers one for each of us. By the middle here was a round table and chairs so that we could do our homework there AND sheer bliss, a lovely big bathroom, with basin as well as a bidet. It was magical!

Now we could see as well as hear the soldiers in the nearby barracks doing their drill and parading to the band music. Before when we were downstairs someone would eventually take us across the road and leave us sitting on a low wall inside the military area. We were fascinated with all the exercising and marching of the soldiers and often enough would copy them. Now with the magnificent view we had from home we did not often go across but if we saw a formation making its way down the hill we would run downstairs and wait for the parade to pass by as we walked down the hill on the footpath in time to the music. Sometimes their goat mascot would also accompany the soldiers and then we clapped and cheered them no end.

Auntie Lottie had returned to Gibraltar with Granny Elena to marry her Chinese Doctor, Chito Chan, I was too young to remember anything about this event. She then went away to British North Borneo and when she discovered she was having a baby some time around 1935 she returned on holiday and for Granny Elena to accompany her back. I remember going on board this lovely ship and thinking that one day I too would go away and travel like this. Granny Elena spent so much time away that up to then I hardly knew her. They did return a short time before World War II together with our little cousin Charlie who had an amah to look after him and it caused quite a stir in such a small town as ours. However when Aunty Lottie, Charlie and the amah returned to Borneo, Granny remained with us for the rest of her life.

There was never a dull moment. Dad was always telling us the importance of speaking English just like people did in the Mother Country and we went through a selection of nannies who were inevitably caught talking in Spanish and asked to leave. Eventually Miss Sylvia Mifsud came and then we were not able to get into disgrace with Dad through speaking in Spanish. Although Clementina and I were taken to school by either one of the parents we were often picked up by Miss Sylvia. She was a lovely, good looking person and we soon learned to love and respect her. Some days we had dancing classes with Miss Valarino while on others piano lessons with Miss Bossano. During these days we were picked up by either one of our parents and Miss Sylvia took my youngest sisters out to play at the Alameda gardens. On returning home she would supervise our homework, make us read in English and then go home. It was all very well organized and it was only after I became nine years of age that my sister and I were allowed to either take the bus or walk home. We loved this feeling of independence and often walked up by the Theatre Royal steps where there was a magnificent ice cream shop belonging to the Balloqui family. We loved treating ourselves to a big cone. It was quite a different story if the fleet was in. Main Street would come alive with bar music becoming louder and the women inside singing   even louder to attract the attention of the sailors passing by. There were quite a number of Military Police around but when drunk the sailors and soldiers would be argumentative and often pursued the local girls. We were too young ourselves to have any unpleasantness focused on us but our parents deemed the situation dangerous so we had to phone home to be picked up as many a time a drunken sailor would be literally thrown out of the bars into the street by the hefty bouncers.

I remember one Valentine Day a boy gave me a box of Turkish delight and because I did not like him that way (or even the idea of being a friend to him) I rudely threw the box down and trampled on the sweets. I have never been able to see Turkish delight without thinking of poor Domingo.

By the time I was ten and for a while before this, on Sundays after going to church with Dad, he would return home and I was made responsible for my sisters to keep them amused. We would go down to the Alameda Gardens where opposite the Assembly Rooms there was a kiosk that sold all sorts of goodies and we would spend all the pocket money, consisting of pennies Dad and Grandad Danino gave us. I was supposed to keep my sisters from eating everything but sometimes it was not possible and on arriving home I would get told off. I always thought it most unfair to be given so much responsibility when I was still so very young. Parents don't seem to realize that even an older sister can still be too young and inadequate if anything really bad happens. I heard about a younger brother who climbed a tree, fell and was killed. The elder sister was blamed by the mother for not taking enough care of him. The girl was traumatized for the rest of her life. On Sundays the nanny did not work, the maids were off and Clara would be busy with granny Elena or mummy cooking our Sunday lunch.

Food at home was always delicious. Normally there would be some stew made for the servants while mum insisted that whoever the new cook was, she had to make us delicacies we did not really enjoy as she was determined that we acquired a taste for what she considered 'refined' food. We preferred the thick soups and minestrone made for the servants instead of what was supposed to be the ideal food for us. Often enough we (spoilt as we were), would have a new menu cooked for us. Mum would object but granny Elena would say "Who knows what is in store for them, Clemencia, let them have what they want!" Life continued with its routine, which was never boring, and we were growing up happy.

Granny Elena was in charge of buying the food and going to the Market. When she allowed anyone of us to accompany her it was fun and extremely educational too. Those visits are strongly engraved in my mind. Granny loved fresh fish and although the fisherman came daily to our front door carrying a huge laden basket on top of his head she made a point of going to the fish market whenever she wanted something special. The fish were displayed by each individual fisherman on top of stone tables. When not busy the vendors would start singing out their wares. Granny would first go round the area looking at what was available and when interested she would go straight to the fish and examine its eyes, its firmness and colour. The smell was not very pleasant and the ground was always wet but there used to be a certain magic in all this.

The second stop would be the Moroccan stalls on the side of the market. It was rather gruesome to see granny sticking her finger up the poor chicken's behind to feel if there were any eggs. She would choose her bird and eggs and then depart to the vegetable and fruit section. The stall owners and their helpers were colourfully dressed, some with funny baggy trousers, others with their kaftans. Granny would not worry too much over the fruit and vegetable section as each morning the vendor from Spain would come right to our front door with his donkey and cart carrying a vast selection.

Usually on Saturdays or Sundays when there was any good football match or horse racing my parents loved to go. Clem and I were lucky enough to accompany them particularly to the races. Mummy always dressed up beautifully and made sure we, the children, were appropriately dressed. Our clothes were brought from Montgomery Ward Chicago catalogue and were very different from anything you could get in Gibraltar. Unfortunately although my sister Clem always looked like a doll with the fancy dresses with ruffles, bows, ribbons or little flower posies, I always felt terrible in them. I was tall, slim and had extremely straight hair which mummy insisted on trying to curl and which left the ends of my hair looking more like the piglets' little tails. I hated it but soon forgot my looks when we met other friends and enjoyed lovely teas and ices. If the weather was good and there were no races we would sometimes go to the same Victoria Gardens where the race course was and had picnics and gathered wild flowers with which to make necklaces.

Chapter 4

THE WAR YEARS

Suddenly things began to change. My parents whispered worriedly, they gathered around the radio to listen to the news. Granny cried, thinking of Auntie Lottie, and we were being constantly told off. One day dad came and told us that war had been declared and that we would have to leave our beautiful home. At first we could not believe this was possible but then my parents started to pack up things and they told us we were leaving for Morocco. The sea journey that normally took hours took us much longer and I remembered my mother being extremely sick all the way there. When we arrived the Red Cross people were there offering us comfort and refreshment. I remember being surprised at them, as I did not consider any of us as being in need; we had all left nice homes in Gibraltar only a few days earlier. After a few days in Tangiers, Dad who was helping with the evacuees took us over to Casablanca where we stayed in a flat owned by a Gibraltarian family and rented to Dad. It was here that I discovered that mum's illness had been due to her expecting another child.

It seemed we had just arrived in Casablanca when we were informed that we had twenty four hours to get our things together and leave. The French were no longer our allies and we had to leave the territory. We returned home to Gibraltar and were so delighted to be back with all our things around us but it was never the same for us. A few days after our return the sirens went off and I remember Mum crying and Granny, who found walking difficult, telling her to stop being silly and come down to the doorway downstairs. Suddenly we were all holding on to their skirts and crying ourselves as a bomb fell nearby our house and the whole house shook and window panes crashed. After this, Dad took us to live in the Continental Hotel downtown near an air raid shelter. As children we all thought this great fun having already forgotten the bomb experience. Naturally at this time there were no maids or Miss Mifsud who herself had been evacuated somewhere else. Only Clara remained with us.

Granny Elena was a lovely person. She had a great sense of humour and was all out for us to enjoy life to the full. She was a woman born ahead of her time, wise and kind who loved us all very much. Ever since she returned from North Borneo we got to know her very well and loved her dearly. She was a bit overweight and had been told at the age of forty-two she had to follow a very strict diet if she wanted to live to a ripe old age. Granny saw things differently, she wanted quality and not quantity of life and therefore pleased herself in every way. She was game for anything. During this time mature women usually dressed in dark colours and granny loved colourful things. Mum made her wear clothes in dark green, navy blue, black and brown. She compromised by wearing lovely scarves of many colours, big jewellery that suited her or flowers. Sometimes she would put flowers in her hair and with her walking stick up in the air and short of breath she would hum 'Over the Waves', waltz and dance. We clapped and laughed. She was so kind and helpful and our greatest chaperone (A duenna, who would supervise and control that you behaved correctly and did not disgrace the family.)

One day the doctor told her that sea bathing would be very good for her rheumatism so she asked Dad if she could buy a swimsuit to go swimming with us all. Dad was very sympathetic and quickly offered to buy her one. That lunch time when all the family gathered together at table Granny informed us all she had bought her swimsuit and next day would be able to start her swimming. "Dani", she said, "would you like to see my bathing suit?" Dad always thoughtful and kind said

"Yes, Dona Elena, please show us all." We had never expected granny to wear it but lo and behold there she was in all her glory with the most colourful swimsuit anyone could imagine. It had all the colours of the rainbow. We, the children, cheered and clapped while Mum and Dad stared in astonishment, speechless. Now, in time of war all those lovely moments were just happy memories.

Once again we were to pack up and go. People were being taken to many different places. Some, amazingly enough to England, others to Northern Ireland, and some remained in Morocco but in Tangiers which was then an International Zone, others went to Jamaica and Madeira, those that went privately. Once again Dad arranged for us all to go to the latter place, a paradise island in the Atlantic, which was to be our home for five beautiful years. There was to be one other ship going there after us with Gibraltarians.

On arrival at Funchal, in Madeira we went to a downtown hotel nearby the Golden Gate coffee house where all the Gibraltarians got together to discuss each day's happenings. Dad eventually looked for a Quinta up in the hills where he thought we would all have plenty of room to enjoy ourselves. Mum was by then quite pregnant. We all thought the Quinta was lovely. A huge rambling house with lots of fruit trees, plus the different kinds of banana trees and vegetables, we thought it great. However, after spending a sleepless night killing cockroaches Mum decided we would not stay and we returned to the hotel for a little longer until another house, this time one in the centre of town, was found. It was a huge house situated next to a river and quite close to the market where we often went with Granny. It was quite different from at home as all the flower sellers were dressed in their national costumes and everything was extremely exciting. Very close too was the Bazaar do Povo which for us children appeared to be the biggest shop ever seen.

Soon after we moved to this house I had a terrifying experience. I had gone to the toilet and on drying myself I found the paper covered in blood. Frightened, I got up, looked in the WC and to my horror and dismay I discovered that instead of urine I had passed blood. I started to cry and scream. Granny Elena came rushing in, for even with the walking stick it was usually Granny who first appeared when needed. Sweetly as she always used to be, she asked "Now Lydia why are you crying, we are all very busy". I showed her all the blood. Suddenly she was embracing me and kissing me.

Thinking that I was dying I cried even louder and by the time my parents came in, kissing me and all excited, I was in hysterics. I had absolutely no idea that as they put it later on 'I had become a young lady' and what had happened to me was a normal thing as you develop and grow up   My father, looking a little embarrassed said "Chamaca, if any boy comes near you, this is what you do." He lifted up his knee as if to knock me. I had no idea why I should do that. This episode made me promise to myself never, if I ever married, which I had no intention to do, would I let my children be ignorant and have them so frightened.

On the 5th of October 1940 our brother Winston Dominic was born. Dad, who was with Mummy at the time of his birth when told that a son, the well desired boy had been born, could not believe it. The doctor brought the baby out and showing his 'signature' proudly said "See, Mr. Danino, it IS a boy". Dad cried of happiness, his dream had come true. At the time I was eleven and a few months old so that baby named after dad's hero Winston Churchill became my very own beloved 'toy' to look after and love.

My parents, like all the other evacuees thought that the war would not last very long. Dad had us all to keep and feed without any money coming in. Soon he found that our finances were quickly dwindling and had to ask for a Government subsidy. It meant our leaving the downtown huge rambling house where Mummy loved to tell us frightening stories that kept us quietly in one section of the house, to go to an 'out of town' villa belonging to the Hotel Savoy.

The upstairs of the villa was already occupied by the Ramagge family, Dona Rosa, the matriarch and grandmother, her daughter-in-law Eliza and the children whom we already knew and were school friends with from the Loreto Convent in Gibraltar. Rosina the eldest was my age followed by Lally my sister Clem's age, then Natalia, Lottie's age, Pepe a little older than my young sister Lena and their 'baby' Maurice born just before war started.

We were allocated the ground floor area which consisted of a little sitting room as we entered the house on the left side, on the right a small room which was given to me and my Granny Elena. (This, however, did not last for long.) Mum had told me that I had to keep an eye on Granny Elena as she had a bad heart. Consequently whenever I woke up I would look to see if her breath was coming as her chest went up and down. One day when she neither made any breathing noise nor could I see any movement I got up from bed and I was very busy trying to listen when she woke up. Poor Granny, all she could see was a head over her body so she gave a huge scream. On hearing this I jumped up terrified. I almost caused her to have a heart attack so I was quickly shifted to my sister's room (while Clara took my place with Granny}. Next was my sister's room where Clara usually slept and next to it was my parents' room.   There was a huge bathroom, a dining room and veranda as well as a great big kitchen which soon became Clara's and Granny's domain.

The hotel provided us with food which was brought over by Ruffino a big smiling waiter who also loved to cook. Sometimes we would not eat the food and so Dad, who knew the owner quite well, made the arrangement to get everything raw and the cooking was done by the family members. There was also a man cleaner, Alvaro. Both of them slept upstairs above the Ramagge family. On the ground level there was a garden which belonged to us as well.

Dad soon found himself working with the Government, taking care of business regarding the evacuees and we led a normal exciting life on a beautiful island without a care in the world. We were too young to remember what it had been like. The British School for Gibraltar Children was opened to continue giving an education to the many children now living in Madeira. Some of the expatriate children who had been studying in England had returned to Funchal and they too joined us.

A beautiful big house with lovely surroundings situated up in the hills enjoying a fabulous view was rented and equipped. Buses were provided for transportation. The buses stopped a little way from the school and we often went to a small shop nearby to buy biscuits. There used to be a man always sitting by the window and eventually we struck up a friendship. He would correct my Portuguese and ask all sorts of questions. I discovered that he was paralysed and did not go out anywhere.

Funchal then was not a rich place, tourism had stopped and the Madeirense tried to make a living as best they could. One day I did not find my friend there but saw a lot of people going into the house. I did not hesitate and joined the crowd. To my dismay I discovered my poor friend lying on the bed dead, people wailing around him. He had committed suicide. It was then I truly realised what being dead and going to Heaven really meant. I could see my friend's body there but where was HE who talked to me? I left crying for him, my family and myself too. I knew I did not want to die, not then or ever. I left running and made my way home still sobbing, forgetting about school. On arrival there I did not want my family to see me so I ran up the stairs to the attic. The matriarch of the Ramagge family saw me and slowly climbed up the rather narrow stairs. "What are you doing there? Are you OK" "No, no, I don't want to die" "But you are young, you are not going to die so stop being silly and come downstairs with me." "No, I don't want to die ever." "That is funny" she said, "you see as you get old and all your loved ones start going and you get decrepit it really doesn't matter." I looked at her in amazement for she was so old that surely she would be dying any time now and SHE did not care.

Occasionally ships came and brought in survivors from wrecks. We all tried to make their stay on the island better by making them feel welcome. Every so often there would be an open air fete held at the Casino de Madeira for the Red Cross and practically everyone who could do anything participated. We (my sister Clementina and I), were often asked to dance at these events and at other charity affairs. My parents too participated by working behind the restaurant counter serving drinks and food. They like every person participating wore Spanish dress costumes to give it the true verbena ambiance.

Sometimes we would find Granny Elena crying and talking softly. If there was a moon, no matter how small, big or bright it was then she would carry on a full conversation telling Auntie Lottie all she had done during the day and other messages. Lottie had always been her favourite daughter. After Lottie had returned with her son Charles to British North Borneo we heard from her regularly even during the first part of the war. However her correspondence stopped suddenly and we were able to find out through the British Red Cross that she, her husband and son were prisoners of war of the Japanese. Granny felt that by talking to the moon she was keeping her alive and giving her strength, so she never failed to do so.

Although the children and the women seemed happy with life in Madeira the men were generally bored and some like Dad took up a hobby. Dad's hobby was more like hard work as he joined a German owned charcuterie factory where he worked without payment just so as to learn how to make the many delicacies they specialized in. (Portugal, being neutral, allowed German businesses to remain open). Life took on some normality although by now we had to give up our piano lessons with Miss Martinez another of the evacuees there and the dance lessons with Mrs Rosario Cruz. We did however continue with our French lessons with Mlle Isabelinha. Mlle was a very old fragile looking lady who loved knowing what we had done and eaten during the day. Dad was very particular about us learning this language that for some unknown reason he loved and thought very important. Mlle loved the high teas my granny prepared for her and always accepted happily any leftovers. Sometimes she would go to spend a penny and as she took so long we would go and look for her. She never closed the toilet door, she was so petite that her feet did not reach the ground and there she would be fast asleep! We loved her and always behaved with her.

Mummy loved being smartly dressed and performed miracles. She had Dad's suits turned inside out and remade either for her or for one of us. Her dresses were made small and she was for ever crocheting us something or knitting. She also would go to the drapers and buy cheaply their material sample catalogues which she would join together most artistically in patchwork and make us skirts, blouses and so on. By then Dad and Mummy had made friends and contacts and we were often invited by the Cine Parque owner for a film viewing or show. Every so often when there was a children's film we, and other school friends, would go sitting two to each seat. We had difficulties but we took it all in our stride since there was food, good weather, the Hotel's swimming pool and even tennis courts where I often played with Dad.

We enjoyed going to school and we sang in the bus, usually songs relating to our being there during the war. A gentleman, Mr. Cubi, wrote a song about us and we often sang this one in our outings. Boys and girls were in separate classes and books were shared out between us. Boys had the mathematic books while we had the French literature books and so on as we did not have enough for individual ownership. Unfortunately all my books borrowed by the boys were returned with 'La fille a la grande bouche' written across the front covers.

At school we were four inseparable friends Rosina, Muriel, Eileen and me. At break time we would either sing or dance. Muriel and her sister Eileen who occasionally joined us would sing, while I would be directing and dancing with the others. We were also quite naughty and loved to 'fence' in our class room whenever the teacher left the room. We had all been Loreto Convent girls and wore our uniforms but while fencing we would put our skirts inside our bloomers which were pulled down as far as we could and with pointer and ruler we would begin attacking and defending. One day I was caught with one of my friends and was made to stand at the front of the office where boys and girls could see us dressed in such ridiculous manner. If one of us did not know the lesson she would suddenly get 'sick'. Sent to the toilet chalk would be used to whiten the face – another friend would offer to accompany the 'sick' girl home. This worked fine until one day that

Dad returned home before being expected and concerned about my pale looks decided to give me some horrible medicine.

There was a 'leader' in the class room who was always inventing how we could make life difficult for some of the teachers. Whether we liked it or not we had to agree and participate or otherwise face the consequences outside school. Some days we were 'ordered' to wear head scarves and sunglasses for the reading class. Others to speak in a squeaky voice just like one of the teachers while other days this particular girl would bring stink bombs. This however backfired as the teacher had a bad cold, couldn't smell, but in order to 'help' us made us close the windows! I think she was a very wise teacher!

I knew I was supposed to be the ugly duckling of the family but I hated having the boys writing 'la fille a la grande bouche'. I became more aware of my big mouth and usually covered it with my hand and never dared laugh or smile when in a boy's company. At this time it was fashionable to be petite like Hedy Lamarr, Vivien Leigh and so forth. One day, when school had been a little harder than usual on me, when I returned home feeling very sorry for myself, I ran down to the swimming pool area verandah and started to cry. I didn't see a young Portuguese man approaching me. Seeing I was crying he stopped and inquired why my tears. "You know I have a big mouth but I did not choose to be like this. My mother and my father made me like this and everyone makes fun of me." He looked at me and said "But you are not ugly, you are a very beautiful girl, look at your wonderful eyes, why do you want to have lovely features if nothing comes from the inside? That kind of beauty will fade and go away, yours will grow more every day." I thought he was kind but very mad. I knew what I looked like; I looked at myself often enough every day before going out. The mirror showed me with my big mouth which always wanted to smile, aristocratic Roman nose, oval shape face which seemed too small for my mouth and YES, I did have lovely, warm, smiling eyes just like my dad, eyes that showed kindness and warmth. Fernando Rebello's words made me feel much better.

Since I could not be a beautiful woman (and by now Rita Hayworth had come on the scene) I could have a splendid body so I cut out all the information I could lay my hands on and tried each and every exercise. It was lovely when finally one day I heard a 'wolf' whistle and looking back I found a boy a couple of years older than me describing my body with his hands. I was overawed and delighted. But it wasn't until another friend, this time a girl, told me "Lydia as long as you show that they upset you the boys will not stop teasing you, so when a boy says something derogative about your mouth just turn round and say something positive" "Positive?" I asked "Yes, like, isn't it wonderful to be generous and not mean?" I took Nita's advice and by the age of sixteen no one remembered my mouth.

Dad was becoming frantic about our financial situation; he wanted to return to Gibraltar and was finding it practically impossible since sailing dates were erratic and ships usually full. At the end a local friend in the business was able to get him on board a cargo ship to Lisbon and from there he made his way home to Gibraltar with quite a lot of difficulty. I was devastated to see Dad go; he was my very dear friend and support. We shared so much and he did so much for me.

My birthdays were, I don't know why, very important to me and I always loved celebrating them. Dad always contrived to help me get my way. He had a son but he never stopped saying "If only you, Chamaca had been my first born son". Dad was not with me for my sixteenth birthday but somehow he got friends to give a party for me. Even as far away as Gibraltar he had not forgotten me.

Chapter 5

TEENS

The War finished and many of my friends returned home. Since my dad had been with us most of the time we were to remain there longer. The villa was empty and we were moved into the Hotel Savoy itself. The home life style was at an end as we had to take our meals in the hotel dining-room and eat whatever was given us. The school closed down and Funchal was practically empty. I had my sixteenth birthday in May and by July we had returned home. I had left Gibraltar for Funchal aged eleven and now I was a young woman of sixteen. It was wonderful to see Dad again, we ran towards him laughing and crying at the same time, embracing him never wanting to let him go. The house seemed so strange. People had stolen a lot of our things, the walls were shabby, and repairs were urgently needed but Dad, dear Daddy, had plenty of lovely food for us and had done his best to make everything comfortable. The government too was sending some of the Italian prisoners of war to paint and do all the repairs needed. Our house had been requisitioned during the war years. At first Grandad Danino had stayed in the house with our dog Blackie but then he too had to go to Spain as all non essential civilians were forced to leave Gibraltar.

Dad's sister, Auntie Mariquita, who had also been in Funchal where her little son Charles had been born at the same time as my brother had also returned and since she had no other home to go to Dad had given her the downstairs flat where we had lived before moving upstairs. Grandad Danino had also returned from Spain and slept in a downstairs room too so at last the family was reunited.

As I had not taken my School Leaving Certificate in Madeira I should have gone back to school. However, Dad asked me if I would help since fortunately he was very busy in the shop and needed someone to answer the phone, take orders, and see that no one went out of the shop without paying. Business was excellent, the shop would fill up to the door and people went mad on the food they bought, well, the locals did; the expatriates were quite content with the 'two slices of liver and quarter pound of bacon,' or such small portions. I could not get accustomed to my father's prompt attention to any of the expatriate Brits that entered the shop often leaving the locals who were spending much more money waiting. I complained about this and was told "But they are from the Mother Country!" Were the English from Great Britain all super people, I wondered?

When we first returned home all the friends used to meet together at one of the homes and we had 'parties' which meant having each girl take a dish with some food and the hostess providing the drinks which was usually a bottle of port wine and lemonade plus other soft drinks. Coca Cola had not yet arrived in Gibraltar. The gang comprised more or less equal numbers of boys and girls all locals and all just friends who liked to laugh, dance and enjoy playing charades or musical chairs, all great fun but very mild compared with today's teenager activities.

One day Dad came home and said he wanted me to meet a young man, a friend of the family. Apparently this boy's family had been very good to my Dad when he was a youngster. John Peter was a very lovely young man in his 20's. He had beautiful eyes and a caring manner. He was to become my very best friend with a very special place in my heart. It was with him that I could relate and talk about all my dreams and ambitions. Unlike most of my friends who all they seemed to want was to find themselves a boyfriend to get married I wanted to study, do things, and be someone in my own right. I used to have long talks with JP and he would listen and never laugh at my desires and life dreams. Dad, who saw how well we got along one day, asked me "Chamaca do you like JP?" "Yes Dad, he is a lovely man" "Are you going to marry him?" When I would say no he would very seriously demand "but if you like him and go out with him why don't you want to marry him?" This was a procedure that I was faced with every time I ventured out on a twosome with anyone else even if it was just when I was only being accompanied back home. It seemed poor Dad could not understand why if I liked someone I would not be considering making the relationship a serious one.

My life now changed. I was no longer a little girl but someone with some responsibilities. In the mornings I would be in the shop. In the afternoons I would attend private lessons with a lovely teacher downtown who was preparing me for my school leaving examinations. After lessons I would meet my friends at the Imperial Tea Rooms which was exactly opposite where I had my lessons. From there we would make plans for the following day. Sometimes we would go to the cinema. There was always quite a choice, the Rialto which usually showed Spanish films, the Theatre Royal, the Naval Trust Cinema and the Gymnasium Cinema in the South. For me, who loved dancing, there was the occasional tea dance at the Assembly Rooms. We had no television but we always seemed to be busy and able to have good fun. I also found a new Spanish dance teacher, el Maestro España, so as soon as I could I also started classes with him.

In July the La Línea fair took place and Dad took us all there. While my sister Clementina loved bullfighting (as did my parents) I hated it. I had been there before but shouted instructions to both the matador not to get too close and the bull to keep away and practically fainted when the picador put his lance into the bull's back. I could hear the crunching and feel the pain while he turned the lance into the animal's wound. It was too much. So, I chose to stay with my grandmother Elena and some friends in an ice cream shop at the fair grounds. Too busy eating ice cream which I adore, Granny pointed and said "That young man sitting near us cannot take his eyes off you." I turned to look and saw this nice looking man staring but he was definitely not my type since he was on the plump side and wearing a double breasted suit, very obviously someone from the 'Mother Country'. Later I found out that when he saw me at the ice cream shop he had said to his Company colleagues "See that girl? She is the one I am going to marry!" Although by this stage I had learned to like boys, my type was quite different. I liked boys tall, much taller than me, not too nice looking, rather like the rugged macho look AND they HAD to be good dancers! I completely ignored him and after finishing eating I set forth with Rosina to meet other friends and enjoy the fair's many activities.

Since Dad had been alone and most of the time spent in the business he had not bothered to have a telephone extension put into the house so we, my sisters and I, knowing that after business hours calls would be for one of us would run down to the shop which was situated on the ground floor of the building to answer it. This day it was my turn to do so and as I ran down jumping at each step hoping the phone would not stop ringing when a young man coming up the hill stopped, looking rather amazed and bewildered, and just stared at me. My first reaction was to laugh as I looked at his astonished face, then I wondered what could have been the cause of such behaviour. Opening the shop's door I answered the phone and forgot all that had happened before.

A few days later a lady employed as housekeeper for the Cable and Wireless Mess came to Dad's business and told him that there was a young man at her Mess who was in love with one of his daughters. Dad was intrigued since his eldest, myself, was only sixteen and my next sister Clementina was two and half years younger. He asked "Which daughter?" "The one who plays the piano and sings" Mrs Joyce replied. Dad was rather surprised as I only played the piano and danced, it was my sister who played the piano and sang. When he came home and we all sat at table for lunch Dad related the story and we all looked at Clementina and laughed. Granny wanted to know more and eventually she found out he was a Cable and Wireless man who had a similar ranking and uniform as a lieutenant in the army. Eventually she even discovered what he looked like and whenever she spotted him going or returning from work, which was nearby our home she would call my sister saying "Your captain is here!"

One day, in August as my sister and I were returning from the Montagu Sea Bathing Pavilion and were walking back home a young man who we recognized as 'Jack, the boy from Cable and Wireless' passed us by and said "Hello, may I walk with you?" Since it was improper to speak to boys to whom we had not been properly introduced we ignored him, so slowly and looking rather sad he passed us. "Clem," I said, "we know who he is and that he is a nice person, he looks so upset, why not answer him?" We hastened our steps and as we levelled up with him we both said "Hello". He then looked at me and said "Your name is Lydia?" "Yes," I said "but it is Clementina who you want!" He did not budge and instead of going to my sister's side he remained next to me. As we walked back home it was obvious that it was I he was interested in. Not my type, as he was very nice looking, slightly taller than me and rather plump and wearing the wrong kind of clothes, not like my local friends wore!

Jack did not give up. It appeared he was the 'young man' at the fair my Granny had told me about. He had thought me to be Spanish and had gone looking for me in neighbouring La Linea. No wonder he was so surprised to see me running down the hill. He lived right opposite our house too. One day a friend of mine who was supposed to be meeting me at the Theatre Royal had not turned up after fifteen minutes of the appointed time so even with the tickets, annoyed as I was, I started to walk back home. Jack was coming towards me so on the spur of the moment I asked "I have two tickets for the cinema, would you like to come with me?" needless to say he did.

After this, we were having one of the parties and I invited him. The local boys did not take too well to this new member of the clan; he was a foreigner, not one of us Gibraltarians. The music started and before any of the others could ask me to dance there was Jack holding me, the problem was that he could not dance a step and did not move at all, but hold on to me he did, and tightly too. My friends were very upset for they were unable to dance with me all night. The following day, when Jack phoned to get a date with me I told him that I did not go out with boys who could not dance as dancing was my passion and hobby. His answer was "Well then, you teach me!" It was obvious he would not give up. We finally agreed on a time and place to do our dancing and after getting permission from my parents I went over to the Mess with my sister Clem. Lessons were great fun and successful and we were able to dance together whenever my parents allowed me to attend the Mess dances. The proviso was that my sister had to accompany me as chaperone. Since I was only sixteen and Clementina so much younger and still wearing white socks it was rather difficult to find someone who would want to partner her.

During the dance classes Jack found out that I was going to private classes in order to sit for my Senior Cambridge School Leaving Certificate. I went to Miss Eliza Carboni twice a week. He quickly offered to help me with my studies and so whenever he was off duty during the afternoons he would come and help me with my studies. My parents knew that I was seeing Jack and although they had absolutely nothing personal against him the fact that he came from abroad, was a 'foreigner' did not make it too comfortable for him. We met downstairs by the house entrance and sat on one of the steps. My Aunt Mariquita was very upset about this as she had got to know Jack personally and liked him very much even though she could hardly understand what he said to her as she barely spoke any English. She took it upon herself to go and visit my mother and there and then told her that if Jack was not permitted to visit me in Mum's house she would allow us to sit and work in hers!

Because of Auntie's help Jack was then allowed to come and visit me at home. Somehow the fact that this was happening made my father constantly ask "Chamaca are YOU going to marry him?" "Dad", I would patiently reply, "he is only my friend, I have no sweetheart, I am not going to get married for a long time!" Granny loved Jack from the very start and was always trying to feed him. In the summer months she would bring out home made lemonade and biscuits and during the cold season hot cocoa, or tea with the tiniest of sandwiches. Jack reciprocated by spoiling her with sweets, chocolate biscuits etc.

Callos (tripe) made the local way, was a very tiresome meal so consequently whenever it was prepared at home it was cooked in great quantities as all the extended family was invited. The tripe had to be cleaned by the cook and then Granny herself cooked it. Chickpeas, chorizos (Spanish sausages) ham, wine, tomatoes, plenty of garlic etc was added. I never ate this as I could not even stand the smell. That particular day Jack arrived home as usual and he kept smelling and asking "What are you cooking, it all smells so good." My mother on hearing him said "que dice el ingles?" (What is the Englishman saying?) When told she gave a huge smile and said "Ah, he knows what is good for him, he likes garlic too. We will invite him too to eat with us!" It was the first time ever Mum had bothered to speak to him. I really hated the thought of what the invitation would turn out to be. Would Jack REALLY like this food? The following day Jack sat at the table with us all and between ahs and ohs he ate a huge serving of the local delicacy. Mum was over the moon and even tried her best to converse with him in English. At table we spoke Spanish except when directing ourselves to Jack. We all looked at him as he ate, spoke a few words, and laughed. Jack decided there and then to take up Spanish classes so that he could understand what everyone was saying!

From this occasion Jack was accepted much better by my parents, eating this food obviously made him more like one of us to them. Jack loved being with the family and occasionally he was invited in for a meal or ride out in the car with us all. Dad owned a Citroen car which could seat nine of us so there were always some guests! On January 25, 1946 Jack had his nineteenth birthday and soon afterwards he received news that the company was transferring him to Massawa in Eritrea. He was most distressed. We were all very fond of him by then and the thought of his going away saddened us all.

One day one of the Company's expatriate wives came and commiserated with me about my 'boyfriend' being sent away. When I asked her what she meant she replied "He is going away most probably because he is seeing too much of you, a native girl!" I looked up and down at her and said "But you too are a native girl, a native from England, so what is the problem?" "Company's rules, I suppose" is what she said.

Our friendship became more intense. Both Jack and I were so aware that soon he would be leaving Gibraltar and we tried to be together as much as possible. Perhaps because of this one day he put his arms around me pressed me hard to his chest, caressed my face and then gently kissed me on my lips. I was surprised and stirred deeply; it was my very first kiss and had feelings never experienced before. The first kiss was followed by others and then I remembered Dad's words a long time before in Madeira when I had become a young lady and realized that perhaps what we were doing so close together was not correct. I started to cry. Bewildered Jack asked "What is wrong, what have I done, why are you crying?" "Look. We must not kiss or get near each other, it is all wrong, I might get pregnant and Dad would kill me!" Jack, who really had only been kissing me, was astounded. The next day he turned up with a little book 'Red Light, Stop' which explained all about our bodies and sex. No one had bothered to tell us anything about the birds and the bees and of course in those days you could not ask anyone of the family. Jack also said that he loved me and that he would marry me one day. Since it was left with no date I did not object. Soon after he told Dad that he had serious intentions with me and that he would be returning and someday we would marry. Jack left in March 1946.

Somehow I had not realised how much I would miss him and how lonely I felt. I occupied myself with my studies and sat for my exams which I passed. Later I continued studying for my London matriculation and on hearing that scholarships were being granted I applied for one. Dad was most upset. Why did I want to go and study medicine if I already had a boyfriend? Wasn't I going to get married? He refused to let me go on with it and instead he sent me to Cushi Dix, a Cuban lady married to another expatriate from the Company, to learn cooking. She taught me to make delicious rolls, cakes and desserts but by the time I was starting with full meals she and her family were transferred as well.

It became obvious that Dad took Jack's words of our getting married one day too seriously and he restricted my going out in mixed company, other than with JP who Dad liked very much. I was forbidden to go dancing and even to take part in the shows that I had previously been able to. On the other hand Jack not only went out with girls but also sent me snaps of them. This annoyed me a lot as I had, without realising it, got myself into a position I did not welcome, I was only seventeen! It did not take long for us to realize that our characters did not coincide as Jack put it and although we remained pen friends we broke up.

Soon after we received a letter from The Red Cross informing us that Auntie Lottie, Uncle Chito and their son Charlie were alive and in Australia and would soon be repatriated. As can be imagined we were all overwhelmed with happiness. Poor Granny Elena kept on crying and laughing and saying! "I knew it, I knew it". We just had to wait for them to notify us when to expect them back home. The rooms downstairs which we had used for partying were now being prepared for them.

Auntie Lottie returned only with her son. Uncle had been asked to return to British North Borneo as Acting Governor (coincidentally he came across the guard who had helped them escape and who was now a prisoner himself). It was lovely seeing them and looking so well. Apparently they had received care in Australia after being picked up in the sea. We were told very little of the hell the family lived while prisoners of war of the Japanese. Auntie Lottie preferred to put it out of her mind and start afresh.

However it appeared that one of the guards that had somehow befriended Charlie had warned his parents that they were the next one on the captain's list to be killed, and it was recommended they make a bid for freedom and get away. Uneasy wondering whether it was an excuse the guards were making to kill them 'while escaping' they did put things together with the help of everyone in the camp and in the middle of the night they got on a raft which they pushed towards the sea. They were in God's hands!

Without food and only water they were carried out to sea. On the third day they heard an aeroplane and too scared to look up into the sky they waited. The plane circled a couple of times but there was no fire. My uncle asked my aunt, who was a natural blonde, to take off the hood she wore. The plane came lower and then dropped down food to them and a note saying a Red Cross ship was around the area, to hold on and they would be picked up. A few days later they were taken aboard the ship and then off to Australia where they received medical attention and aid.

The house seemed changed with Auntie Lottie's return. Granny was so happy she now sang and tried to dance ever so often throughout the day. Our cousin was found a school and life continued with my aunt looking for a home where they would install themselves once uncle returned from Borneo.

I loved being with my aunt and listening to her travel adventures. It was what I would like to do myself. But my life continued with helping Dad at the shop where I was now given more responsibilities. After successfully passing my London matriculation exams Dad could see that I was getting restless and upset because I was not being allowed to go to the University. He promised he would get a cashier and I could go to study dance in Sevilla. It was a way to keep me quiet. By then my sister Clementina was also helping Dad as much as she could whenever free.

I went off to Sevilla where I stayed as a boarder with friends of the family Dona Carmen the mother, and Mercedes the daughter. The latter was much older than me but we became good friends. I started my dance classes with Enrique Jimenez de Mendoza better known as 'El Cojo' (because he limped) every morning and with Eloisa Albeniz every afternoon. It was hard work but a lot of fun. Since I was a British student I automatically became the English girl and because I loved a prank I made believe I could not speak any Spanish. It was a riot. Whenever I made a mistake or did not get the style correct I could hear and understand the teachers grumbling under their breath and making rude remarks about my ability or stance. It was hard work but I was soon able to cope with the best of students. It was here that I met the Duquesa de Alba, Dona Cayetana, when she herself was a student but whereas she was learning for the pleasure of dancing I was for teaching purposes.

My stay in Sevilla was a lot of fun and for the first time ever I was away from the whole family but well supervised by Mama Carmen who, like my parents in Gibraltar, would not let me go out alone in the evenings. Mercedes became my chaperone. I always thought it strange that during the day a chaperone was not needed unless going out with a boy - but come evening it was an entirely different matter. My parents came a couple of times to visit for a weekend and my very good friend JP as well. Traditions and customs were different from home as well as the food but it was more carefree. It was a shame when I had to return home which happened when a talent agent offered me a contract to dance at the Pasapoga Night Club in Madrid. I was delighted and thrilled but when I phoned my parents to give them the good news they quickly came to fetch me to return home! Dad kept on saying "Chamaca, I am sorry but I am not going to allow a daughter of mine to entertain anyone. First the admirers will send you flowers and gifts but then they will expect something from you in exchange!" Why would they do that? That was the end of the matter. Instead, once home, he had the area above what had been the laundry and was now the servants quarters extended to connect with the 'sotea'. There they gained more space where a studio with dressing room and bathroom was built for me to start giving my lessons. I became much happier with all my young pupils and particularly when I was able to put on shows for the Church and St. Vincent of Paul.

On my eighteenth birthday I had two big surprises. Fernando Rebello wrote to me asking me to be his official girlfriend and promised to visit Gibraltar but I turned him down. Dad gave me a Renault Juvaquatre car and paid for my driving lessons. I was ecstatic. There were provisions and rules to be followed of course. I was not to go over to Spain on my own at any time. There were to be no boys on board and so on but it was great having my own means of transportation. Soon after I was given military permission to enter a number of places not admissible for the locals as whenever Dad's driver did not come I would now take over the delivery van and with two young Spanish boys to carry the orders and set off to where the army people lived. My sister Clem had finished school and so she too had to help in Dad's business.

It seemed that eighteen was the age for local boys to make their marriage proposals and a couple of them that belonged to the clan (or had been a little more special) proposed. I remembered one who was rather persistent who, while walking me home, said he wanted to marry me. I never answered him, I just took off running and never again went out with him. It was nothing personal except that I did not want to get married or even give it a thought.

By now Dad had converted what had been stables at the far side of the house under the sotea into a meat factory where he made all kinds of sausages, salami, pressed tongues, brawn etc. People like Tyrone Power and Errol Flynn came in their Yachts to Gibraltar and took many pounds of special sausages as well as Italian delicacies. Dad did well from what he learned in Madeira. Sometimes, if Dad was away for any reason and a big order for sausages was received I was the one who mixed all the ingredients with the help of Grandad Danino. I would mix everything myself so that Dad's butchers would not learn the secret of the recipe. I did not enjoy this very much but understood the necessity. Once mixed the butchers would continue with their tasks. The shop although in the same building was lower down the hill. It covered the same area as the ground floor and beside the retail shop he had the biggest privately owned refrigerating plants in Gibraltar. Unlike before the Spanish War and Second World War meat was now imported directly from Argentina, Brazil, and New Zealand and some other countries. Animals were not slaughtered any more locally. Whole sides of beef were brought in and the butchers had to cut and prepare for sale. Not like nowadays where everything is pre-packed and cut.

Whenever a ship with meat arrived if Dad was at home he would go to the docks to make sure that all ordered was correct. I would be down in the shop counting once again to verify the delivery. More often than not the ships were unloaded late at night or very early in the mornings and if Dad was travelling it was left to me to go to the docks while Grandad and the butchers were in the shop. I worked hard and it was hardly the sort of job I was educated for, but I loved my father dearly and supported him in any way I could.

Chapter 6

PREPARATION

Eventually with my sister Clementina taking over, we received a letter from Jack's parents inviting me to go and visit them as Jack was going to be there on leave. Dad allowed me to travel to the UK with my aunt so that I would visit what he considered to be the main cities in Europe and see how the Armstrongs lived and what they were like, just in case. We left by ship which was still repatriating army personnel, it was not luxurious like cruise ships nowadays but I was very excited to be on board a ship once again. In England my aunt took me to Aintree for the Grand National and there I had the shock of my life. Didn't Dad say all English people were educated – ladies and gentlemen, well I had a very different experience as I was pushed and shoved, hat all over the place, in order that the locals could have a better view. I realized that in England like anywhere else there were rude people as well as educated ones and that the idea we colonials had of the Mother Country was very different indeed in the reality.

Girls were much more forward than we in Gibraltar and I often saw them lying on the grass cuddling and kissing their boy friends. In Gibraltar it would have been unheard of. It took ages before you let a boy hold your hand and even more before allowing a kiss. In the UK newly married girls worked and went out with their friends. In Gibraltar it was very different. You married and you ceased to be your parents' property to become your husband and his family's. They controlled how you dressed, who you went out with and usually you went out with your sisters or in-laws while the men lead their lives as they liked.

I knew men finished working and went to their respective clubs where women were then not allowed – they actually lived like bachelors exchanging their mother for their wife who did everything, plus sex, for them. It became very evident why I had never considered marriage. I worked and was as capable as any man or maybe more so and I was not going to allow any man to tell me what to do or not to do. I was as good as any of them and when and if I married it would have to be a 50/50 affair. By proving to my dad that in spite of my being a girl I was as capable as any son could be he made me have ideas of marriage very different to the local girls. And that was really the reason why I had behaved the way I did with the local suitors.

From Aintree my aunt took me to Leeds to visit some of her friends there. Then came the bombshell, she would not go with me to Durham to visit Jack and his people. What would my dad say when he found out that I would be travelling on my own? I did have all the details as how to get there so Auntie took me to the railway station, bought me a first class ticket — in Spain no one in their right mind would travel in economy, and with all the instructions in my hand being read and re read I left for the unknown!

On arrival at the station, while debating as to which side of the road I was to take the bus from a young man walked towards me and said "Hi there Ly!" It was Jack, but a very changed Jack. He had lost weight and had the lean and angry look I liked in a man but he was also a complete stranger, it was like meeting each other for the first time. He took over straight away picking up my case and getting into the bus which was to take us to his home. I felt shy and tongue tied. He took my hand into his and said "Come on Ly, relax!"

The Armstrong home was a bungalow quite close to the bus stop so we just had to walk across the road. Panic struck me — visiting people

I did not know, having to speak English all the time and the weather being so cold for me too. What a disaster! It was with some trepidation that I entered the house .The front door opened on to a long carpeted corridor. On the left side there was one big bedroom which was where Jack and his two brothers slept. Next to it was the parents' bedroom. On the right hand side was a huge sitting room which was referred to as 'the front room' then a square hall leading to a pantry on the left. This little room with all kinds of food tucked away was something we in Gibraltar did not have, we usually kept the food in a sideboard in the dining-room, kitchen cupboards and fridge. There was a window in the centre facing the yard and to the right a big dining-room with a big fireplace and some comfortable armchairs on each side. It was a most cheerful and warm room. The table was set and loaded with all kinds of sandwiches, cakes, jelly, tinned fruit and cream. On seeing all this I exclaimed to Mr and Mrs Armstrong standing by the kitchen door "Oh, you are having a party!" The words came out before I had time to realise. It was their usual tea.

Soon after Jack's younger brother Jeffrey as well as his Aunt and Uncle joined us. I was told that their second son Len was unable to join us as he was an apprentice somewhere. Jack's Aunt Dora and Uncle George turned out to be really friendly. They insisted I called them like Jack did and Aunt Dora kept on looking at me, holding my hand, and saying "Oh but you are a funny one!" I never knew what to make of this. When they went I was taken to the front room which was where I was to sleep, a fireplace in the middle of the wall facing the door, a huge clock on the mantelpiece, beautifully polished brass railings, bucket with coal and fireplace accessories on the sides. Two beautiful antique statues of women guarded the fireplace. A big carpet covered the front of the fireplace. There was a selection of armchairs and settees with scattered tables in strategic positions. To the left of the door there was an organ all dark and sinister, and next to it a tall piece of furniture with a "His Master's Voice" old fashioned gramophone on top. Next to it a grandfather clock was tick-tocking all the time. Above the doorway was a cuckoo clock. I had never seen so many different clocks together in my life. A huge bay window was right opposite where my bed stood.

To my horror there was a tremendous photograph of Durham Cathedral almost as big as the subject, with a heavy carved mahogany frame above where my head would lie and on the side two big oval photographs also in heavy mahogany frames of Jack's granny and grandad. Their eyes followed me wherever I went. It was all so drab after my parents' colourful bright home. I was horrified to think I would be sleeping here and all alone too. My fears were confirmed. The clocks were not synchronized, the floor squeaked, every time a car or bus passed by their headlamps shone into the room and I quickly would look to see if the damned pictures were still looking at me. It was too much and I started to scream!

I shall never forget what followed. Jack, his brother and the parents all appeared by my doorway in their night apparel. I could see by the senior member's faces that I had disgraced myself. Jeff thought it very funny while Jack was most concerned.
Comforted they left me having promised to lock the front door which was normally left unlocked to prove that I would be safe.

The next day, Sunday, I left the house for church with Jack after hearing Dad's opinion about religion; he did not share my Catholic one! After mass Jack took me for a walk to Penshaw Hill monument relating stories as to their tradition of rolling hardboiled eggs down the hill at Easter time and the story of how this monument was built by the people in honour of John George Lambton in 1844. He was the first Earl of Durham (1792 to 1840) and Governor General of Canada in 1838. It was built after the style of the Temple of Theseus.

After this long and interesting walk we went back to the house for Sunday lunch. In 1947 Gibraltar had no supermarket, there was no television and people's customs and traditions were not so internationally known as they are today. In Gibraltar the vegetables were limited to what was brought in from Spain. When anyone mentioned 'pudding' it meant they were talking about a sweet dish, a dessert. So when we sat down for what was referred to by them as Sunday dinner I had no idea as to what to expect! Already in the morning I had been rather surprised that eggs and bacon (what we in Gibraltar considered the typical English breakfast) had not been offered me. Instead they served toasted tea cakes. Now at table 'Mum' turning to me sweetly asked "Will you have some Yorkshire pudding, pet?" My God, I thought, the English start with their desserts first. I had seemingly disgraced myself already by my previous night's behaviour so I would be brave and do as they did. "Yes, please, Mrs Armstrong" I said meekly. To my further astonishment she picked up a jug and again asked "Would you like it with your meat and vegetables or by itself?" My stomach turned, how could people mix food like this, I wondered. "No, no, I shall have it alone please". Pointing at the jug in her hand she said "Gravy?" "No thanks" what had I got myself into I wondered. When everyone had been served I picked up my fork and cut a tiny piece, it was not sweet, and without realizing it I had made this remark aloud. Looking strangely at me she asked "Do you want some sugar, pet?"(I can well imagine what she thought of me this time) "No, thank you, I think I will change my mind and have gravy instead." When this was finished Dad carved the meat placing it carefully on the heated plate. Then Jack's Mum dished out the vegetables. Roast potatoes, mashed potatoes, boiled potatoes and my goodness, what the heck was she giving me? I had never ever in my life seen such small cabbages (Brussels sprouts) and of these she put quite a number of them on my dish together with mushy peas (never seen or heard of this before) carrots, cauliflower, parsnips, turnips and God alone knows what more. As usual with the candour that characterizes me I said "No, thank you, 1 only want the meat, roast potatoes and one vegetable. Mr. Armstrong who had been a Regimental Sergeant Major with the Durham Light Infantry got up, pointed to my plate with food mounting said "You EAT this!" Never in my life had anyone spoken to me with such authority. I meekly took the plate and started eating when they were all served, passing some of the vegetables to anyone on either side whenever I could. My instinct told me that Mr. Armstrong did not think too highly of this spoilt foreigner his son had brought home and I wondered whether I would ever be able to fit into such a family should I want to.

Aunt Dora loved to tell me stories regarding from where they had all come. I was amazed to hear the different countries they had descended from. They were almost as much Heinz 57 varieties as I was and yet they were supposed to be pure bred English people! Anyway Aunt Dora was a great story teller and I enjoyed the way she described the family history. Jack's family came from Scotland to settle down in the North of England; The Armstrongs originally were named Fairbairn but according to historians the name was changed by an ancient king of Scotland having had his horse killed under him in battle, was immediately re-mounted by Fairbairn, his armour- bearer, on his own horse. For this timely assistance he amply rewarded him with lands on the borders, and to perpetuate the memory of so important a service, as well as the manner in which it was performed (for Fairbairn took the king by his thigh, and set him on the saddle), his royal master gave him the appellation of Armstrong.

Jack's father's mother's maiden name was Ryder from Kilkenny in Ireland and supposedly the adopted surname of the Markey and Markahan families; Apparently Marcach is the Irish for rider. They too came to live in Yorkshire where first records appeared on the census rolls taken by the early Kings of Britain to determine the rate of taxation of their subjects. Eventually they went further north settling down in Co. Durham as well.

Mrs. Armstrong's maiden name was Emily Dowell and her mother's maiden name was Barrass. The Barrass family originated in France, later moving to Ireland and eventually to the North of England. The Dowells hailed from Inverness, Scotland and eventually came to Philadelphia, Co Durham. It was in the North that they met and married.

Things at the Armstrong home went from bad to worse - the toilet was at the back of the house near the kitchen and the bath was under the kitchen table. This last 1 did not know until I asked for a bath. The chaos it brought was quite horrendous and from then on I washed as well as I could in front of the kitchen fireplace at least I was warm. At home, a maid washed my hair or I went to the hairdressers, here I tried to do it by myself and once again it turned out to be another nightmare. Wanting to show that at least I was trying I decided to do my own laundry. Mrs. Armstrong had a huge laundry place with some funny contraption which she used to pound the clothes with and then having hand rinsed, she would put each individual garment through a mangle. It seemed like torture. At home we had the laundry woman who would hand wash with a board to rub the clothes on before the war and a washing machine later. I had not, until then, realized how lucky we were on the good old Rock. Well I successfully did my few pieces and then hung them on the line. This we held with wooden round pegs which I had never seen before. By the time I went to pick up my clothes they were full of black spots which I foolishly tried to rub off. It was the soot from the coalmines. I had to redo all my laundry once again. Nothing I did seemed to go right and when it was time to travel to London to meet with my aunt once again I was only too pleased to leave the North. What an experience!

As Jack had to report to the London Head Office he decided to travel with me. He would be staying with friends in Wimbledon while I would be joining my Aunt Lottie. The trip by train was great and then we arrived at King's Cross Station. Everyone was hurrying everywhere; I had never seen such traffic. We followed the crowd and then came to the stairs. I stopped suddenly looking at the moving steps and was too frightened to get on them. Jack, not realizing this was all new to me, was already at the bottom. Someone behind me made up my mind by pushing me on-to the steps. As we got nearer the end I wondered how I would get off in time. 1 jumped off the steps to the landing and almost fell down dropping my case with a crash!

I had noticed in the Underground many posters advertising something saying 'Friday Night is Amami Night.' Curious, I asked Jack what it meant. "Oh, it is a shampoo they are advertising" Surprised, I asked "Do the English only wash their hair on Fridays?" "Heck, Ly, I don't think so, any night is just as good." "Then why say Friday?" "Perhaps because everyone stops working for the weekend and they like to look fresh and smart" said he. (As soon as I could I bought Amami — it was really a lovely fresh pine smell!)

I had found the more mature Jack rather fun to be with and when he asked that we continue being special friends I promised I would give it a real good thought. I knew I would not make anything official for then I would be most restricted once again but would give our future together some serious consideration. After all, we would not be living in the North!

Jack left me with my aunt, promising to come and see us in London before leaving for Southern Rhodesia, where he was then stationed. Auntie Lottie booked us in a quiet elegant hotel and off we went to unpack for the week we would be staying there. That same evening, hungry as I was, we left the hotel to go to a little Italian restaurant Auntie knew opposite the Windmill Theatre. London was so terribly exciting and so very big. Dad had not been too happy about my visiting this city as in Gibraltar we often received news about street attacks; sexual harassment etc. so we were actually discussing this while walking when out of the blue came a hysterical woman who grabbed my handbag and started to pull it away from me. I held on for sheer life, while Auntie pushed her off me. No one stopped to help us though there were many people walking by. At last a man who turned out to be a Spaniard came to our aid and more or less at the same time so did the police. It was horrific. I was wearing a red hat with a very long red feather and a tweed coat. Auntie was smartly dressed with a fur coat over a dress. As soon as the police arrived the woman fainted and then the Black Maria arrived on the spot as if by magic and the four of us were thrown in and taken to Bow Street Police Station. It turned out the woman was a habitual of the police, she suffered from persecution mania and when the police did not take her in after a while she would get into trouble so as to be arrested. We were informed that we would need to go to court and that they would see it would be within the time we had in the City. I never expected to make it in the newspaper but the News of the World came out with the story describing me as the girl with a red feather in her hat!! My father never found out.

The police were very kind after the first shock and they gave us transportation back to the hotel. When we arrived back in the police car we were met by horrified stares. We felt so bad that we decided to change hotel notifying the police first. When Jack was told he laughed and kept on saying that we women could not be left alone.

Jack had become very special. I felt jealous at the thought that he might be having other girl friends - and perhaps doing things with them. I could not understand how if he loved me, he would want to make love to another girl. Aunt Lottie laughed and said "Lydia. men are like that. Whereas we women need to be in love and have a relationship men see to their sexual needs without having to love!" "You mean to say he can have an erection without loving the person?" "Grow up.child. Men are just that, men, and if he did do 'it' it would not mean anything to him."

The court case finally over Aunt and I left London for Paris, France. Once Dad had allowed me to travel he felt my education would be more complete if I visited what he considered to be the most important capitals in Europe- London, Paris, and Madrid. Aunt and I left by ferry boat and stayed in a private hotel centrally situated with easy access to transportation. Because of the extra time spent in the UK we had to shorten our stay to only four days but we managed to occupy ourselves all the time. I could not get over the lovely little bistros, the Eiffel Tower, Notre Dame de Paris Cathedral and oh, so many other beautiful sights. It was difficult to leave this lovely city where like in London, girls were so very much more modern and freer than we in Gibraltar.

Our trip by train was total luxury. We had a sleeping compartment and there was a wonderful restaurant on board. This was much more exciting than the way we had travelled to the UK. The countryside was beautiful and it was with sadness that we left the train and some of the fellow passengers we had met and whose company we had enjoyed very much.

Madrid was amazingly exciting. Although my parents had visited there very often with my brother and a couple of my sisters I had never been so lucky. Now I was able to enjoy the shows and shops they had often talked about. Madrid was a lovely city but girls seemed to be even more controlled than in Gibraltar. Although not so bad it reminded me of my visits to Alhama de Granada, the spa my grandmother visited every year for her rheumatism, and how narrow minded people were. At Alhama there were many older people with their young companions, and since there was nothing much to do, the young people got together most days for walks along the river or to sing at night. There used to be many priests at the spa as well as the Bishop of Malaga. One day, I had the idea of organizing a dance at the hotel where we were and inviting the town's young people. When the priests found out I was admonished and told that I would be sinning. Unable to comprehend their attitude, after all in Gibraltar the Legion of Mary to which I belonged, often held parties where Fr Grech or Fr.Devlin would preside and we would all sing and dance. There was nothing wrong. We, the young people went ahead with our plans and many of the locals were only too thrilled to come and enjoy the fun. Up till then I had danced without noticing anything but then, made aware by the priests' words, I realized how sometimes the hand wandered, or you were being brought closer to your partner and so on.

The next day the young priests were once again chastising me. Angry as I was I turned round and said "Yes. It was a simulated embrace but I never noticed or had disturbing thoughts until YOU said it. It is not my sin but yours!" Of course the priests were furious and told me I was not to go to the local church - I was a bad woman! With tears running down my face I ran to my grandmother who was sitting in the courtyard with the Bishop. The Bishop on hearing my story told me "Don't be so upset, these young priests are the soldiers of the church and take things too much to heart!"

Spain in Franco's days was really very narrow-minded and strict. When bathing in the sea women had to wear a skirt over their swim suit while men could not go to the beach unless the top was covered with a T-Shirt. When going to any church service you had to wear long sleeves inside the church (and some churches provided them for you to wear temporarily). Low neckline was also considered to be too provocative. In fact it was no joy to leave our more open minded Gibraltar to do anything else but visit places of interest and to eat out as well as shop.

Madrid had some beautiful clothes. There were two big stores that we particularly enjoyed visiting, El Corte Inglés and Corte Fiel. Both sold their goods at much more accessible prices than the shops in Gibraltar.

We managed to go to see a 'Zarzuela' a show like an operetta with great, lively music. In Madrid we also enjoyed our meal times much better as it was more like what we were really accustomed.

It was with enthusiasm that I returned home. My mind was clearer than ever before and for once I felt I knew what I wanted. JP was happy to see me and hear all about my experiences abroad. When we met and he heard all that had happened we shared much laughter. JP was the first to know that I was seriously considering marriage with Jack who with patience and understanding had made me fall in love with him.

Correspondence in those days took a long time as the mail came by sea. Jack's first letter after his return to Rhodesia was to formally ask me in marriage. My answer was that I would get engaged only when he knew when we would marry. I did not want to have my life restricted once again similarly to when Jack first left Gibraltar and Dad would not let me go out. I had felt like a prisoner and thought it most unfair.

At about this time the Revd Father Mondejar, a Jesuit priest, came to Gibraltar to give his sermons. Everybody went to listen to his lively lectures regarding human frailties and the way he gave advice to keep relationships intact. I loved Fr. Mondejar who I thought particularly charming and bright. In his native Malaga, Spain, Fr. Mondejar gave many young people a chance for a better life by giving them a home and education. The church was usually packed. Men and women loved listening to him. He would go to the pulpit and with good humour he would proceed to talk in a down to earth manner. He related how parents had to wake up to their children's doing. One of his stories went like this. "A mother was going out with all the family and her teenage daughter said she was not feeling too well and wanted to stay at home. The mother wanted to call the doctor but the girl would not let her, instead, she would stay in bed. Mother and her whole family left. Soon after, the girl all dressed up, opened the door to her boyfriend. They kissed, they caressed. Then they heard the family return so the boyfriend exited hurriedly. The mother entered the girl's room and found her all hot and bothered, touched her forehead, the girl was feverish, so there and then mother called the doctor. The doctor came, checked the girl and then said 'She needs iron' 'What, in vitamins?' asked the mother. 'No, not in vitamins, in door locks!"

With regard to marriage he would say "My children, hear me well. The woman is the best policeman of the husband. Your husband wants to go out. You get dressed up and go with him. With you there the others won't have the chance to take him away. Look at your husband as if you did not know him, look at him as if you were a woman without a man and then instead of being fed up with him, you will see him as a most desirable man." His best story however was "When your husband gets up to go to work he doesn't want to remember you with your curlers on and looking frumpish so, my girls, you get up before he does. Dress yourself nicely, comb your hair and perfume yourself, give him his breakfast, send him off with a big kiss. The image he will have of you will stay all day. Then, if you want to go back to bed, do so!"

I was already twenty years of age. I already told Dad that Jack and 1 wanted to get engaged to marry in November of that same year 1949. My sister Clementina was helping Dad full time at his business while I was running a new business, a Charcuterie which Dad had opened a little higher up the hill from the butcher shop. We served teas and coffees as well as soft drinks and any kind of sandwiches and something that used to be the military peoples' special, pigs trotters! Somehow I think Dad was hoping that when married, Jack and I might settle in Gibraltar.

My sister Lottie, as soon as she finished her High School education, was invited by the Loreto Convent to join their teaching staff and she found herself at seventeen teaching girls of her own age and a couple older than her. Lena was still at school. Winston, who had not been a very strong child, was being tutored at home. My friend Muriel was now in England in a Teacher Training College. Rosina and Yvonne, another childhood friend who had been evacuated to Jamaica, all were at home. These were the years when girls did not go out to work unless they were teaching, helping in their family business or had their own enterprise.

Jack and I continued writing regularly to each other and the idea of getting married sounded more and more exciting and wonderful. We both wanted to get engaged and make it all official. My parents were happy because they had grown to like Jack and the idea of his becoming a member of our family but sad at my having to leave home. Grandad Danino thought of a perfect solution. I could get married and stay behind while Jack would come and go. The fact that Rhodesia was thousands of miles away never entered his head! The engagement was announced and as there was not to be too long for the wedding I was thrown into a whirl of preparations. A big wedding was to be arranged for I was the first and the eldest of the Danino sisters to get married. I must wear white. Mum took charge of everything. The wedding dress was to be made by her dress designer Eugenia Valarino in accordance with what Mummy thought was fashionable. Mum also had all my trousseaux made, beautiful lacy, hand embroidered underwear and nighties, everything you could imagine. I would have much rather have had a small wedding. I would have also much preferred to have been able to decide on my own wedding dress instead of the one chosen for me with a Juliet cap to wear under the veil and which I hated. Ironically, the one who had not been interested in getting married would be the first of my group to do so!

Jack was to have arrived two or three days before the wedding day but unfortunately with the irregularity of transportation and the bad weather he was delayed in London so he made it home only the night before our wedding day. My parents did not allow me to go to the airport to meet him 'for I might have got too excited and kissed in front of everybody'. Jack was rushed to Algeciras, our neighbouring town, to try his morning suit as all had to be perfect. When I finally saw him it was late in the evening. My cousin Pepe Gache who was my first dancing partner in Madeira was ill in the hospital with tuberculosis and we both wanted to see him before our wedding day. Just as I was descending the stairs Dad came and asked "Where do you think you are going?" "To see Pepe." "What, alone with Jack?" "But Dad, we are getting married tomorrow morning" "Tonight Chamaca, you are still my daughter. Tomorrow you will be Jack's wife and you can go wherever you want, but not tonight." Clara, our governess and housekeeper, had to accompany us.

Emilio Gallego Ibanez

Elena Nuza Luz and daughter
Clemencia Gallego

Villa Mosaico

James Danino and Ana Baro

Below: Papa Rosendo, Mama Carlota, Granny Elena, Dad, Mum, Clara, sisters Clementina and Lottie. myself and driver

Domingo and Clemencia Dani-no's wedding day

Below: School girls in Madeira

The Danino family with Granny Elena in Madeira, 1944

Ana Lydia - age 16

Jack - age 18

My wedding day

The Armstrong family in County Durham 1948

Part Two

A New Beginning 1949 - 1956

Chapter 7

MARRIAGE

The next day November 17th 1949 Jack and I got married at St Joseph's Church where my parents had married and where we were all baptised, made our First Holy Communion and were confirmed. The Reverend Father Grech who had married my parents married us. As I had anticipated Dad asked Jack to remain in Gibraltar and take over the new business but Jack refused. He was a telecommunications man and that was what he enjoyed and what he wanted to do.

We were married in the morning and after a champagne breakfast celebration at the Imperial Tea Rooms in Main Street, Gibraltar, we were driven to Sevilla for the first part of our honeymoon. My parents and all my friends knew that once the honeymoon was over we would not be returning home as from then on home would be wherever Jack would be and at this time it was Salisbury, Southern Rhodesia. Friends and family were both happy to see me married and sad to know that we would be separated for a good while.

In Sevilla we stayed at the Hotel Inglaterra where we enjoyed a lovely suite. All the friends I had made while studying dancing there gave us a lovely party and we were having a lovely time. Being married was terribly exciting. I enjoyed lovemaking and discovering my sensuality. We were free to do what we wanted and as we pleased. It was a great sensation. To our surprise and embarrassment my parents turned up on the third day of our honeymoon and took the room adjoining ours! Two days later they accompanied us for a while on our way to Madrid. We stopped the cars and embraced for the last time with my parents gallantly smiling while tears came down their faces. Dad handed me an envelope saying "Chamaca, this is in case things get difficult and you wish to return home". As we returned to our car I too was crying and wondering whether I was doing the right thing going so far away from all I had loved and knew.

1 broke down in the car and a startled Jack tried to console me as best he could. In Madrid we stayed at the Gredos Hotel on the Gran Via. In the bedroom we were given a huge four poster bed which was very high off the ground. We found this rather funny as once we got into it we were quite reluctant to get out particularly in the middle of the night in complete darkness.

We left Madrid for Paris where we remained only two days and crossed in the ferry to England. Jack checked in with the Head Office and since none of Jack's parents or other members of the family had come to our wedding, we made our way North by train. Everyone was most polite and Jack's parents asked me to call them Mum and Dad but I could sense that neither one of them were too thrilled to have a foreigner for a daughter-in-law. Some of the younger friends were in fact quite rude asking me what I had done or used to catch Jack. (This was hilarious for poor Jack had had a tough time convincing me to get married!) One girl asked "In Gibraltar, do you live in caravans or caves?" "Actually we live in caves" I answered "We grow our hair very long and part it by the side of our ears so that we can cover ourselves: you see we do not wear any clothes!" For a stupid question a more stupid answer. But, you should have seen their faces. Those were the days when the package tour deals did not exist and there was no television and of course the English people then thought they were still the only civilized nation where people lived well!

Back in London the chartered air-line Sudair informed us that we would have to fly in a small five passenger plane to Paris as there were no other passengers travelling from England, and their big plane, a Vickers Viking, would start from France. I was not aware what was awaiting me but when I saw the narrow canvas covered little plane I almost had a heart attack. I was all dressed up and wearing high heeled shoes. As I entered the plane Jack warned me to make sure not to step on the canvas and to step on the pieces of wood serving as a gangway. Believing him I tiptoed to my seat and again following his advice I sat still, looking ahead of me into the pilot's head, to thus assure the plane's stability. Eventually the pilot asked me to stop boring holes in his head! I was most embarrassed and thought Jack's sense of humour was definitely peculiar. On arrival we were met by the airline representative who said we were to go to the King George V Hotel near the Place de l'Opéra as we would not be leaving for a couple of days. In fact we stayed two nights and one day.

When we finally boarded the plane we discovered that instead of going to Rome as scheduled we would be flying directly to Athens as once again there were no passengers to be picked up. The plane would only fly during the day and since the cabin was not pressurised it could not fly too high as we found out for ourselves when we flew over the Alps and the lack of oxygen made us all rather light headed. A strange sensation!

In Athens we arrived with sufficient time to go and explore the city and enjoy the sights with the friendly crew before going to our hotel. The following morning we left for Tel-Aviv to pick up some passengers. Here we were allowed to disembark and go for a walk inside the airport. Back in the plane we set off once again. I looked out of the window and noticed a flash of fire. I quietly asked Jack if this was OK. When Jack saw what was happening he called the air hostess who closed the curtain and quickly went to the pilot's cabin. The plane started to lose height and began turning. The Captain then informed us all that we were returning to Tel Aviv.

I was terrified. I did not want to die so young. Wanting to be prepared for any eventuality I turned to Jack and asked "Where is my parachute?" "Parachute" said Jack "what for?" "So I can be prepared to jump when required!" I answered. "My God, Ly, there are no parachutes!" I was speechless. I did not want to die and there was nothing I could do to help myself except to remain seated. By the time we landed I was in a state of shock and unable to say a word for quite some time. The landing by the way was smooth and wonderful as if there had been nothing wrong with the plane.

We remained at the airport terminal while the plane was being checked and repaired but when the crew came to call us for re-boarding I refused but finally consented when I realized that there would be no other means of transportation. I either went with people I already knew or faced going in another plane. So off I went as meek as a lamb.

We arrived in Khartoum and as usual went to our hotel where we were informed that we would be remaining for a while as the plane was picking up some pilgrims for Jeddah. When the plane returned we were faced with another delay as it had to be disinfected and de-flead, a job that was not so well done seeing that most of us passengers spent our time scratching ourselves practically all the way to our next overnight stop at Entebbe. Stewart Granger was at that time filming King Solomon's Mines and all the passengers were wondering whether we would come across any of the film stars as they were staying in our hotel, however we had no such luck. At breakfast we were served papaya, a fruit which I had never seen before. Since it looked like a melon I started to eat it with knife and fork, when suddenly the waiter in a dazzling white kaftan and red fez handed me a spoon saying "You eat with spoon memsahib, not knife and fork!" After breakfast we departed for N'dola in Northern Rhodesia, the last stop before Salisbury, Southern Rhodesia. It was already December 9th 1949.

I did not know what to expect. The Africa I knew was the one of the films where all the black people wore horns and cavorted half naked. Therefore I was very surprised when the few black men I saw at the airport were dressed European style. From the airport we were driven directly to the house which Jack had rented. It was situated in Cranborne, a pleasant suburb of Salisbury about three miles from the town centre. This area had housed many Royal Air Force personnel as there had been an air training camp there. Awaiting our arrival were two men servants, Shilling the houseboy and Shadrek the gardener. They both greeted me with big smiles and they really seemed friendly enough.

Until this moment being married had been thrilling and lovely but on finding myself in the house and so far away from home and all I knew well, I realised that I had taken on a responsibility and I wasn't too sure as to how I would cope. I suddenly felt very homesick, and why not admit it, frightened too.

We were busy unpacking when I heard humming and clapping as well as banging and then voices half singing half talking. "Jack, what is going on?" I asked. Jack laughed "Its OK honey, don't worry, it's the boys giving you a welcome song. They are making up stories about you and how happy we shall be!" Apparently this was their way to show they approved of their master's choice.

Chapter 8

RHODESIA

After a few days with Jack at home he had to return to work. It was then that on my own I did not know how to react with Shilling and Shadrek. They lived in a little house in the back garden. Our kitchen door to the back was left unlocked during the day but the door to the dining-room and the rest of the house was locked and I would not open unless they answered me in Spanish what I had taught them to say so that I would be sure they were my own servants. The dining-room led to a comfortable sitting-room and then there was another door locking off the sleeping quarters. This seemed to be the norm in all the houses.

We had very little money, in fact, we were rather poor. Jack had broken one of the Company's rules by marrying before he was twenty five years of age and so we were not entitled to a home or any of the married couples' perks. I suggested that since we did not have money we could dispense with the servants. "We cannot do that, Ly honey, we are Europeans and we have to keep the standard!" said Jack. Although had I asked my father for financial help and I knew he would have given it to us, I felt that since we had decided to get married it was up to us to be able to sustain ourselves.

Christmas was drawing near but I still looked at jobs available in the newspapers. It was rather difficult for me since I had had no professional training in the business world and what I had done previously was to help Dad in all he asked after he explained what I had to do. One day I finally saw something I thought I could easily do. When I showed Jack the newspaper he read records clerk wanted for Rhodesia Oxygen and Acetylene Co. "Do you know how to do this?" he asked "Why Jack, anyone can put records on the gramophone and play the music!" I answered. "No, no, you twerp, it has nothing to do with gramophones or music. Keeping records means taking note of whatever goes out of the company or comes in. It means taking notes!" "Well, I think I can do that!" I applied and was accepted.

The sunsets in Africa have to be seen to be believed. There is nothing so beautiful, the still of the night, the background of silence, where every chirp of the birds or falling of a leaf was heard and there were splendid reds with flashes of bright yellow and purples. At times it looked as if the sky was on fire. It was excitingly beautiful but also rather scary if you happened to be alone.

As Christmas Day drew nearer the faint beatings of the drums, claps and humming became more noticeable. You could close your eyes and imagine all sorts of exotic and adventurous happenings. Eventually on Christmas Day we were met with singing and clanging of bells. We opened the front door and there were our two boys with some other friends. They stood on two tins strapped to their feet and around their legs and up to their knees they had tied more empty tins hanging from a string. They shuffled along making the tins hit each other and ring. It was a thrilling experience. Then our two boys grinning like Cheshire cats came to us and said "Morning Master, morning Missy, Christmas baksheesh!" "Oh. You think you deserve some?" I asked "Yes Missy, ten shillings please!" Jack and I had already made out their Christmas presents and we had been much more generous than what they seemed to anticipate. "Just a minute, Shilling, I go get your present." On my return I held the two envelopes in my hand and said "Ten shillings, is that what you want?" They nodded still smiling broadly "Ah well, I better open the envelopes and take out what you do not want" I said.

"No, no, Missy we are both good boys!" Laughing we handed out our gifts and then they were off for the rest of the day.

One day when I got my laundry back from Shilling I discovered to my horror that my beautiful silk nightdress had been scorched. I called Shilling and asked what had happened for I had cautioned him to be careful as it was a very precious garment. He just stood there smiling and shrugging his shoulders. His attitude upset me and without realising it I started to tell him off in Spanish. Seeing that he remained unconcerned I told him to go and I went into my bedroom to lie down. Then I heard what appeared to be me talking, and laughter. I went to the window and to my amazement found Shilling mimicking me and talking gibberish that sounded Spanish. When Jack came home I told him what had happened "Oh my God, I shall now have to go and reprimand and punish him!" "What do you mean punish him?" "Well, it is what he expects of me!" As soon as Jack called Shilling he appeared, stood very straight and still while being told off and being taller than Jack went down the kitchen step so that Jack could slap him on his face. I stared in shock and then Shilling saluted smartly and said "God Save the King." Later he was heard telling all his friends what a strong, good boss he had!

Jack and I had been asked out for Christmas lunch at one of his friends. He explained to me that he had baby sat for them, for their little girl June. The first shock was when we arrived at their home and I found that little June had bigger boobs than me. I had the first of many bouts of jealousy and Jack only laughed and could not see why I was so annoyed. We sat down on their stoop (back porch) for drinks. The houseboy dressed in sparkling white came to announce food was ready and the hostess turned to me and said "Would you like to powder your nose?" "Why, is it shining?" I asked. We got up and once again she questioned me "Would you like to see George?" "Who is George?" I asked. Silence! Then I said "Would you mind if I go to the bathroom please?" Jack turned round and said "Ly, honey that is what they have been asking you all the time." "Is it rude in the English language to call a bathroom a bathroom?" Why could the English not call a spade a spade I wondered?

It was at such happenings that I realised how different we all were. Traditions, customs and background all had so much to do in a relationship. Although I spoke English at this time 1 did not think in English. I translated what I had to say from Spanish and did the same with the English spoken to me and at times the translation was extremely rude!

At the beginning of the year I started work. I was picked up every morning and brought home from work. The company offices were at some distance from the town so they provided us with a cafeteria run by the head lady, a Mrs King. The job turned out to be just as Jack had explained and I found I learned quickly and enjoyed it very much. There were six or seven other European ladies (the African women were hardly ever seen in town or in business, they remained in their up-country homes looking after their vegetable plots and piccanins) all very nice and helpful.

At the office one day I said at meal time that I had to return a dinner invitation to a number of people and I did not know what to do. I could make delicious desserts, cakes and bread but not main course. I had had a number of contretemps when left to cook for Jack. One day he told me he would be home for lunch. Up to then we had been eating out. When I told him I did not know what to cook I followed his advice, put a small piece of meat he had bought with a lot of vegetables from our back garden to make a stew however it turned out to be a nice soup which he ate, but not me. Another time I had tried to cook rice and I started with the smallest pan and ended with the biggest one in the kitchen and rice was still rising. So how was I going to cope for guests?! Mrs King came to the rescue giving me a complete menu and step by step on how to cook everything. Fortunately all came out quite well and it encouraged me to be more adventurous with my everyday cooking. Shilling, the house boy did not cook anything except the English breakfast that we often had for dinners as I could not fry an egg without breaking it.

Usually we stayed at home enjoying each others company. We listened to Jack's classical music and danced to my Spanish pasodobles, tangos and music of those days. Sometimes we just played noughts and crosses and others I would spend baking. One of Jack's friends, Johnny, loved my home-made cookies and cakes and was more often than not at home those days. Whenever he was there after my working all afternoon I would find only a couple of cakes left as both Jack and he had devoured them. This somehow frustrated me as I loved seeing all I had baked before it was eaten. Although I objected, nothing changed.

One day we went visiting Johnny and when I saw he had a great collection of books I asked if I could borrow a couple of them. "This is not a public library, you know, Lydia" he said. I saw red. "Why, you son of a bitch"- my English was improving -"my house is not a public cake shop and you gorge all my baking" I thought. I kept very quiet and on our way home I told Jack I did not want to see Johnny at home and explained why I was upset. "Ly, honey, Johnny did not mean anything, he was just being funny. It is the English sense of humour." "If humour is what you call rudeness, OK, but I mean what I have said," I answered.

I had already been working for over two months when a couple of the other girls told me that I was being given more work than the previous employee had had and in fact I was doing two peoples' jobs. I was most upset to hear this so I marched into Mrs King's office and told her that I believed I was doing two jobs but getting only one salary. When I started and the first month I received my wages I had been rather embarrassed and upset for previously I had been the one who paid all my father's workers and now I was at the other end receiving wages. Now I had changed. I worked and I wanted to be paid for what I did.

Mrs King smiled and told me that once I had completed my three months probation period and I became a permanent member of the staff my salary would be renegotiated. A few days later Mrs King called me into her office and told me that she had to fill in some forms with personal information in order to promote me to the permanent staff. She started to ask me questions which I answered to the best of my ability but then she asked me something about St. Vitus Dance. Surprised, I wondered why on earth a company such as this one would want to know anything about dances. "Mrs King," I said, "I don't know why this dance is so important. I do flamenco and classical Spanish dancing as well as folklorical and ballroom and if it is necessary I will learn this one." Mrs King's face was a picture. She went red, covered her mouth and stood up. I knew that something I had said was wrong but did not know what. Then Mrs King said "Come, come in with me and tell the Manager what you have said." Somehow I distrusted her and I said "Not now Mrs King, I must go to the toilet. You can tell him" and I left. As soon as I arrived home I asked Jack why I felt so bad and what had I done wrong. "Oh my God Ly, St Vitus Dance is a disease, an illness." "Illness? Ah! It is el mal de San Vito! Now I know but in Spanish it is not called a dance!" Although up to now I had liked Mrs King the fact that she had tried to ridicule me in front of the boss was unforgivable and there and then I decided I would not return to work. Mrs King came for me, apologized and asked me to reconsider and only when she saw I was adamant about my decision did she come later with the wages due to me.

In a way it was the best thing that could have happened to me. We had been considering leaving Cranborne for a house nearer to the town centre from where we could walk into town, go to the park on Sundays where the band usually played, without having to spend money on transportation and thus be able to treat ourselves to the icecreams we so much enjoyed. We found a house in Eastleigh which was much smaller and did not need any gardener. The one condition was that we had to look after Penny, a small Pekinese dog, the owner had perpetually carried under her arm. There were conditions, Penny had to be fed liver once a week and eggs twice a week, she was not to be bathed nor allowed to have sex with another dog; she also had to sleep in our bedroom. She did, but only for a couple of nights, and certainly not after poor Jack had got up and put his foot right into a present she had left by the bed! To get some liver I practically had to make love to the butcher. They slaughtered cows to get plenty of different cuts of meat but only a small piece of liver and couple of kidneys to sell, offal was therefore a delicacy — so Penny had to do with other things. I also bathed her and she became lovely and fluffy more like a dog should be and eventually when she got on heat we sent her to the kennels but the ungrateful bitch would not mate yet at home she tried with a bull terrier from the next door neighbour that was too tall to do any damage.

At Roselea Cottage in Eastleigh, our new home, we only needed the one houseboy Mischek who was a tall capable boy with a wonderful sense of humour and a strong unusual personality always adding some funny chapters to our lives that broke the monotony of a tight budget and heavy working schedule. I shall always remember the day he offered to do the shopping for me as I was too tired. Off he went to the store for a few urgent purchases and we waited and waited but he just did not return. The police were notified, investigations made at the hospital, but Mischek had disappeared leaving all his belongings and wages behind. After a week and with no news from him we decided to replace him with young James. Things were soon back to normal until suddenly three months later James came in, most indignant, almost in tears to say "Why hadn't missy told him that she had another boy?" I replied "Nonsense, you are my only boy." But once again he argued that an older boy had told him to leave the house. Imagine my surprise, and yes, even delight, just to find our Mischek approaching grinning from ear to ear, all the purchases in a bag. . . three months to do a little shopping. Where had he been? Loftily he explained "Mischek had met some friends and so Mischek had gone for a walk with them!" No other explanations were necessary, this was Mischek.

Once installed in the new house I started to look for another job. Jack heard that the owner of the driving school where he had been taught needed a receptionist secretary and made arrangements for me to meet with him. Mr Kollman, an Austrian Jew interviewed me and then very solemnly said "Mrs Armstrong, I vill give you the job, you know for vhy? You are like me, a bloody foreigner!" I thanked him and left. Jack who was waiting for me asked "Well Ly, how did it go?" "He gave me the job but I am not going to take it. He was very rude. He said I was like him and called me a bloody foreigner!" Jack laughed "You silly girl, everyone uses the word bloody here, it does not mean anything."

My job at the school was much more fun than in the previous one. Mr Kollman turned out to be much nicer than he looked. He was a huge rather fat man with big round red face and balding head but very kind. Working for him was more like working for Dad. I answered the phone, made appointments for the students, kept the petty cash book, taught the rules of the road and even accompanied students for their driving tests. Most students were Africans who were trying to better themselves by getting employment as lorry drivers. There were two African teachers, Wilbert and James. They were always smiling and helpful. I found the Africans to be very gentle, naïve and kind people. There was one particular student M'Bongo who would walk in bowing and never turned his back on me. Most of them had no idea of their ages and they would tell me of an historical happening so that I could guess how old they were. Others would open their mouth and show me their teeth.

My big problem with Mr Kollman was his accent, he would ask me to call Mr Verth on the phone, I would take some time trying to find the name and number to discover that his "w's" were always pronounced as "v's". Since the office was situated in the centre of town I was able to meet with Jack and go to lunch at Johnny's friend, Agnes, who did home meals at her house. All in all my life was improving since I was meeting some of the young Rhodesians and other foreigners with whom I had much more in common. I also had more time and I began to plan starting dancing and fitness classes.

I went to the local church to which we belonged and the priest would not accept my proposal that to start with I would pay only a percentage of what I received. He was adamant about charging me a straight fee from the start which, without students, I could ill afford. I was commenting this at the office when some of my boss's friends who also had offices next to us heard me. A couple of days later, Sancta Pelham whose husband had one of the offices, came in to ours and very excitedly told me that she had arranged for me to give classes at the Sephardic Hall at no charge and she already had ten pupils willing to start with me. You can well imagine my delight — I was going to start dancing again.

I started giving lessons after office hours and once people heard of me I was invited to take part in shows which made me feel alive and happy once again. The Joan Turner School of Dancing also invited me to teach Spanish dances and join the Dance Teachers Association for which I had to learn the basics of ballet, tap dancing and musical comedy and I was off in a big style. I was much happier than I had ever been since arriving in Salisbury and financially we were much better off although now we were aiming at buying an old jalopy to get around to the many beautiful places Jack had visited prior to our marriage. Jack had sold his car in order to get together some cash for our honeymoon expenses.

A frequent visitor to the driving school was a Jewish friend of Mr Kollman who approached me one day and said he knew I loved dancing. True. Would I like to go with him to a dinner dance? In my naiveté I thought Jack was being included but I was amazed to discover that it was just a solo invitation. "What will I do with Jack?" I still don't know what made me say this, except that at times I find it extremely difficult to control that horrible imp that makes me do and say the things that I afterwards regret. Mr Kollman's friend left saying he would soon return. Half an hour later he appeared and in his hand which he extended, there were two small white tablets. These, he said, I was to give to my husband with his meal and he would come over to fetch me at 10pm. I had no intention of going, but why did I again accept his plan so quietly? I got home, had dinner and then Jack, who always loved his bed, yawned and stated as usual his wish to retire for the night. The devil in me said "Ha, ha, so the tablets are really effective". Then I related my experience, poor darling Jack, he didn't dare believe me even when I showed him the innocent pills still in my keeping. He was wild and desperate, made himself sick and sat waiting for 10.pm. When this gentleman arrived, a very much awake and furious Jack was there to meet him. I have never seen a man drive off so quickly. My suitor was short, ugly, middle aged, insignificant looking but very rich and I heard later that he had been on intimate terms with Hedy Lamarr at the beginning of her career in Europe.

When I was single I had looked forward so much to coming of age. Twenty-one was going to be magical for I would then be able to go out into the world and do things I could never achieve in Gibraltar. Now here I was in Salisbury and married. We celebrated my birthday with a visit to the cinema and a huge icecream. Even going to the cinema was a bore for us Europeans as we had to wear evening dress on Fridays and Saturdays. Here we were in evening dress either walking or going in the bus to the cinema. To me it all seemed so false and artificial and I hated this way of living. Jack promised me that we would eventually celebrate my twenty first birthday in the style I had been accustomed.

Our contract up for the Eastleigh house we decided that we would go and live in Cranborne once again but instead of renting a house go to the hostel there. The hostel was a government subsidized residential community that had once been RAF barracks for the training camp during the Second World War. The hostel consisted of rows of wooden bungalows each divided into four small rooms, two persons to a room. The toilets and bathrooms were in separate buildings. There was a big communal dining room and if lucky, you just shared your table with one other couple. If you arrived late, the places left were normally at the bigger and longer tables. We always preferred going to the same table so that our waiter would get to know us and consequently give us better service. Everything including the cleaning of the room was charged for very reasonably. So in spite of the room being very small, only a single bed fitted in and not much space for anything else, we decided to take it.

We learned to hate the tunes then in fashion 'I love chewing gum' and 'Between two trees' — which somehow used to smooth the nerves of our neighbour in the adjoining room. She pacified her intense desire for her homeland by playing her favourites day in day out time and time again. This plus the excitement of wondering when Mr Smith was going to meet with Mr. Jones, Mrs Smith's assiduous admirer, with the extra bit thrown in (for luck) of close up sounds of slaps and thrashings through the thin dividing walls slowly made me a nervous wreck. I could not even enjoy bathing in peace, for often whilst I lay enjoying the peaceful relaxation of a hot bath, just lying in contentment, some young lads would start giggling and there they would be sitting on top of the dividing walls looking down on me and enjoying a free Follies Bergere show at my expense.

With reduced expenses we were now able to afford a second hand car, a Hillman Minx which we named Petergas. It had a leaking radiator which we could not afford to have fixed but we got accustomed to having the trunk always loaded with a couple of petrol tins full of water. We enjoyed the freedom that the car afforded us and we were no longer restrained to the town centre for entertainment.

At weekends we would pack poor Petergas up with pillows, blankets, food and water and go off to the different places. This included Mermaids Pool, a lovely picnic spot on a river with a gorgeous waterfall, where all the young European people would meet. Other times it would be Domboshawa with interesting caves, Mazoe Dam, and a mission station with magnificent rock formations. On local holidays we would go further afield.

On 'Rhodes and Founders,' a two day local holiday, a time when all Rhodesians went investigating and viewing nature's wonders, we followed suit. We packed up Petergas with all the water tins, food, etc and off we went - what joy, what relaxation! George, the giraffe, followed by his partner and little one, smooth, graceful, occasionally stopping for a sweet juicy leaf, then the herds of antelopes, close to the zebras and elephants just staring at us while the ugly hippos rolled in contentment in the horrid muddy waters. We would camp by the river side in a secluded spot which we would think absolutely safe only to find that we were on the animals' drinking tracks near their favourite water-hole.

My first hot-dog was at Shorty's mobile stand, such simple pleasures and yet we were so happy (at that time neither hot dogs nor hamburgers were known in Gibraltar.). The Rhodesian highways in themselves were exciting; no electric lights, in the middle of the "bundu", just two narrow strips of tarmac, with the lovely twinkling stars far ahead and the murmurs of the birds. Then all of a sudden it would start to rain, in bucketfuls, falling and roaring down like stones in a river, carrying away all the dirt and leaving behind just mud, glorious gooey mud, no tarmac tracks, pebbles or anything to hold the car steady. Poor dilapidated Petergas, its windscreen wipers would not work, and the headlamps were giving up on us. It was terrifying to hear the birds blinded by the rainfall crash into our car, making thunderous thumps. Other birds those happy to have escaped from such a death, hooted in different tones giving a very eerie effect. In the midst of all this, our engine started to smoke and splutter until it finally burst into flames. Jack, always on the alert but better at giving orders than carrying them out himself, shouted "Put out the ruddy fire". Automatically, and without giving a thought to the inclemency of the weather outside our warm, dry car, I opened the door to slide and fall into the ghastly mud. My language would have given credit to any old trooper; my English had at long last reached the ultimate. I must say that Jack kept a straight face as he said "Come on, Clot, open the bonnet" I did. "Where is the water, Jack?" "Oh, honey, just pour on the ruddy mud before it explodes!" Charming thought! Back in the car, full of the sticky mess, we continued towards Bulawayo, with nothing but a hand torch to light our way. At long last civilization, there was beautiful and tranquil Bulawayo awaiting us! We were very dirty and tired and just had to have the luxury of a hotel room and bath.

Saturday night, every one in their evening suits and dresses, and in we trundled like characters out of a Hitchcock movie; carting all our belongings as we could not lock Petergas. The hotel was unfortunately (for our pockets and circumstances) one of the better class, as the smaller pensions were all fully booked. As anticipated we were met with horrifying stares and frozen silence. We were grateful to a kind porter and receptionist who on seeing how tired we looked condescended to let us have a room and whisked us out of the elegant guests' sight. After a much deserved and appreciated bath we ate our corned beef sandwich washed down by the last of the coffee in our thermos flask.

Life in the hostel was really not very easy. The food was not too appetising. There was no privacy whatsoever and although able to enjoy more of the beautiful countryside I found the style of living very stressful. When one day I received the news that Grandad Danino had died I became anxious and fretful as I thought I would never see any of my family again.

Jack very generously said he would cash an insurance policy he had so that I could return home to Gibraltar if I felt so strongly about it, Dad's present for an emergency having been spent long before this. I was torn between going and leaving. Jack and I were very much in love but I still was not very confident and wondered whether Jack would stray away. I knew if he was unfaithful I would not want to be with him again. I did not deserve this behaviour since I had always been a good caring wife and carried out all Fr. Mondejar's teachings in every respect. At the end with misapprehension I decided to take Jack's offer, I needed a real good change and to see the family again.

We also started to save all we could so that we could also go and visit a few other beauty spots before my departure. By then Jack like all the expatriate staff had been given the option to stay and become naturalized Rhodesian when the government had nationalized the telegraph company. So from now onwards we would always have to pay for any travelling abroad we wished to do. Rhodesia would be our permanent home.

Jack decided that it would be wonderful to take me to Umtali and to see the Zimbabwe ruins where legend says a pygmy people lived long ago. It was mysterious and astonishing. Walking through those very narrow roads circling and zigzagging around the very tall walls gave you a most eerie and peculiar sensation as if those inhabitants were still living there. I also wanted to see the Victoria Falls before leaving the country. So once again we made use of accumulated holiday and set forth on what was to be a most unbelievable and magnificent adventure.

The beauty of the Victoria Falls left me in awe and wonderment. The peace and quiet and yet the murmurs of the rippling waters in a syncopation of music. The birds were humming and hooting flying around enjoying their freedom, and the idle chatters of the hundreds of spirited young monkeys, priming themselves so that we could take their photos. Finally thunderous noise and heavy cascade of water forced us to stop the car. We had reached the Victoria Falls and were getting soaking wet. The sight was exciting and unforgettable. Oh, the beautiful majestic uncontrolled mysterious Africa!

Soon after our return I told Mr. Kollman that I was going to travel home to visit my family and handed in my resignation. "Missy is going, missy is going" The teachers and students all wanted to know why and where. "I am going very far away" I explained. To my astonishment the African boys started to bring me a lovely selection of goodies, mealies (maize), bananas by the branches, goat meat etc., "Oh, this is very kind of you all but why are you doing this?" I enquired "Missy, we want you to have enough to eat for as long as your trip takes!" Their kindness and thoughtfulness touched me. I would come back to see them on my return and maybe if possible get my job back. I also discovered that I had more friends than I had realized, and that it was more difficult to leave them than I had anticipated.

Chapter 9

HOMEWARDS

A couple of days before embarkation day which was November 17th 1951 Jack and I arrived in Beira, Portuguese East Africa. We booked into a nice little hotel and that night when we walked into the dining-room the orchestra started to play 'Here comes the bride.' I turned round and said "Oh, they must have a wedding party down below." We had been seated in an alcove above from where we could see all the diners and dancing. Two drinks with fire sparklers were brought to us compliments of the house. When we went to pay we were given a big discount. On Jack asking why this had been done the receptionist said "The hotel wishes you all the best. You only get married once. Enjoy your honeymoon!" "But we are not newly married" we both answered him. He smiled disbelieving us.

The Llangibby Castle was a freighter/passenger ship, nothing like the cruise liners you have today. There were two classes. First class where older and expenses paid passengers travelled and the tourist class usually used by the real 'traveller for pleasure' passenger. Since the company was not paying for me I travelled in the latter. The cabins had four bunks and there was only one hand basin. The toilets and bathroom were located in the middle of the ship and you had to book your bath so that the bathroom steward would have it ready for you. The bath water was salt water and you were provided with the soap to be used with it. On top of a stand you would also find a small bath, just like a child's bath, full of fresh water so that once you had lathered and cleansed yourself you would rinse off the salt water. It was all very new for me. Other than the occasional film show or dance there was no entertainment. Passengers got together, played deck games during the day and cards or just talked during the night. Since the ship also carried cargo it was to be a leisurely voyage for we remained at port whatever time it took to load and unload goods.

I shared my cabin with a middle aged lady, an assiduous traveller who kept us amused with her tales. Besides Mrs Ryan, two sisters, Karenza and Loveday Code-Lewis who were going to a very elite business school in London, made up the cabin's occupancy. There were four other young women passengers who were part of the sister's group and we all soon became good friends, and companions. We were all about the same age but I was the only married one and travelling alone. Somehow this seemed to attract the men's attention and I had to get Mrs Ryan to temporarily 'adopt' me and thus give me the respectability I seemed to lack just because I had a ring round my finger and travelling alone. Loveday did everything she could to make me participate in all the onboard activities. We both enjoyed listening to Billy Graham, the well known evangelist who was also a passenger. Every time I attended these meetings some Catholic priests on board would be waiting outside in an attempt to stop us from attending!

Our first port of call was Dar-es-Salaam in Tanganyika. Jack had taken the trouble to notify his ex-Company friends stationed there (and throughout the whole journey) to meet with me and when they discovered all the young women companions it was like a party all the time. Zanzibar, a fragrant island, where all the spices come from was the next port on our journey. The unforgettable smell of cloves pervaded the coconut plantation where many of the local people made their living, not only packing and processing the different spices, but also with the coconuts, making copra which was then shipped all over the world. It was the first time I had seen the coconuts as they grow with a thick fibrous outside cover which was pierced with a sharp short spear-like object stuck into the ground. These carcasses were torn apart to let out the brown coconut which we see in the shops. Every section of this fruit was put to good use.

Mombasa came next with its lovely harbour with exotically dressed skippers on the many dhows peacefully floating in the calm sea together with the commercial fishing fleet. It was all so different from what I had seen before. The lovely White Sands Hotel stood amidst the coconut trees and the exotic tropical flowers under a brilliant sun.

Then there was Aden, Port Sudan and Suez where we were always met and shown around and taken shopping. In Aden we were also invited to the Company Mess for lunch, a lovely old house and with many servants who seemed to slide noiselessly on the polished wooden floors. Here, when using the bathrooms, we roared with laughter as they were known as thunder boxes; everything you did reverberated for everyone to hear. One evening our ship group was invited to go out to dinner, it was quite a pleasant enough restaurant in the open air. Some of us ordered chicken and others steak, neither looked very appetising, both meats, being darker and tougher than usual. Whether seriously or in jest our hosts said we were eating camel meat and black birds! You should have seen our faces! These last places were not scenically significant but we always enjoyed going ashore and seeing for ourselves how different cultures lived.

By the time we had reached Port Sudan only the faithful Loveday accompanied me. The other girls had by now found themselves male company on board the ship and they preferred to do their own thing. Jack's friend, a six foot gawky young man came to fetch us in his old sports car to go to the market square for sight seeing. I had often heard of the 'Fuzzy Wuzzies', but thought they were an invention of a fertile mind. Now, they were there in swarms, clad with loose clay coloured blankets, long curly hair all matted. Each and every one of them who was not participating at what we thought was a warrior dance, continuously scratched their heads and bodies with a long handled wooden fork. We were enthralled by the spectacle and without realising we started to perform some of their dancing steps. Hell broke loose, we were chased away by screaming enraged people and how we ran!

Unaware, we had interfered in their religious dance. We jumped into the car, started the car and accelerated far away from all the upheaval. We laughed but we had been scared stiff at the time. On our return on board we too were itchy and scratching and quickly made our way to book baths.

After passing through the Suez Canal it was a leisurely trip to Genoa. Genoa the land of my forefathers was beautiful after the bareness of the last places. The people here were lively and friendly. It was interesting to see that several businesses carried my father's family name. Marseilles was the last port of call before arriving in Gibraltar. At Gibraltar the ship did not dock and when the tender boat appeared there were several passengers. I recognized my parents and my sister Clementina but I had no idea who the two other sophisticated young ladies were. My younger sisters Lottie and Lena had blossomed and were now using makeup and were stylishly dressed and here I was still without using any make up and in my dirndl skirt! My Mummy's greeting of "My goodness Lydia, you look like a missionary!" did not make me overjoyed! Whereas all my sisters were made up and groomed I still had my thick eyebrows that practically joined above my nose and the shadow of a moustache showed on my upper lip. I had been described in Rhodesia as petite, raven-haired and attractive, but when I looked at myself in the mirror I could see a frankly startling face, very dark eyes that somehow did not seem to balance properly although they were friendly, warm and perhaps mischievous, rather a long somewhat crooked nose and a very generous mouth which was eternally smiling.
To top it all I was now conscious and very aware of my hairy self.

I loved being home again and with the family but I no longer really belonged in the spoiled childish world I had left two years before. The hardships and small budget had turned me into a woman.

Mummy was determined to modernize me and before I knew what was happening she had engaged some beautician to come home to take my hairs away. This lady made some kind of concoction with sugar and lemon to which she added some of her spit and turned it into a sort of waxy dough. She took bits and stuck them on my upper lip pulling all my hairs away. Although it hurt there was just a couple of sharp pulls and the result was rather astonishing. Then out came some tweezers and she started to pull the hair off my eyebrows, my nose started running and my eyes watering. I did not think much of all this. Then the lady started to do my legs and no matter how much I screamed and called for help she continued, relishing her work. My cries were heard by the people in the street and the soldiers from the barrack who all came to see who was being murdered. I ended up with a lovely smooth right leg and a very hairy left leg that had to be shaved instead and although free of hair was not as smooth as the other one. Fortunately I had had my hair beautifully cut on board the ship in a fashionable way so I did not have to put up with any more fancy ideas. With my new look I had to have a new wardrobe and this I looked forward to as I only had a couple of new dresses I had made myself. The problem was that they were made so tight and narrow at the bottom so that if I wanted to go to the loo I had to undress completely and what was worse I could barely walk. I was no longer comfortable but Mummy and my sisters were delighted.

Christmas was wonderful. All the family together; the lovely festive season food, the friends coming to see me and the lovely happy feeling of belonging once again. It was great to be back at home but I missed Jack. Two letters a week came regularly telling me all he had been doing. Knowing how he hated writing, for since we married I had had to take over all correspondence (including to his family) I reckoned he must really love me and be missing me.

Dad's attitude was absolutely ridiculous. My friend JP had married a few months after I did and he was already a happy dad. One day soon after my arrival, I had gone to the bank for Dad. JP was there and delighted to see me .He was always asking my family after me and concerned for my happiness. He walked me to the car park nearby wanting to know how my trip home had been. As soon as I arrived back home both my parents asked me where I had been. "To the bank and nowhere else, why?" "But you have been with JP!" I had forgotten what it was like in Gibraltar. Someone had seen me as I walked from the bank to the car park and had rung my parents! From then on I was only able to go out with them, my sisters and my friend Yvonne, and even then I noticed that if I went to the cinema Dad would always need to go into town and thus take us and then by coincidence always be at the door when the film was over. One day when the film we had gone to see was boring Yvonne and I decided to go to the Assembly Rooms where there was a tea dance. Having been an assiduous visitor there before my marriage I had many acquaintances and one of them asked me to dance. I was dancing when Dad appeared and made me go home with him! I had been on board the ship on my own and now a married woman I once again had to have a chaperone! I vowed I would never return to Gibraltar on my own again. I knew I was not doing anything wrong and I never cared nor bothered as to what the people might say so I could not understand Dad's behaviour.

Jack wrote that as he was already twenty five and of 'marriageable age' he had started negotiations with his old Company and if his application was accepted we would be transferred somewhere else. I was sad that I would not be able to see the many friends that I had made in Rhodesia again, in particular Agnes and Johnny with whom we had shared a lot of our time. But I hadn't been really happy there. So I was keeping my fingers crossed and wishing hard that Jack could be re-instated. Finally, after three months in Gibraltar I received a telegram — no computers then - saying "Well, are you coming back to me? We are going to Nairobi, Kenya." I quickly made preparations to join him and once again travelled on one of the Union Castle Line ships. There was an elderly South African couple that befriended me and I often sat with them. One day there was a dance on deck and the Paul Jones music started to play. We had to make two circles, the ladies on the outside going clockwise and the gentlemen inside going anti-clockwise. When the music stopped, you had to dance with whomever was in front of you. It happened that I had an African gentleman and I danced for a while with him. He was very nice and educated but when I returned to sit with the South African couple they told me to go and have a bath before I could join them once again! Such a rude and abhorrent attitude put me off them completely. Later on I was told they were Afrikaners mainly of Dutch descent and that was the way they behaved in their apartheid. It had not been that bad in Rhodesia.

Chapter 10

KENYA

Jack was waiting for me in Mombasa and it was so funny to see his face when he saw me. "What have they done to you Ly?" he asked me when he noticed how sexily dressed and made up I was. On the train to Nairobi I was brought up to date as to what had happened and the way I had to act in accordance with the Company rules and regulations. I needed to have visiting cards printed and once this was done I must call both on the manager's wife and the chief engineer's wife, leave the cards and then they would ask me to tea. That day I would need to take them a bouquet of flowers!

We had a house for the time being while some older and more established members of the staff were away on leave. Once the family returned we would have to vacate. I listened and agreed to all. We were both so happy to be together under the great, clear skies of Africa where the far away noises of the tom-toms mingled with the birds twitting and the frogs croaking as if preparing like Gigli, the famous Italian tenor, for an opening night. You felt a tingling sensation, excitement and awareness here; somehow, I felt I would be very happy.

The house allocated to us was lovely and had a big garden. The two servants, one a cook/houseboy Moya, and the other a shamva/laundry boy Simon were smiling and friendly. In Nairobi they spoke Swahili while in Rhodesia it was 'kitchen kaffir' which was really like pigeon English and easy to understand, Nairobi was much more sophisticated and modern too. There were many hotels and clubs whereas Salisbury only had one wonderful super deluxe five star hotel Meikles (almost as well known as Raffles Hotel in Singapore) and the hotel store which was the equivalent of a Harrods in Africa. Unfortunately we had never been able to afford even a soft drink there. "Are you married or do you live in Kenya?" was the fashionable question in Nairobi which somewhat illustrated what life was like.

Our house in Dagoreti Corner was lovely, nicely furnished with a gorgeous garden beautifully kept by dedicated Simon. My problem was that if I really wanted to make myself understood I would have to learn Swahili. It was also the way I could bargain whenever I went to the market which was apparently the 'sport' expected. I loved it here and all the junior members of the staff were very friendly too. Our finances had improved tremendously but I had very little to do and was bored so I found myself a job at a second hand store and car hire firm. It was a privately owned business belonging to Mr. Kerr, an Englishman as was Mr. Wallwork, the chief salesman,with three African boys and me in the office. I enjoyed my work.

The Company Jack worked for was structured very much like the Army. Jack and I were at the very bottom end of the ranks. Although Jack had been recruited at the age of sixteen, and had worked until he was just over twenty two with the Company, he had lost all his seniority when the Company was nationalized in Rhodesia so his working time counted only from age twenty five. We were often asked out to parties and as was the custom in Gibraltar, I used to serve Jack with all the things I liked before serving myself. The other wives objected to this and since Jack sometimes complained that he had missed some delicacy he liked I stopped doing this and made him get his own food.

One evening we were asked by one of the senior employees to dinner at his home. His wife was very uncouth, had no table manners and poked the knife into her mouth. I was aghast since by what Jack had told me, she had the right to come into my house and if necessary correct me! How could she when she had no culture or manners? As soon as we got home I asked Jack what he had to do to get on in the Company. "I have to take a Company exam, one section covering their rules and regulations. "Well, get them and we shall study them. I do not intend having people like these telling me what to do" I said. Jack was beginning to object when I continued "Better not think about it too much for I shall not stay here with you!"

With all the books at home Jack started his studies and I often helped him out by asking questions and so forth. I too was learning all we were entitled to. We both discovered that in accordance with these rules when Mr Sylam, the previous tenant of our house, went away on leave he had ceased to have any rights to the house. The house should have been ours to keep throughout our stay. However, since Jack had accepted the arrangements there was nothing we could do.

One day, while both Jack and I were at work (Jack did rotation duties) Mr Sylam had returned and by the time we both got home he was installed in our spare room. I hated the idea of sharing the house with a strange man and most particularly when both boy servants started to follow his orders and not mine. I kept objecting to this intrusion and asked Jack to do something about it. I waited patiently, until one morning while Jack was on night duty and not yet home, I met Mr Sylam in his underpants going to the bathroom. As Father Mondejar used to say about me I was very nice if happy but when annoyed there was no stopping me. Somehow I used to gain strength and courage that pushed me to do what had to be done. I got into the car and drove to the manager's office and asked to be seen.

No doubt surprised, for he was a feared man who very few junior members liked, he condescended to see me. I entered his office. He was writing and continued to do so never answering my morning greetings. I stood in front of his desk. He looked up and said "Put your arms behind your back while talking to me." "Why, I am not a school girl" I replied. "You are very rude, to what school did you go?" "To a private school the English call a public school like most probably you too went to. I speak English, Spanish, French and Portuguese. I had a nanny, took dancing and piano lessons" I replied. Astounded by my answer he looked up and said "What do you want?" "I want Mr Sylam to leave the house or different accommodation for us" I replied. He then said "When my wife and I got married…." I did not let him continue "Excuse me, sir, perhaps in the English tradition and education it is accepted to have a young married woman left while the husband is on night duty to sleep where another man, a stranger, is next door. I also do not like seeing strange men in their underpants which I saw this morning. Why, I have never ever seen my father like that. In any case, according to the rule book Mr. Sylam should have forfeited his house when he went on leave." The stern look on his face made me tremble but I stood my ground anxiously waiting to hear what he would say "Um, very well Mrs Armstrong, I shall see what can be done." To my surprise he got up walked to the door, opened it for me and said goodbye.

When I returned home from work and told Jack what I had done he was most angry with me. "What have you done? What repercussion will there be?" and so on. I did not see much of Mr Sylam for the next few days. Shortly afterwards Jack was told that the manager wanted to see him. When Jack arrived at the office in a different area from where he worked he was greeted with "How is your wife, is she feeling better? I am happy to inform you that alternative provisional accommodation has been found for you at the Woodlands Hotel. You can move any time you want". A thrilled Jack rang me at the office and that very same day we moved into our new home.

Woodlands Hotel was privately owned by Dr and Mrs. Thornton, whose daughter Elizabeth was a dance pupil of mine as I already had started giving lessons. The hotel stood in beautifully kept grounds. We had been allocated a lovely big bedroom with bathroom ensuite. The room had two bay windows facing the grounds. It was quiet and peaceful. The premises had a big comfortable lounge, dining-room and bar where all the guests met for sundowners. During weekdays we had breakfast and dinner while at weekends and holidays we would have all meals. If by any chance we were not to be in for meals we had to notify reception. The guests staying there were all extremely friendly and nice. We enjoyed the sense of humour of a Scottish woman doctor and Irene

Richter a South African lady slightly older than me who worked for the American Embassy and her visiting boy friend Sam Rose who was a bookmaker, and a charming person. We were to become firm friends.

Not feeling very well I went to the Company's doctor, a lovely young, good looking Irish man. I had pains in my chest. The nurse helped me out of my blouse and brassiere. I quickly covered my breasts. "My dear, Dr Mark will have to look at you!" Blushing profusely going all hot and bothered I meekly agreed. I could not look at the Doctor's face. "How many children have you got Mrs. Armstrong?" he asked. "Why doctor, I have none" I replied. "Shame on you. You are too much of a woman not to have children!" he replied. "And what do I do if they don't come doctor?" 1 inquired. "You mean to say you do want them?" "Of course we do!" "Well, let me check you!" "Oh no you won't, you are too young and too nice looking!" "OK then, I will send my older brother to check you!" When the older brother came I nearly passed out, he was better looking than his brother and with mischievous twinkling eyes. Reluctantly I took off my clothing and since I was so terribly embarrassed covered up my face with the pillow. Once the examination ended I had to stay still for a while until I settled down. I was covered with red blotches all over my chest and face. The doctor could not understand why I had not conceived since other than a slight prolapse of the womb all was fine with me. I was strong and healthy. Apparently only the breast glands were swollen.

When I got home Jack wanted to know what had happened and when 1 told him he wanted to have a look and see what the doctor had seen. When I refused saying that he was not a doctor, he kept on reminding me he was my husband but no matter what he said I was adamant.

On my twenty-third birthday Jack, remembering his promise, arranged a twenty-first birthday party for me at Chez Dave, a lovely night club. By then I had many young Kenyan friends who came to my dance and fitness classes which I held at the Casa de Portugal, and they all came to celebrate with us. It was a wonderful treat and I honestly believed I was two years younger than I really was.

Soon after I started my dance classes I was asked to dance at one of the leading hotels there. Jack had agreed that I could participate as long as he too was able to attend and was not on night duty. I went to see the organizer and once all was confirmed he asked me what was my fee. Surprised, I asked him how much would he pay. The amount he stated was almost as much as my office salary. "Fifty pounds?" I exclaimed. "Well, OK, make it sixty pounds and a table for four!" Without even trying I had become 'The Brilliant Spanish Dancer Ana Lydia' and a professional too. From then on I participated in many shows at Chez Dave, The Stanley Hotel and The National Theatre. I loved being recognized and known.

Dr Mark called Jack and I to his surgery. As we had been trying to start a family without success he suggested that perhaps I should undergo surgery. Jack would not hear of it. He could not stand the thought of my going to hospital! I was devastated and felt that I was a failure as a woman, I was useless. Fortunately I always rally round quickly from adversity and I was soon real busy and more active at regular dancing appearances.

Unfortunately the situation in Nairobi was rapidly changing. Villages were being ravaged by the Mau Mau; houses were being robbed and people, both Africans and whites were being killed. It was no longer safe to go to all the beautiful places such as the Rift Valley past a little church that was built by the Italian prisoners of war while actually building the road and where we often went for picnics, Lake Naivasha the home of thousands of beautiful Flamingos in different shades of pink, Thika slightly closer to where we lived for our Sunday tea, or to the Langa Langa car races which Jack was always keen to go to.

On one occasion, while at work in the office a couple with a young child came in. The child was enjoying with relish a lollipop and I had to control myself from actually grabbing the sweet to eat it myself. When they left, I told Mr. Kerr who suggested for me to go and buy one if I felt so strongly about it. To my amazement I felt I only wanted the girl's. Another time in the middle of the night I woke up Jack to tell him I fancied some artichokes. He was really rude and uncaring I thought, so unlike myself I started to cry. The next day I went to the market, bought artichokes, borrowed the office kettle and when at the hotel cooked and ate them. I was revoltingly sick. Next day at the office in spite of my having washed the kettle very well several times I could not drink the tea or coffee finding the taste disgusting. What was even more astonishing was the fact that I, who adored ice-cream, no longer wanted any and instead I would wait eagerly for the bar to open to get and drink a beer.

I decided to talk this over with Irene who said that I might be having a false pregnancy. I then asked the woman doctor who recommended I went to see my doctor. Dr. Mark examined me and then said "Congratulations Mrs Armstrong we are pregnant!" "But how can I, you said I would need surgery" I said. He started asking questions and finally worked out that I was four months pregnant but he wanted me to go for weekly checkups. Jack felt so contrite that he had lost his temper with my peculiar behaviour and did not know what to do for me to make up for it. When the hotel guests started congratulating us and management found out we were very kindly told that no children or animals were allowed there so eventually we would need to go to other accommodation. We informed the Company who agreed to look for a house for us.

There was no telephone service to Gibraltar at that time but Jack somehow managed with Head Office and Spanish cooperation to get a line through to my parents. It was lovely hearing them but the emotions and bad line did not make it easy for them to understand and so we followed up by sending a telegram, the only means of quick communication at that time. My parents replied overjoyed and saying that a member of the family would be coming over for the event.

Our friends Sam and Irene made it possible for us to find and get a house which was situated in Kabete district. Sam, aware that we needed the holding deposit to secure the house came and said he had bet on a horse in our name and it had won. No matter how much I refused the money, as I had not given him any to make the bet, he insisted it was ours. The house stood in some lovely grounds on top of an incline with tall impressive iron gates making the premises all very quiet and secluded. We felt quite safe. We had a houseboy/cook named Edward and a shamva/kitchen and laundry help Miles. Edward was a friendly, happy person who loved dressing up according to the job he was undertaking. He wore a long green coat during the day time; and for housework it was covered with a huge striped apron. He loved playing the radiogram while he polished the wooden floors with sheepskins tied onto his feet. He would sway and twirl as if on skates; imitating a ballet dancer doing his jetes and arabesques. This operation was a pleasure to watch; he was so quick, skilled and graceful. When Edward cooked, he did so almost to cordon bleu standard, undertaking any kind of recipe which I had demonstrated once before or read to him. Edward was unable to read but he had the most brilliant memory I have come across. He liked to wear a tall cook's hat and a snow white apron, and fortunately was impeccably clean. At nights, after he had finished his housework including the dhobi, he would change into a long white coat and hat, or don a red fez with a black pompom, just as his moods dictated. He was always such a vain and dandy person.

Chapter 11

OFFSPRING

I was seven months pregnant when my sister Clementina arrived at Mombasa where I had travelled to meet her. When I left Nairobi I had had a scarcely noticeable tummy, but by the time I got to the docks I looked quite affluent. My sister took a look at me and laughed. I had always been so vain about my figure! When I informed Mr. Kerr that I was having a baby and that my sister was coming to Nairobi he suggested that if Clementina was willing I could train her and she could take over from me. Mr. Kerr had a very good friend and client John Berigliano. He was the chef in the Avenue Hotel and perhaps because he was Italian he became very friendly with both Jack and I. He had been married to an English woman who had one day run away with an Indian boyfriend. He had then befriended a pregnant lady who had been deserted by her husband so John was taking care of her as he wanted to have a family.

She gave birth to a baby boy but after John had spent so much money on her over the pregnancy and birth of the baby, her husband re- appeared and took them both away. John was devastated but took comfort on seeing Jack so happy and our baby due in a short time. He told me "My girl, if the baby is a boy I, John Berigliano, will be his godfather. OK?" I just laughed. Clementina took over from me at the office but I continued to give my private classes until practically the last moment.

A couple of months before my baby was due Edward came, said goodbye, and left without any explanation. We were very sorry as we had all become very fond of him. A week or so later he appeared accompanied by an askari who showed us my husband's old watch and asked if it was ours. It seemed that our Edward had appropriated the watch and although we did not want to pursue the matter, the policeman politely but firmly informed us that we had to go to court. Unfortunately Edward was taken away for a short term as Her Majesty's guest, grinning happily he said "Never mind, and do not worry Memsahib and Bwana, Edward will soon come back and be your good boy again!" A new boy James replaced Edward and although he said he could cook he was really disastrous. Asked if he knew how to make bread and butter pudding he said yes but when he brought it to the table pieces of bread were floating in the milk. He had forgotten to put in the eggs! Another day he roasted a chicken before he had gutted it. It was brought to the table all golden brown and appeared very appetizing. We thought he had stuffed it and were commenting that things were indeed improving when Jack on starting to carve realized that James had left in all the entrails. We would have sacked him on the spot but since I was getting nearer to the birth of my child and he was otherwise a good, honest boy and hard working too, we kept him on.

When John found out what had happened he thoroughly enjoyed the joke but then became very worried. I was to be a mother soon and mothers-to-be had to be well fed so as to have good (and plenty) milk for the baby. From then on everyday either he or one of his employees would come and deliver delicious food to the house and no matter how often we told him not to do so, the lobsters, roast cuts, ham etc continued to arrive.

Clementina enjoyed life in Africa and I suppose the freedom she would never have had in Gibraltar. John, who was in his mid forties and divorced, started to date her. We liked John very much and thought him to be a good man but not as a date for my barely twenty-one-year-old sister. He actually reminded me physically of my Dad as he was of the same stature and build and had the same kind of smile and twinkle in his eyes. John however had a broken nose from his boxing days. He also spoke with an accent even though he boasted proudly he was the first English Italian. His parents had emigrated to England and he was born there! He had a terrific sense of humour and was a lot of fun so I could understand Clementina wanting to go out with him. I really need not have worried for soon after there were many young suitors hanging around and all was fine.

One morning, when we were peacefully enjoying some music, we heard lots of noise, people running, whistles blowing. Jack, followed by his women, opened the door and looked to see what was happening. The police in force with a fleet of cars were there, English police officers and local Askaris. "What is happening?" asked Jack.

"Go in, we are raiding the area. Don't worry, everything is fine!" they said. We stood by the window looking. The houseboys were all running about with the police chasing them, quite a lot of activity. When normality returned, the officer in charge rang our bell and asked Jack to go with him. We were all surprised when we learned that although our boys were not involved in any Mau Mau activities they were involved in making skokian, a very potent drink, at the back of our garden and next to their living quarters. No wonder our servants had had so many friends and visitors! The making of this drink was forbidden. We promised the authorities we would keep an eye on the boys and make sure it would not happen again. We heard later that this raid, the first down town was part of Operation Anvil. The Mau Mau situation, now already causing damage in the town area, had in fact got so out of control that troops from the UK under General Sir George Erskine were now in Kenya.

In the early hours of the morning of March 30th, 1953 while Jack was still away on night duty I started to have labour pains. Now the time was near I panicked even though I had gone through the natural birth course, the first patient to do so in Nairobi, I forgot what to do. With my sister Clementina comforting me we waited for Jack's arrival. Poor Jack, tired as he was from his night duty did not know what to do or say. Eventually he took me to Dr. Mark who checked me and told me to go back home, have a bath, take some lunch and go for a walk.

I did as he said and when I reached the bottom of the driveway just by the gates, I could not move any more. It was 2.30pm. A nervous Jack and sister drove me to the Princess Elizabeth Hospital where, in the delivery room, I was guarded by four special policemen. Terrorism had struck the country in full, and all the mothers and new-born were given extra protection, as killing and abduction of same for use in their final Mau Mau oaths and rites was a primary requisite. The Mau Mau would cut up certain parts of the women and particularly babies bodies and proceed to eat them afterwards. Thus they turned to cannibalism, ceasing to remain civilized and thus commit the atrocities they did. They took six oaths and this was the final one of them.

By five o'clock in the afternoon our beautiful daughter was born. Tired but extremely happy I waited for Jack to come and see me. He had been in such a state that I asked my sister to take him home. When he walked into my room he looked awful. When the hospital Sister jokingly said "Mr. Armstrong, it was not you who had the baby!" My sister in all seriousness replied "He has been going through awful pains all the time!" The first visitor I had was John Berigliano carrying a bouquet of flowers bigger than him. He looked at our daughter and then said "Never mind, it is a girl. I, John, will not be her godfather but I shall give her christening party."

A friend of ours, a chief inspector of police in charge of the dogs training department came with a lovely Alsatian dog, Lancer. Lancer had proved to be too friendly, playful but no good for the work required by the police. His appearance was quite fierce and he would prove useful to frighten away intruders. Lancer was really a silly dog, but tremendously good and affectionate with our baby who was to find in him a faithful protector and playful friend. It was rather amusing to see Lancer, so inoffensive, barking playfully at some unknown caller who on seeing him would run away in fearful haste. Should the pursued suddenly stop and turn round he would have seen poor Lancer come to an immediate halt using his rear end as a brake; and then he himself would give a loud howl as he returned to the safety of home, his tail between his legs.

Every week I had to take the baby to The Lady Northey Home for check ups and it was like this that I befriended another young mother Betty, who had also been at the Princess Elizabeth hospital with me having her baby son. Her husband Philip was in the colonial service and like Jack, was a junior too. We had lots in common and often went to each others homes for tea and other social activities.

After much thought and discussion we finally agreed on our baby's names. She was to be named Lyana Patricia Mary (Lyana composed by Jack with the Ly from the first two letters of Lydia and Ana my first name). Father McCambridge of St Austin's Parish Church would be christening her. John quickly reminded us that he would be providing the christening party and that all I had to order was her christening cake. His generosity knew no bounds. Having asked a number of friends from the Company, the business circle, and artistic group to our home I was quite petrified when by the time we left for the church no food or drinks had arrived. What, just a cake for so many people? I should not have worried. By the time we returned we were greeted by a maitre'd in tails greeting me and the guests and showing us into the house. John excelled himself. There was plenty of champagne and delicious little canapes, cakes and sweets. Our manager was astounded at such abundance and exclaimed that this lovely get together was like the old Company had been. He was very friendly after this. Fr. McCambridge came to the party with Fr. McGoldrick, a jolly Irish priest. When this latter one was asked what he wanted to drink and he said whisky, he was poured a glass and then handed the bottle which he jokingly placed inside his cassock pocket. He then retrieved it but we laughed and told him to keep it and drink to our daughter's health.

One of Jack's Company friends started coming over to our house quite regularly always with some excuse regarding work or sport. He was an athlete and also played football as goalkeeper for a local team. His name was Bill. What we did not realise was that he was interested in my sister, and was trying to get into our good books. My sister also liked him and after their first date alone together, she informed us on her return, that Bill had asked her to marry him and that she had said yes. We had to tell our parents. Dad was concerned and asked Jack to find out all concerning his future brother-in-law. Jack's attitude was rather logical, if the chief engineer had wanted Bill for his daughter, he must be good enough for Clementina! So their wedding followed the christening. Once again it was Fr.McCambridge who officiated and the reception was held at home in great style.

The owners of our house who up to now had lived in Thika wished to return to their house in Kabete where they felt they would be safer and once again we had to start looking for a house. This time we were in luck and found a lovely, rambling house on magnificent grounds in Hurlingham Road. Unfortunately there weren't as many neighbours as in Kabete but it suited us with Lyana and her playful dog Lancer. We named it The Barn because of its simple lines but it was certainly bigger than the previous one. As always Irene and Sam were only too willing to help since Clementina now had her own home and a new husband to take care of.

James did not want to come with us to the new house and frankly with his lack of culinary know-how I wasn't too sorry to see him go. Miles, by now quite fond of the m'toto (Lyana) and enjoying pranks with Lancer did not hesitate to come.

Later my sister took James as her servant since she knew he was an honest person. In fact he took great care of her when she was having problems with her pregnancy and had to stay at home requiring a lot of rest. It was therefore with surprise that we had her visit our home saying that there had been another raid and that the police had taken James away. Jack and I accompanied her to the police station and saw the inspector in charge. My sister was very upset that he had been taken away and explained like we did what a good and caring person he was. The inspector looked strangely at us and said "Instead of asking for James' release you should all go to church and thank God that you are all well and alive. You have all been very lucky as we have found all seven scars on James' foot that proves he is a fully fledged Mau Mau and he didn't kill you because he didn't get the order to do so".

Justin was our new cook/houseboy. He was not a Kikuyu from the tribe that was predominant in the Mau Mau so we felt more at ease with him. Justin was an excellent cook, he could read and was therefore able to follow some of our Gibraltarian recipes. We had a very good Gibraltarian friend Alberto who was stationed there as the Attorney General. We loved having him visit us as he always had great stories to tell and would entertain us and the other guests. Alberto's favourite meal, kidneys with sherry, was Justin's piece-de-resistance so one night we had it prepared for the main course. I wanted everything to be welcoming and nice so I told Justin that a bwana mkubwa sana (a big man, meaning important) was our main guest for dinner. When the door bell rang and Justin answered, he opened but quickly shut the door. As no one came in I asked what had happened. Justin replied "Memsahib, hapana bwana mkubwa sana, bwana kidogo sana!" (M'am it was not a big man but a very small man!) When I opened the door there was Alberto in all his official regalia, pin striped trousers, dark jacket, bowler hat and rolled umbrella on his arm. Alberto is not a tall man; he is lovely and chubby with a marvellous sense of humour and an electric personality. He was the first one to laugh at why our house boy had closed the door in his face.

Alberto told us the following story regarding the Africans and their superstition and how they would believe anything that had been told them, whether bad or good, so intensely so that with their power of auto-suggestion they would make it happen.

One of Alberto's servants, Szusu, had been told that the following Friday at three in the afternoon he would be dead from a wasting fever. The boy was at the time healthy. Alberto was told of the prediction. When Szusu did not return to the house for his chores, Alberto went to investigate and found him making preparations for his death. Alberto reiterated that nothing would happen to him, he was fine and strong, but a few days later, Szusu ceased to eat and had an extremely high fever. Alberto was shocked, how could an otherwise sensible boy have become a victim of such auto-suggestion?! Alberto was determined to do something about it and went to see a local friend used to such happenings who would help him.

A big crowd of mourners-to-be had accumulated by Szusu's quarters at the back of the house waiting for the poor sick man to die at the time forecast. Alberto and his friend marched into the servants' quarters and sent everyone away saying "It is a lot of nonsense your being here; it has been proved that Szusu will not die; so ku-enda upesi, ku-fanya kazi- -go away and get on with your work." The spectators did not move. Alberto then said "Szusu was supposed to die at three o'clock and it is already four and he is fine!" Everyone spoke at once. Then one rushed to the sick man's side and found him breathing with difficulty but still alive. Szusu, in a weak voice and fully content to pass away; pointed to his watch, "Such little time left" he wailed. Alberto and his friend marched in and in a strict voice ordered Szusu to stop that nonsense. "Your watch has stopped, you can see Big Ben (the grandfather clock in the hall) it is already after four!" Szusu was not to be deceived so he asked his friend to go and check the Big Ben clock that was always so reliable. The hour was confirmed: and lo and behold, there was Szusu up and about laughing and so happy at having discovered the announced prophesy wrong. Alberto had to remember to put his clock back an hour that night.

Just before Christmas 1953, when I had returned to my dancing and keep fit classes, I could then take Lyana with me, I got very sick with amoebic dysentery. The cure at that time was a liquid diet, M&B tablets and bed. People from the Company rallied round and took Lyana out and also visited me, often coming for tea or sundowners with Jack. Lyana herself got very sick with vomiting and diarrhoea but at first it was thought to be teething. She already had four teeth by her third month, but it turned out to be poisoning from some pods that had fallen into her pram and which she had sucked. She had to be taken to the Children's Hospital as she was dehydrated. Lyana returned home before she was completely cured. There had been a polio outbreak and a couple of children had been taken into hospital. A couple of days later my sister took me to Dr Mark for a check up. I was weak and was dragging my leg; I had also been suffering from bad headaches. Dr Mark saw me, went out of his office and returned with his brother and another doctor. They made all sorts of tests on my leg, hitting it with a small rubber hammer and quietly informed me that I had polio.

I could not believe them. Dr Mark stopped all my complaints and procrastination by telling me that unless I behaved, went home, and did all he told me, I would be sent to the Infectious Diseases Hospital. I went crazy. Here I was at the height of my dancing career, young with a lovely baby. It could not be happening to me.

It is funny how you never appreciate all you have until something goes wrong with your life. All I now wanted was to get well. My illness had repercussions with many members of the staff who, including my husband, had to go into quarantine as they had been visiting me when the disease was at its worst. A physiotherapist came regularly, friends sent flowers and magazines and for once I did everything I was ordered to do. Poor Jack carried me to the bathroom, and did everything he could to make my life easier. I promised that if I walked and danced again I would produce a benefit show for the Red Cross Polio Fund.

At long last I was convalescing. I was allowed to go into the garden and enjoy the sunshine and fresh air. I had been left with a slightly dropped foot and thinner calf. Justin had arranged the daily menus himself and Miles had cooperated with him helping in the kitchen. I noticed however, that a bottle of liquor was missing and after commenting it to Jack I decided to tackle the boys. I had already noticed the visitors' half full glasses quickly disappearing as soon as they were put down and suspected that one or both boys were hoarding all the remains together.

I called Justin and Miles and asked where the missing bottle was. No one knew anything about bottles. "Very well, I shall soon find out." They stood there disbelieving and grinning mischievously "O.K. Memsahib Mkubwa will speak to the White Spirits and they will tell me who has taken the bottle." They were now looking rather uncomfortable. I went to the kitchen and half filled a glass of water, then with great ceremony I laid two pieces of white thread on the surface, and again, two pieces of black thread across the white ones. Alongside I put a candle holder with two red candles which I proceeded to light while chanting "Eenie meenie mynie mo, tell me white spirit who's to go." By then neither one of them was looking too happy, Miles had a funny colour too. 1

turned round to him sharply and before I could say anything else he said "Stop, memsahib, I found it, I found it, I will bring it back upesi, upesi."

When I told Jack he laughed but then forbade me to do any such thing again. I did not mean any harm and only made up in a rather theatrical way what I thought would impress them after hearing Alberto's tale. I accepted Jack's advice and then I realised my folly when I became quite a celebrity with my boys telling all their friends that I was a witch doctor and wanting me to make white magic.

After telling my dance pupils and some of my artist friends who had previously performed with me, my intention of putting on a show for the Red Cross they all rallied round to help me. We started by making a competition for the poster that would be used. It was going to be a musical production of a journey to different countries at fiesta time, so what better name than to call it 'Gay Fiesta' which in those days had a completely different connotation from nowadays. I had a lovely English gentleman Michael Watson directing it, Yvonne Faithful, Benny Goodman (not the dance band leader) and Fred Hicks taking the principal parts with me. Jack as always when I danced helped in everything he could, including biting his nails, while I performed. I think he knew my dances as well as I did! Opening night had all the dignitaries who although invited guests donated a good sum of money. We gave several other performances which made up a tidy amount of money for a good cause.

.

After this show I was asked to perform for the army. A lot of young soldiers had also been stricken with polio and they thought that seeing me dance again would stimulate them. General Sir George Erskine was there too with his staff officers. I never had such a great audience. I came out with a rose in my hand to do my version of 'Carmen.' I stamped and twirled, played the castanets while I held the rose between my teeth, and then as the music ended, I kissed the rose and threw it to the audience. As the General himself caught it, his men went crazy clapping, whistling and calling "Ana, show us your leg!" The General, a very handsome gentleman, with beautiful green eyes, came back stage and when introduced to me, got hold of my hand, and looking straight into my eyes, kissed it. I thought I would faint. Young and silly as I was I did not want to wash my hand after the General's kiss.

The Mau Mau were getting more and more daring, killing their own people as well as white. They were getting closer to town and we were issued police whistles and a gun. It was fine while Jack was at home but the week he was on night duty and I had the gun I could barely sleep. I kept checking to see if the safety catch was on. The whistle hanging round my neck, I would get up time and time again to ascertain that I had double locked the door from the living area to the sleeping area. We were told that our servants would not come to our aid because if they left their quarters they would be the first to die. So I would be on my own. During the daytime if we were in the garden and saw a group of Africans we were warned to go inside the house straight away and lock everything up. It was a stressful way to live.

The old, strict, but by now friendly — at least with us – manager had one day left his home full of vigour to play a game of golf and right in the middle of the game had had a stroke. He was taken to the hospital but he never recovered. It was quite a shock and sad to see how few of the Company's people attended the funeral. The new manager and his wife were quite nice and life continued just the same. The King is dead, long live the King!

Our time in Kenya was slowly coming to an end; and then to my surprise and happiness I discovered I was pregnant again. I was still dancing professionally, Irene and Sam usually coming with us to make the foursome. John Berigliano came to visit us regularly. One afternoon he arrived with a brand new, red sports car. He had given up his job at the hotel and now instead of him 'spending money on silly young girls, he had an older woman who was keeping him!' He had been given a Rolex watch, a diamond ring and pin. We had to laugh and could not believe him to be serious. His happiness did not last long. It was obvious that the lady who was spending so much on him also expected him to be her faithful lover and friend. Too jealous she did not let him out of her sight so he was unable to go anywhere or do anything.

The next time we saw him he had no car or any of his finery but was again his happy self. "Lydia" he said, "No matter what I covered up, everything was still old!" Every so often things happened that proved the different backgrounds that Jack and I belonged to. In Gibraltar men were never seen carrying baskets with groceries or pushing prams. These were women things. Yet Jack loved and enjoyed helping me with my shopping and most particularly taking care of his little girl whom he adored.

Lyana was a lovely little girl, very solemn looking and with gorgeous, big black eyes with long curly eyelashes. She was a good baby and other than the time when she had to go to the hospital she was a healthy happy child. When she started to crawl she did it backwards and she was very quick to learn how to stand up, look at you in a superior manner and then laugh. It took her a while to speak other than 'Papa' and 'Mama' but when she finally did it was long sentences and not the usual baby talk. She loved romping about with Lancer, who never left her side. The poor dog allowed her to make sand castles on his back, and put up with practically anything she wanted to do. When he finally had had enough he would roll over, stand up, shake himself, and start running. He ran lifting his four paws in the air, as if jumping, looking more like a deer than a dog.

Our police friend, Terry, often called at our home. He loved Lyana and of course he kept an eye on his silly but nice dog Lancer. This time he came with a huge basket of delicious mangoes. How I enjoy this fruit and what fun reminiscing on the first time I was introduced to it on arrival in Nairobi. I remember Jack telling me, "Look at this lovely fruit, you have to eat it over the bath tub!" "Good Lord, why is that?" I remember peeling the fruit and cutting some slices but the stone had lots of flesh. "Use your hands, Ly, use your hands, see? Like this!" said Jack, showing me. The fruit juices oozed down my chin, I now knew the reason why he had said what he had.

One day Terry sat with us on the back porch, Lyana with her inseparable partner Lancer, squatted with both Justin and Miles. Lyana thought the world of Justin who always came to her rescue. In Kenya there was a fly that laid eggs on the clothing hanging out to dry and these eggs would filter into the skin, particularly the babies', leaving dreadful bumps, nasty looking, full of puss and more eggs which would spread further, so all her clothing had to be ironed on both sides. Justin would lovingly do it for his m'toto as when I started to do it he was upset that I did not trust him. Lyana loved to follow and touch the different insects she saw crawling on the ground, insects that we had never come across before. One day she put her finger in an ant's nest and a red warrior ant bit her. I tried to pull it off but only made her finger bleed. The claws, like a lobster's, tightened even more. Justin came and burned it off with a lighted match. He always seemed to know what to do. It was he who also cut one of those fly lumps off Jack. The three of them made a peculiar picture, Lyana listening to her companions and repeating words, the boys laughing. "Listen, listen, Lyana is having a conversation with the servants!" Terry said. We laughed and answered "Yes, she mimics them very well!" Terry turned round and looked at us with surprise "No, she is speaking Swahili and very well too!" We had not realized it.

One evening while 1 was on my own, poor Lancer started to bark ferociously and then whine in great earnest and once again to bark loudly. This was definitely not the usual barking and growling. I got up to investigate and realized he was outside Lyana's bedroom window. He was barking at someone. I distinctly heard sounds of footsteps and running on the gravel around the house. Suddenly there was a thunderous noise which left nothing to my imagination, bodies crashing against my front door in a joint effort to push it down. I rushed to the window, stuck my head between the iron bars which we had reinforced for protection, and shouted "Taka nini?" On hearing my voice asking "What do you want?" I realized the stupidity of my action. Thoughts, dreadful thoughts, went through my mind. I had not come to Kenya to be killed. I did not want anything to happen to my beautiful daughter. I had forgotten my gun as I rushed to the wardrobe to pick up a wooden clothes hanger, left my bedroom, locking it behind me and rushed to Lyana's locking it too. Then I started to blow the whistle and scream like I had never done before in my life. Soon I heard from outside more whistles blowing, running steps and shouts. The Home Guard had come to my rescue! I was in no state to be left alone. Jack would not be returning from work until early morning, the station could not be left on its own, he was the only one manning it, so an Askari (African policeman) was posted outside the house.

This event marked me. The police said the groups attacking the house had only come to steal. They did take everything they could find and all the fruit and vegetables we grew in our plot, but I knew it had been a failed Mau Mau attack. I was too nervous to enjoy the simple pleasures like before this event. I loved walking around the house after heavy rainfall smelling and enjoying the wet fresh earth, a smell that you never forgot or stopped enjoying particularly after a long dry spell. 1 was too frightened to go far from the house even while still on our own property. My sister Clementina had had a Mau Mau killed in her front garden so all I could think of was to leave and get back to civilization again even though I loved Africa so much.

Soon after this experience I did not feel so well. Dr Mark was worried in case I would miscarry, gave me an injection and said 1 was to stay in bed. He would come and visit me next morning as I had started to bleed a little. The following day, as I got up to fetch Lyana I felt something strange down my leg. I put my daughter back to bed, looked down and saw a little blood and something else. I had had no pain and was not aware of what had really happened. I picked up everything in a towel, dressed myself and Lyana and then drove down to the doctor's surgery. Dr. Mark was really annoyed with me. I had miscarried my baby boy! This was obviously the last straw. Emotionally I was a wreck; I was fine if Jack was with me but in hysterics if left alone particularly at nights. My friend Loveday from Rhodesia came to stay for a couple of weeks. She wanted to see Lyana and keep me company. Then Irene, who had by this time married Sam, offered to put Lyana and me up whenever Jack was on night duty. They lived in an apartment building which offered more safety. This happened for a couple of months and then, finally, came our departure date with all the farewell parties. No matter what has happened it is always sad to leave a place where in spite of everything I had been very happy, had had my daughter, made so many friends and achieved so many things. I was also leaving my sister and her husband behind.

Our entire luggage packed, and sad goodbyes said to our last but very faithful servants we left Nairobi for Mombasa by train. Even our grocer came to the station loaded with presents. At this point I was so preoccupied. Were we really getting away? Would we reach Mombasa without any mishaps? Half way to Mombasa - Why, oh why, had the train stopped? On investigating we found that a herd of elephants had decided to rest across the railway tracks forcing the engine to stop and wait until they departed. At last Mombasa where we had often driven to on long weekend holidays and enjoyed the smooth white sands and clear blue waters of the Indian Ocean at Nyali Beach Hotel. We went straight from the railway station to the port where we embarked on the 'Warwick Castle' for an eight weeks trip round South Africa.

Chapter 12

SPAIN

The journey was a wonderful tonic for us all. We had forgotten what it was like to relax, to go to bed without having to worry about ghastly things happening. By this time I found I really could not sleep well. I woke up at the slightest noise but by the time we arrived in England my nerves were calmer and I had regained some of my spirit and joy for living.

The trip South from Mombasa took us to Zanzibar, Dar-es-Salaam, Mozambique City, Beira, Lourenco Marques, Durban and a special trip to the impressive Valley of a Thousand Hills in Zululand. We continued to East London and Port Elizabeth before a few days spent in Cape Town where we visited the majestic Table Mountain. Once we had rounded the Cape into the South Atlantic we headed to the picturesque island of St Helena, where Napoleon spent his last years in exile. There we were met by another Gibraltarian girl, Denise, married to a friend of Jack's also working for the Company. We were there for only a few hours but it made for a very welcoming stop over. At Ascension Island no passengers were allowed ashore. However, the ship was invaded by visitors from the island to buy items from the ship's shop and for the ladies to have their hair done as all the ship's facilities remained open. These were special arrangements made for the islanders, all of them Company employees, many of them Jack's colleagues, as the infrequent calls of passenger ships were the only physical communication with the outside world. There was only one further stop at Las Palmas in the Canary Islands before reaching England.

In England, we went to the North to visit Jack's family. Dad Armstrong was especially delighted with his little granddaughter. They had lost their one and only daughter when she was seven years of age and I think this made our child particularly precious. Lyana looked very much an Armstrong and her appearance was similar to Pat, the lost daughter. We had gained quite a long spell of leave and planned to return to London for orders and then make our way to Gibraltar.

We had brought our slightly used Morris Oxford with us from Nairobi on the ship from Mombasa. It was a reliable car and held many happy memories for us; though never a patch on our old dilapidated Petargas that had given us so much pleasure and excitement in Rhodesia. Once in London, Head Office informed Jack that our next station would be Vigo, Galicia, Northern Spain. Knowing then that we would not be returning to England we stayed at the Company's Exiles Club in Twickenham making arrangements for our main luggage to be sent directly to Spain while we would tour Europe on our way home to Gibraltar.

We crossed to France on the ferry and then motored leisurely, finding accommodation wherever it took our fancy. We normally stayed at the 'Routieres' which were clean, comfortable and served excellent food at affordable prices but were rather primitive, generally used by the French lorry drivers, thus their name. I had a funny experience once when I asked for the toilets and following instructions I went in and could not find any. I asked the landlady again and she took me herself, I still could not see any. It was just a hole in the ground with two small platforms to stand on. I found it so difficult that I had to go out into the countryside and find a secluded spot. Sometimes we even stayed at camping sites in our car. But we enjoyed the freedom of travelling as far as we wanted.

It was a pleasure to be back in Spain and knowing that soon we would be seeing the family and showing off our little girl. Lyana was no yet two. Approaching the crossroads at San Roque we noticed a car parked on the other side of the road and a couple of people stopping the cars going our way. Imagine our surprise to find it was my parents who had not been able to resist the temptation of coming and meeting us on the way. Poor Lyana, who could not speak any Spanish, just heard what she thought were screams and started to cry; mummy, all emotional, got hold of her and would not let her go. It was obvious we had reached home!

Finally we decided to drive on to a little restaurant nearby where everyone calmed down and things were more or less normal again. I had forgotten how excitable and noisy the Latins were! When we finally reached my parent's home it was late and we were too tired to do anything else but have baths and go to bed. In Gibraltar we spent the better part of our five months long holiday. The weather was excellent and my parents had plenty of room for us all to be comfortable.

Clementina had remained in Nairobi, and Lena was in Manchester studying physiotherapy and going out seriously with Jon, an Englishman from Devon, who had been evacuated during the war to Canada. Lottie was still teaching at the Loreto Convent and already engaged to her childhood sweetheart James, born and bred in Gibraltar. My brother Winston was already a teenager and still at home. Granny was enthusiastic and loved seeing both Jack and her great granddaughter who took to her immediately. Unfortunately Lyana was very confused with her Granny Danino who was always very demonstrative and excited. Lyana, not understanding any Spanish, was always in doubt as to whether she was being loved or chastised. Auntie Lottie Chan had bought an apartment house just across the road from my parents and lived there with her son.

We engaged a young girl, a school leaver, Angeles, who together with my brother Winston kept Lyana happy and entertained. We all loved going together to the beach and the Alameda Gardens. It was usually in the evenings that Jack and I had quite a hectic social calendar. We also enjoyed the night shows at the Assembly Rooms where some Cubans with very little clothing were performing, all terribly sophisticated for Gibraltar. Lyana went early to bed as was the English custom, something Mummy could not understand and which she criticised continuously by saying "Fancy putting the child to sleep with the sun still shining!"

With the La Linea fair starting in July, mummy insisted on taking her granddaughter. Since it was an evening outing I was very hesitant but finally relented and let Lyana go. They had gone to a late variety show and when they returned in the early hours of the morning Lyana was past her sleep, and so wide awake she would not let us rest. The next time Mum decided to take her out again I accepted as long as Lyana's crib (she had just turned two) would be moved into their bedroom! Mum never asked to take her out again in the evenings!

Unfortunately I started to feel unwell. I was losing weight but my skirts and trousers could not be buttoned up, the waist line was bigger and occasionally I had discomfort and bled. I visited my parent's doctor who, without being a gynaecologist for at the time there were none in Gibraltar, suggested I had a D & C. I felt too bad for the diagnosis to be correct. I went across the border and saw a specialist in La Linea. He diagnosed an ectopic pregnancy and warned that what I had was like having an atom bomb in my pocket ready to explode at any time.

My mother poopood it saying "All the Spanish doctor wants is money!" 1 made enquiries with some friends who gave me the name of a renowned doctor, Doctor Bustamante who had his own private clinic in Malaga. Unknown to Mum I made an appointment and telling her that Jack and I were going to the beach in Spain left for the day. On the way we saw three young men walking in the heat and so stopped and offered them a lift. They were foreign seminarians visiting their Order in Spain for their summer holiday. On the way I started to get bad pains, Jack was worried and told them where we were going. Coincidentally the Nursing Home was very near where they were staying and they helped tremendously by showing us the way beyond Malaga to the clinic. On arrival I was seen by Dr Bustamante himself who said that he would not allow me to return to Gibraltar as I would never reach there. However, if I wanted a Gibraltarian doctor to operate he would allow it. I refused. Blood tests were taken, I was pinned to the bed so that I would not move and they had everything ready to operate even though I wanted to wait for my parents to arrive. The fallopian tube had burst and I was operated on just in time.

I was very well looked after by the nuns and Jack was allowed to stay with me in my room. Fr.Mondejar on hearing I was there came to visit me several times making quite an impression on the nuns who had unsuccessfully tried to get him to visit them. I was not yet fully recovered from the operation when we had to leave in our car for Vigo on the northwest coast of Spain.

We liked the idea of being so close to Gibraltar and we enjoyed Spain. However Vigo was very different from the Andalucia which we loved with beautiful blue skies, and brilliant sunshine during the day, soft breezes and the heavens covered with sparkling stars at night. It was not at all like that. There is no doubt that Vigo and all of Galicia is beautiful. The lovely never ending 'rias' (estuaries) dividing mountains, picturesque scenery, gorgeous sandy beaches, mountains with firs and eucalyptus trees, and fresh air that during the winter penetrated our bodies like knives cutting our flesh.

The finca in Taboada Leal was a beautiful hacienda right in the middle of the grounds that were surrounded by camellias, chestnut trees and marvellous flowers .The stately building stood right in the centre. An apartment here was to be our home for just over a year. The building was divided into five flats and a club house. We also had a swimming pool (that was hardly ever used as it was always rather 'fresh') and tennis courts. The Manager, Mr. Mann, lived in a small but delightful house we all called 'La Casita' in the same area.

One had the feeling in Galicia that it was not Spain where we lived but Scotland with the wailing bagpipes which filled the air with their sad notes making it quite eerie when they played at night. Their dance was the Jota Gallega which again was more like the Highland fling. There were no castanets, no zapateado or clapping and most particularly no 'piropos' the compliments that Andalucians often paid women they did not even know but for some reason or other found attractive. Mind you, sometimes it did not relate to beauty but they were nevertheless funny and usually appreciated. To give you an idea, once when I had just left the hairdressers and thought I looked very good, two young Andalucian gentlemen stopped and looking at me, in their inimitable 'simpatico' way, one said to the other "Que cara, que cara" and I thought, great, at last someone likes my face. But he had not yet finished "Si, que cara esta la vida!" (Cara in Spanish has two meanings - face, expensive — Yes, how expensive life is!)

Mr Mann was a lovely human being, thoughtful and kind. Lyana loved 'Man' as she solemnly called him. Mr Mann was tall and elegant, with a nice kind face and lots of wavy white hair. Lyana was tiny next to him and he enjoyed it when she would run to him and say "Hello, Man". He was nearly at retiring age which was fifty five and he had been living in Vigo for many years. He was well known all over the countryside where he was considered a veritable Father Christmas. He often used to visit people in need to take them goodies and give them financial help. Everyone respected him and gave themselves wholeheartedly to their work. Jack had been posted there to assist Mr Mann in the reorganization of the office, so although financially we were not very prosperous we mixed with a very nice set of people all much above our meagre income level.

Mr Mann was generosity itself. We had a little dinner party to reciprocate the hospitality we had received. All senior members of the expatriate community as well as our Manager came. When the British Consul asked for whisky, which our budget could not provide, Mr Mann getting up from where he sat said "It is OK Armstrong, I will get the drinks" returning shortly after with all the drinks including the whisky on a tray. He had been aware that this guest only drank this beverage and so brought it for us himself. Very frequently he sent us and the other three couples consisting of another junior couple with a child a little older than Lyana, an older couple nearing retirement age themselves and a middle aged couple with a twelve year old daughter, cartloads of firewood, coal and pine for our ancient coal and wood burning kitchen stoves and fuel for our many fireplaces. He made it possible for us to keep warm through the better part of the year. Mr Mann also shared with all of us, including the young bachelors in the Mess, fruit and vegetables from the finca.

When we arrived we inherited Maria the maid, recommended as being a very clean, hard working, capable and reliable person. She was a well made, tall, and strong woman who could cart a whole load of wood or a big shopping bag on her head, balancing everything so placed and walking with great elegance. She could also drink a whole litre of wine with each of her meals! (Which we had to provide in accordance with what she said was the custom there!) She informed me that in Vigo the ladies did not go to the market and that all I had to do was give her a list and in the mornings when she came from her home, she did not sleep in, she would bring everything with her. She was an excellent worker as foretold but she never did what I asked her, politely she would reply "Ah, senoritica, today is not my day for that!" She was so big that I must admit I was rather daunted by her.

The children in the Finca were going to school and Lyana cried wanting to go with them. The other two girls had come straight from England and spoke English only. Lyana having been in Gibraltar was now understanding a lot and speaking a little Spanish. I took her with me to see the nuns at the convent school and they accepted to have her three days a week and would, if I allowed it, use her to interpret for the other two girls? We set off to buy her navy blue uniform, white shirts and panama hat. The shirts with very stiff starched collars gave her rather an old fashioned and grown up appearance. The skirt hung down almost to the ground. She made rather a forlorn picture. Jack and I took her to the school and she went in without looking back even once and leaving me in tears. Our baby was growing up. She hated the days she had to stay home so against my will I asked if she could go all the time. 1 then discovered that most of the time she would slip out of the class unnoticed and go to the playground with whichever class was then enjoying break time!

Although we were always short of cash we were the only staff there to have a car and we generally took Mr. Mann and one other couple for rides in the countryside or to the beach. Every three months we had to leave Spain with our car thus avoiding paying taxes for the automobile. We would cross the border into Portugal and thus kept within the law.

I was discussing with Catherine, an English woman married to a local man, our financial position. When I told her what Jack was earning she was even more amazed, it was more than what they made, she taught English to the Spaniards while Luis taught Spanish to the British people living there and they managed to live very well. How on earth could that be? What did we do? She knew we lead a simple life style. "Ah", she said. "Who does your shopping, how much do you spend on food?" When I told her she was astonished "Why, you are spending daily more or less what I spend for a week!" She then told me to tell Maria I wanted to visit the market with her the next day. What Maria did not know was that Catherine was coming too and taking me to where she did the shopping so that I would get treated properly and not overcharged as perhaps arranged by Maria with them. A week later Maria left our employment and we had plenty of cash to spare!

The next maid was a young woman whom I discovered was ill-treating Lyana. She had a boy friend she wanted to meet with and if Lyana cried wanting to go to the park she would hit her. At home she had been very nice but some of the Spanish neighbours had seen this behaviour and told me about it. There and then, on the spot I asked her to leave.

Finding a servant was not an easy matter as most girls were employed in the factories and fisheries. The priest called us and said that he had an unmarried mother, Josefa, who was desperately looking for work to earn sufficient money to take care of her little boy and old mother. Unfortunately no one would employ her because of her status. He could recommend her, would I give her an opportunity. I agreed and never regretted it; my Spanish neighbours like the baker's wife, drug store employee etc all came to warn me "Senora, do you know who you have given employment to? She, Josefa, is not married and has a boy!"

When I said I did not mind and that we were all very pleased with her they left astounded and in disbelief. How could I take a 'loose woman' into my house?!

The surgery I had had in Malaga took quite a while to heal. No matter what medicine I used the scar was swollen, red, itchy and a great discomfort. I finally found a family doctor, Dr. Requejo, who on seeing it recommended I sunbathe it for a few minutes a day increasing the length of time every two or three days. Weather permitting we would go to the beach but my husband had to stand guard as I wore a blouse and with panties pulled down to bare my tummy to the sun. Once caught like this I was insulted by some old women going by. The Spain of 1955-1956 was a very narrow minded one indeed. One day when I had run out of flour I went to the shop near the finca to buy some. They did not have any and sent me a bit further down the street. Without noticing it I was in the town outskirts wearing my slacks. A group of women obviously realising I was a foreigner and therefore not expecting me to speak Spanish started saying nasty things about me. Their faces were a picture when I told them I was more decent and covered up than they were considering the amount of breast they were showing!

During the time we were in Vigo, both my sisters Lottie and Lena were married in Gibraltar, and Lyana and 1 were lucky enough to attend both weddings and meet again with my sister Clementina who had returned from Nairobi. Jack was also able to spend a Christmas in Gibraltar, the first in six years since I had married, with all the family, as a special gesture from Mr. Mann who had allowed Jack to take a few days off to cover this meaningful season. We weren't to celebrate another family Christmas together for twelve years after this.

A Spanish member of the staff invited us to a dinner party. Jack, who was not in the habit of drinking had one too many and soon was singing flamenco and showing off his bullfighting passes which Dad had taught him. The many Spaniards there cheered and egged him on. I could not believe my eyes, the usual quiet Jack making a show of himself. The worst thing was when next day he came home and very excitedly said that his host who was involved in the organization of local bullfights had told him that they were holding a novillada for charity and wanted Jack to participate. A novillada is a bullfight with young bulls and the bullfighters are not yet master bullfighters. They even had a name for him 'Machaco' which translated into English means 'Mashed'. When I pointed out that they were taking the mickey out of him he argued and made both Lyana and me be the 'bull' by holding coat hangers in our hands and charging towards him. In despair I rang my Dad, "Hi Dad" I said "The Spaniards here are having fun with Jack and want him to bullfight, please have a word with him and stop him". Dad who had been a novillero himself before marrying and wanting one of us to have shown some inclination towards the sport only said "Tell me, tell me where and when, we shall be there!" Fortunately Carlos, the Spanish employee, took him to the farm where they had some young bulls so that Jack could try out before the date of the festival. When Jack returned home he was white and shaking "Ly," he said "The bulls have horns - big horns!" "What the hell did you think they would have, coat hangers?" That was the end of this adventure for Jack but my parents and brother having made the necessary arrangements decided to pay us a visit anyway.

Mum was amazed to see the old fashioned way we had for cooking and heating the bath water, if we did not cook there was no hot water! When I baked anything I had to take it to the bakery next door where for a small fee they would roast my meats or bake my cakes. If only to keep the fire going I needed home help! Mum loved the huge apartment otherwise and the special surroundings. She enjoyed going up to the Castro, a ruined castle on top of the adjoining hill, towering over our finca but mainly she enjoyed the lovely restaurants and shops. My brother, always full of energy romped around the grounds returning with a handful of fruit. "I hope you did not pick them from the tree Winston, we are only supposed to get whatever lies on the ground." "Yes, that is where I got them from" he replied. "Now give me a basket as there are more." When he returned and I saw the amount of fruit in the basket I asked "Are you sure you picked them off the ground? The Manager usually divides what he gets between all of us." Looking a bit shabby, he replied "Well, Lydia, I first shook the tree and then picked the fruit from the ground!" Dad was happy to see that we also had a chicken coop in the grounds. Chickens then were expensive and we used to buy them small and feed them well for our own use. However Josefa had taken time off as the mother had been taken ill and during those ten days Jack and I had to feed the birds. Without intending to we began to call each of them by names, in accordance with their behaviour, so we had a Fatty, a Cocky, and a Bashful and so on. When Dad suggested we took a couple of them to cook with rice he could not understand why we would not eat them!

It was at this time that the Spaniards had brought out on the market very small cars called the Biscuter. This small car weighing only 240 kilos used a motorcycle engine and was Spain's economic 'dream of greatness' in the early 1950's but produced during four years only, being succeeded by the Seat 600. The story goes that once the gear was put in reverse it was impossible to change back and you would often see a stream of these cars all going backwards. From then onwards they became known as 'little Gibraltars' because it was felt that they were 'the shame of Spain'.

Good things soon come to an end, and just shortly after our year was up, we were notified that we were on our way again; this time on transfer to Ascension Island. It was the same place that we passed on our way home from Kenya when I had indiscreetly said "Thank God, we shall not be sent here!" Evidently I had tempted fate! How this unfortunate news came to my notice was rather strange. I was sitting by the kitchen window when the engineer's wife passed by, and after her "Hi there Lydia, how are you doing?" she proceeded to tell me how sorry she was with the news, and before I could ask anything more she had gone off. My next door neighbour was the next one. She came into the house, put her arms around me and said "Oh, Ly, I am so sorry." and quickly left. Mystified I went downstairs where the only telephone was located in the carpenter's shop, and phoned Jack. "Jack, what has happened?" Silence! "Jack, are you there? Has anything happened at home?" "Are you seated?" asked Jack. I really got scared, now I knew it had to be something big. "Ly, we are on the move once again, we are going to Ascension Island!" "What? You must be joking. I know you did engineering work in Nairobi but you are not an engineer and only engineers go there!" "No, it has nothing to do with telegraphy - I think I am going as Harbour Master and Canteen Manager!" In spite of it all I found myself laughing. Jack hated water and did not swim?! When I married I knew full well that we would have to travel around but with a young child and my gynaecological problem where at the first possible notion of being pregnant I would need to consult a specialist I was not too pleased.

Ascension Island then had some 200 inhabitants, all working for the Company. The island is barren, volcanic in origin and situated in the middle of the South Atlantic. The only bit of green was on top of the appropriately named Green Mountain, where there was a small farm where people stationed on the island spent their local ten days holiday a year. Even swimming, my forte was only permitted on certain beaches as there was a great abundance of those toothy creatures, the sharks. The thought of living there was definitely not attractive. I would need to take up sport!

When the local people found out that we were leaving they wanted to write a petition to the manager to stop our going away. We knew from the start that Vigo would be a short stay station, just the sufficient time for Jack to complete the job he had been sent to do. We said our goodbyes to family and friends and left Vigo for England by ship. Mr. Mann and all our friends came to see us off. Just as all the visitors on board were leaving Mr. Mann handed us an envelope saying "God Bless you all and thanks." Imagine our surprise when inside the envelope we found sterling money and a note saying "My dear Armstrong, Just to say thank you for your always cheerful and ready help that you have given — for which I am grateful. I wish you, Lydia and Lyana all happiness in the future. This is for you to buy yourselves something - no thanks please — it is the other way round. Yours very sincerely (and signed) Roderick Mann. PS Don't worry too much about success — go for happiness!"

We were to stay in England for a while as most of the ships gave preference to the 'Round Africa Trip' or to passengers going further than Ascension, so until a suitable vacancy appeared we had to wait. This time we remained in London near the Olympia complex in a private hotel run by a retired army officer and his doctor wife. It was well situated; very comfortable making provisions for a young child, near trains and buses so we were content. Since we were 'in transit', the Company paid all our expenses. For once we had money to spend and enjoy ourselves seeing shows and visiting tourist places. At long last, after a couple of weeks wait it appeared we had been allocated passages on board a Union Castle Line ship. Jack on seeing a public telephone in the foyer of a Cartoon News cinema at Piccadilly Circus took the opportunity to ring up Head Office to get more details. I watched amazed as Jack spoke and did a little dance, a happy look on his face!

We were going to be lucky after all. Someone, clever man, had discovered that Jack spoke Spanish, and so we were to be sent to Rio de Janeiro, Brazil! How very excited and happy about our change of fortune. We thanked God and blessed the chap who had made the language discovery even though it meant that Jack would be faced with an entirely new language, Portuguese! Jack would be going to Brazil in yet another capacity, that of a commercial representative for the Company. By having to learn another language he would then be in a position to take his final exam that would open the door to promotion and a successful future. He had successfully taken his first exam in Nairobi so we were confident that this time he would also achieve his aim. As far as I was concerned I had spoken Portuguese fluently in Madeira so I would only need to practice it. So on a dreary grey day in November 1956 we left England towards the sun and an entirely new life that was to surpass any expectations.

Petargas- the Hillman Minx

At Victoria Falls

Dancing at the Caledonian Society Ball, Salisbury, Rhodesia

Forces Christmas variety show in Nairobi

The Barn-our home during the Mau Mau troubles

Four generations- 1956

ACADEMY OF DANCING
CENTRE OF NAIROBI
ANA LYDIA
E.D.A. CLASSIC: H.J.D.M. FLAMENCO SEVILLA.
C de S. PORTUGUESE

EAST AFRICA COMMAND

presents

LEREVUE

and Devised

...ANT

KENYA
COMMAND THEATRE
EAST AFRICA COMMAND
presents

"TELEREVUE"

—— with ——

CINDY RYDER
ANA LYDIA
WYNN DAVIES
PATRICK POR...

—— with ——

SUPPORTING CAST
FORTY

Nightly at 9

Mon., 31st Mar., to Sat., Apr. 5...

Matinee :

Sat., Apr. 5th. ...

Polio victim
dances to
help others

Four months ago Ana Lydia, a
Spanish dancing teacher, lay in
bed stricken by poliomyelitis
Her right leg was paralysed and
she thought she would never
dance again. She vowed that if
her recovery was more complete one
than then seemed possible, she would do
at the first things she would do
would be to put on a show to
...se money for polio victims,
...rrow Ana Lydia—her
...Mrs. Ana Armstrong
...ain. Her leg is
...red, but it
...le her to

A**s a thank-offering for
her recent return to
health from an attack of poliomyelitis ... Ana Lydia, the
...cer (in private life
...Armstrong, of
...putting her heart
...oject. She intends
...show in aid of the
...d dance in it her-
...f possible, make
...to see some un-
...iri through his

Star Turn

BEAT POLIO TO
DANCE: FULFILS
A VOW

Sunday Mail Reporter

...lt is more to her gai
...ant decision than this. Having
...been through
...the terrible
...mental stress
...engendered by
...her attack of
poliomyelitis, Ana Lydia hopes,
through her example, to spread
hope for, and not fear of, the

...oraltar in there
...time there
...known there
...be name Fi
...be name to

HELP FOR
POLIO
VICTIMS

It's exotic....It's exciting....It's unusual. For it's
artistry by Ana Lydia,
specialist in Spanish dancing
and star turn at the Press
Ball tonight.

OVERSEAS LEAGUE
NAIROBI, KENYA BRANCH
MONTHLY MEMBERS' MEETING
at the
" FLAMINGO "
(By kind permission of the Management)

24th July, 1952

Overseas League:— Monthly meeting, Flamingo Restaurant, 8.30 p.m.
Dancing display with Miss Morea Soutter, Miss Ana Lydia and
Miss Shirin K. Suleman.

...E EAST AND WEST "

136

KENYA NATIONAL THEATRE

MAY 15th to 22nd, 1954

ANA LYDIA

presents

GAY FIESTA

devised and produced by
ANA LYDIA

assisted by
FRED HIGGS and BENNY GOODMAN

continuity and stage direction by
MICHAEL WATSON

CAST

Lola	YVONNE FAITHFULL
Tani	ANA LYDIA
Pepe	FRED HIGGS
Pablo	BENNY GOODMAN

with

Pamela Rose-Innes
Mollie Browse
Betty Whittaker
Pat Davies
Anne Carter
Wanda Sulkowska
Rosuitha Boedeker
Peter Cook
Bill Mooney
Tyson Ponquett
Colin MacDonald

Avril Parry
Vera Gellert
Diane Togosoff
Deirdre Davies
Lyn Broadle
Winnie

Squires, Vi Herbert, Pat
Davies and member
Tyson Ponquett

House
Assistan
Wardrol stress
Stage Manager
Assistant Stage Manager
Lighting
Stage Crew
Production and Publicity Man

Part Three

The Awakening 1956 - 1961

Chapter 13

BRAZIL

The 'Highland Princess' was a lovely ship, bigger and more sophisticated than the previous ones on which we had travelled. First class on such a long trip offered much more improved entertainment so the time taken was yet another enjoyable holiday. We actually arrived in Rio de Janeiro two weeks before Christmas. The Brazilians refer to Rio as the 'Cidade Maravilhosa' and it was indeed the most enchanting of cities. Nature has been more than generous with this very captivating place. Pao de Asucar, Cristo do Corcovado, Copacabana, all were awe inspiring.

The Company found us temporary accommodation in the Guanabara Palace Hotel in the Avenida Presidente Vargas quite close to the Company's main office for Jack to be able to come and go without much difficulty and until a suitable residence was found for us. When we left London the city had been beautifully decorated with Santa Clauses in their red robes, rotund bodies and cherub faces, the bells ringing and the lovely tunes of 'White Christmas' and other appropriate carols being played. Lovely light decorations and window displays. Here in Rio it was all so very different. The whole city trembled with their never ending 'batucadas'. The drum beats and loud carnival music of the escolas de samba all around us. The few more conservative stores played, European style, the softly and enchanting tunes such as 'Silent

Night' but they were quickly lost as they mingled with the tourist shop music also competing with the drum beats as they loudly played 'Jingle Bells' over and over again! It was a startling experience. It was sensational and not comparable to any other place where we had lived either for natural beauty or mode of living.

Our heavy luggage had been unloaded and kept at the customs. The customs officer had opened every single bag and packing case, exactly as we had been forewarned by the Company. We also discovered that according to usual practice almost everything we carried was subject to duty. We therefore waited with bated breath and studied with anxiety every reaction, movement and comment the officer in charge made, expecting the worst. At one point he stopped, faced me and practically undressed me with his eyes, it was quite blatant and obvious that here was someone who found me not only attractive but very desirable. Jack anxiously looked at me fearing I might say the wrong thing. I looked back and smiled as the officer slowly and with what he thought was manly and sensuous movements walked towards me completely ignoring Jack. "Welcome to Rio", he said while strongly shaking my hand and standing a hair breadth away from me. His attitude was so obvious that even I realised what he was after. It was so interesting to see him priming himself like a tom cat and sidling towards my body as if drawn by a magnet, it was so comical that I would have laughed; yet, for once I was being courted as if I were a desirable beauty. Jack stood there shrugging his shoulders and waiting for further developments. No need to worry, we got away with all our belongings without paying a single cent! Jack's colleagues could not believe that we had entered Brazil without paying substantial custom duty and often he was asked what was the secret? If this was the reaction I was going to have on the male population, after being the ugly one of the family all my life, with no one wanting to look like me, and which had left me with such a complex, then, I thought, I would love Brazil!

The hotel provided responsible baby sitters at a fee and we made use of their availability to go to the office welcoming party. When we returned from our outing, we went up to our room and found our daughter gone. We looked everywhere we could think of, phoned the housekeeper's department and the reception. The hotel was in turmoil. The babysitter had been checking on some other child and when she returned Lyana was gone. We thought we would go mad with the anxiety. The hotel was thinking of calling the police when we heard our daughter's voice saying "Up, down, again" repeatedly. We followed to where the sounds were coming from and we found her inside the elevator with the porter who was entertaining her by going up and down to the various floors of the hotel! After this we did not dare leave her alone with anyone again. Wanting to entertain her and ourselves we looked for the films showing in the local cinemas but discovered that no child under five was allowed in. There stood Lyana very attentive at what I was saying "Nana darling, if the man in the cinema asks how old you are, what will you say?" Sticking out three fingers she would say "Three". "If you say that you will not be able to go in, you say five, and open all your hand, it is a game to be allowed in." She had such a solemn grown up way of staring at you. "Alright, mummy" she said. Lyana was very bright and intelligent for her age but rather a small child. We never forgot how when the man there asked her her age she proudly opened all her hand and boldly said "Five" The man was a little dubious, however we were in, to see a musical which we all enjoyed!.

Most of the expatriates lived in Niteroi on the other side of the bay which naturally necessitated crossing by ferry or travelling a long way round by road. We were offered an apartment house in Leblon on the outskirts of Rio further from the centre but nearer to Copacabana and close to the beaches with plenty of public transportation available. We were therefore quite keen to take it and moved in a few days before Christmas. The apartment without any lift and on the fourth floor was a three bedroom, spacious one which had been previously the home of a captain on one of the Company's cableships. It had been empty for some time. We moved in to what at first glance appeared to be a cleaned place. Our luggage was all stacked in the spare room. During the night I got up for drinking water, put on the light and screamed, the whole place was covered with the most horrible huge cockroaches. We spent the night chasing and killing them. Now we knew why the cockroaches were characteristically named 'baratas' — meaning cheap, there were so many of them and they were everywhere. In the streets, cinema, buses, everywhere! The most disgusting thing to illustrate even better the state of hygiene is what happened the day I heated the oven to make a roast - I heard crackling sounds, opened the door and to my horror saw a number of cockroaches newly dead. I should not have been surprised since when thoroughly cleaning the crockery I found cocoons under the saucers stuck to the ridge at the bottom.

After a sleepless night battling these unwanted guests, I got up to prepare breakfast only to find that there wasn't a drop of water available. The water supply had been cut off, something that was to happen regularly for a period of a day to a week throughout all our stay in Brazil. The porter had not been notified of our moving into the apartment, and therefore had not advised us to fill a few pails for emergency to get us by. He did however manage to get all the neighbours to give us some of their saved supply and so alleviate our situation. Our apartment on the top floor of the building was unfortunately the first to be left without water and the last one to get it back due to the way the plumbing had been done. You never saw our bath from then on empty. We used it as a storage tank and instead took showers in the other bathroom.

In Brazil we were going to encounter yet another different style, standard and philosophy of life. Once again everything was new to us. Whereas where we lived it was relatively clean with the exception of crawling insects, huge potholes, mounds of dirt and stones filling the holes in the street, it was a different story in the back streets and downtown where the tourists did not generally go. One never knew what would be thrown out of windows; it could be cigarette ends, empty glass bottles, cans, bed springs, love letters or coffee dregs. Walking was hazardous as not only did you have to look where you placed your feet but also for anything that was being dropped from above.

Definitely this was a land of contrast and extremes. Macumba, their black magic ritual, was mixed up with ceremonious religion and sprinkling of holy water. The people were mostly very rich or very poor. The gorgeous majestic villas and high rise deluxe apartments were a complete contrast to the poverty stricken 'picturesque' favelas on the hillsides where hunger, dirt and passion reigned. You were always advised not to walk into these poorer areas. Not only would you be braving the black waters thrown out of the ill constructed wooden windows but also have all your possessions stolen and possibly be badly injured as well.

Brazil had something good to differentiate it from British East Africa. All the inhabitants of the Portuguese colonies of Mozambique and Angola etc. were not separated because colour discrimination did not exist. Equally here all citizens, regardless of the colour of their skins were Brazilians; they came under the headings of morenos – suntanned, claros – light skinned, mulatos – mixed, and brancos – whites. Everybody lived happily as far as that was concerned and if they chose to mix in marriage or in 'concubinatum' it was their own private affair and business. You could go anywhere and do anything if you had the money to pay.

On the ground floor of our apartment building we found our first friends. Phyllis was a woman of around my mother's age, 'uma balzaquiana gostosa' (a desirable older woman) as Brazilians would describe her. She was an extremely smart, well kept, fashionable woman. Phyllis was legally married to her uncle, her father's brother, an elderly man in his sixties, a real darling full of fun and life, and terribly kind to all of us. His English was perfect. The family all spoke fluent French as well, for although they were born in the Amazonas, they had all gone to Europe when younger and then to Casablanca where they had lived for a long while before moving to France, where some of the brothers still lived. Her nephew Bobbie was an intimate friend of Brigitte Bardot.

I engaged a Portuguese maid called Maria because everyone had warned us that to employ a Brazilian one you would run at least two risks. One, during the Carnival celebrations they would disappear and more often than not did not return. Second, if they got annoyed with you they would use Macumba (witchcraft) against you. Since we had experienced a bit of this in Nairobi we thought it best to pay attention to the advice. Maria was middle-aged and she told me that she could not do any heavy work or climb up and down the four flights of stairs to our apartment too frequently as she had a heart condition. I soon found out that I was committed to almost all the heavy work and shopping on my own, however I felt it was worth it to have a reliable responsible woman to look after my three year old daughter, someone with whom I could leave Lyana without any worries. Because of my fear for her health if she did not answer me as soon as I called her I would start to panic and think something terrible had happened to her. One day when my husband and I returned home and walked into the kitchen we noticed Maria writhing on the ground and holding on to the top of the verandah. We both ran to help her but she motioned us to keep low so as not to be seen and to our dismay we found that two or three buildings away from ours, standing on a bench in front of an open window, a man completely naked was cavorting and making indecent gestures towards our house. Maria was not really a sick woman as we had thought but a cheeky devil that my husband there and then sent away.

Our first Christmas and New Year celebrations were very sad and lonely ones. No one had asked us to their homes and we three celebrated as well as we could by ourselves. It did not seem like Christmas at all as we spent most of the time on the beach eating salads and cold food as it was so frightfully hot. It was so hot that the street tarmac melted and shoes stuck to the ground. Spending the festive season alone affected me for life as from then on I made sure no one from the Company was left on their own at such a meaningful time.

The first person who invited us over to their home in Niteroi was Eva. Eva was married to John, Jack's colleague and friend. She was German born but had gone with her parents to Brazil as a child. At first I did not wish to go to their home but Eva turned out to be the most wonderful friend anyone could have wished for, tall, brunette lively and such a lot of fun. It seemed as if we had always known each other and we shared so many likes and dislikes. From our place in Leblon we had to travel by bus to the ferry station and cross over to the other side. It made an interesting trip which we all enjoyed very much. After talking a while and having a pre lunch drink Eva called us to the table. She had prepared quite a sumptuous meal. First she served succulent shrimp cocktails and then came delicious smelling roast adobo pork, vegetables, white rice and a dish of piping hot black food. This last one caused me some misgivings as other than black pudding I had never seen food this colour. I asked for only a little of it not knowing what I was about to eat. I took a small portion of this black concoction and to my surprise it was quite delicious, without realising it I said "Um it's nice!" and before I had finished speaking Eva plonked a huge helping of it onto my plate. "It's black beans" she said "the typical Brazilian 'feijoada' and very good for you. Eat it!" It reminded me of long ago when Dad Armstrong had uttered similar words to me on my first visit to Jack's family in the North of England!

Without a maid in such terrible heat was absolutely awful so I turned to Phyllis for help as I usually did. She was always available for me and if anything went wrong with Lyana's health or any other problems she always found a solution for them. She asked Aninha, her maid, and I was lucky that her sister Olimpia had recently arrived from Portugal and was looking for a job. This would be quite handy as the sisters would then be close to one another.

Lyana also found two friends in the building, one a Brazilian girl slightly older than her called Elizabeth and the other a lovely blonde American girl called Vicky who lived in the apartment directly beneath us. Lyana spent much time with one or the other. Elizabeth could not speak English but Lyana seemed to make herself understood fine with her Spanish until she eventually spoke quite fluent Portuguese. Languages always seemed easy for her.

Shopping in Leblon was no hardship as we were very close to all kinds of stores, supermarkets and restaurants. The supermarkets were glorified grocery stores. They did not offer much choice of canned goods and most definitely they had never heard of Heinz 57 varieties! The meat was bought at the butcher shops. Meat was of excellent quality, plentiful and reasonably priced. The street market came to our area on Thursday. This too was within walking distance and if I happened to go alone there were always plenty of young lads only too willing to carry the baskets for a few coins. Stalls upon stalls were set up with everything under the sun. On market day you could get meat, fish, cereals, vegetables, fruit, and biscuits, everything there and all so good and fresh. We could eat extremely well without spending too much. I had learnt my lesson only too well in Vigo. Now if Olimpia did the shopping alone I knew exactly how much the bill should come to. It was sad to see the hoards of poor people from the 'favelas' coming down to pick at all the stall holders' leftovers that had fallen to the ground or had been thrown away as unfit for selling. These were very poor people but they were also very happy, smiling and dancing as if life was a celebration.

In Rio we did not have a car. They were very expensive and only the top management enjoyed private transportation. We went on buses or taxis which were reasonable although sometimes very difficult to find especially when it rained! There was a bus stop very near our home so travelling anywhere was no big problem. Jack was now working as a sales representative stationed in downtown Rio so he travelled every day by bus.

Transportation in Rio was quite something. The 'lotacao' or small omnibus was an unimaginable contraption. Almost all were antique models of locomotion that were supposedly able to seat twenty-two passengers and take a standing capacity of eleven. But in reality the bus would tear across the city – almost bursting at the seams with more 'illegal' passengers than 'legal' ones. You could feel or imagine the wheels sighing at the extra weight, while the engine panted in its effort as it went speeding along the not too smooth highways. To travel in a lotacao was an adventure in itself. If you were lucky to get an inside seat with a lady next to you, you would be alright, but, if you had the misfortune of either an outside seat or of standing up with a man next to you, you would soon feel him rubbing his legs or his body against you. If seated you would squeeze into the corner as it was useless saying anything for the male would cheekily complain in a loud voice "que audacia – what audacity, she is trying to pick me up." I found out that the best protection was to carry either a safety pin or hat pin with which to return the gentleman's compliment. The 'papa filas' or 'eating queues' buses were even worse. They were huge, brown, tremendously long buses, their construction inspired by a centipede. What fun to sit on the broad rear seat, especially if you happened to be in line with the passage way and on sudden stops being catapulted to the front. These sudden stops were deliberate – the conductor would then call out "Enter; there is always room for one more".

The other means of transportation was the 'bondinho' or tramway. These were almost prehistoric and you just couldn't squeeze anymore people in than they did. Like the 'old woman who lived in a shoe' they seemed to be ready to burst out like a sausage skin, with people hanging from just about anywhere. One visiting English reporter from the News of the World sightseeing the city on one of these open trams interpreted the destination board 'cidade' (city) as 'suicide' and wrote quite an interesting article about it, although wrong about its true meaning - city – he was right about the final implication. There were many victims of the tramways.

A more 'refined' and comfortable means of transportation was the always available and gallantly offered 'corona' or lifts. If you were looking for excitement, or the unknown, you could accept a courteous offer in a private car. Of course, you never knew how or where it would end. The amorous and passionate Brazilian would take your acceptance as a promise to much better and enjoyable things, in fact in their estimation, a trip to paradise.

Phyllis often had her family over on Sundays and on one occasion she invited the three of us. They were all very well connected, particularly her sister Ruth. When Ruth heard that I had been dancing professionally she was very keen for me to meet Austragesilo Athayde a very important man who had connections to TV Tupi in Urca. He introduced me to Dr. Almeida de Castro, the director who promptly gave me an eight weeks contract and I was soon making my debut in front of the cameras as 'the great exponent of Spanish dancing'. It was great to be back on stage and this time in a completely new media. So very many people would be seeing me dance. I was most excited and happy. Jack would come with me to the rehearsals and on the show days once finished (they were live presentations), we would leave the studios and go home together. It was very successful but my contract was coming to an end and I was called in to Almeida Castro's office. He was a tall rather good looking man, suntanned as most of the Brazilians are, with bright piercing small dark eyes, moustache and well combed and perfumed hair. He was all in white and somehow to me rather sinister looking. He informed me that the sponsors were delighted with me and would be renewing my contract. They would be meeting me for dinner after the show. My answer was quick in coming, I was very pleased they liked my programme but would be unable to attend dinner. Then Mr Castro walked towards me and started playing with a slave bracelet I was accustomed to wear on the upper part of my arm while he tried to convince me in his soft toned voice that "You have to be a nice, understanding girl, you must cooperate, and they would in turn double your fees and give you more promotion in leading magazines like Manchete and O Cruzeiro etc."

I honestly don't know what happened to me but there he was, sleek and perfumed, leering at me and in my mind I could see him doing unwanted things. I started to scream. Mr Castro stood stupefied looking at me, nothing had happened and there I was hysterically screaming my head off. There was pandemonium. The door opened suddenly, people coming in to see and Jack who had heard me, shouting in English "Ly, honey, what have they done to you? Tell me and I'll kill the bastards!" When I answered him "Oh Jack, nothing has happened. I was just frightened at what could have happened!" Jack was awfully mad at me as he took me out and back home. Naturally after this episode, although very amusing afterwards, I kept on seeing poor Castro's startling looks, I gave up my dancing and when I mentioned this happening to Mr Athayde his answer was "Well, Mrs Armstrong, I thought you knew that TV was not a place for ladies!" When I told Ruth what had happened she could not understand why I had reacted as I did. I should have accepted my sponsor's offer "Everybody, but everybody who thinks anything of themselves has 'lovers', just for the heck of it, and here you are turning down not only fun, but being an established star with a lot of financial gain".

Shortly after this the Spanish film producer Cesareo Gonzalez visited Rio de Janeiro together with Spanish film stars Paquita Rico and Luis Escobar, el Marques de las Marismas. We were thrilled to receive an invitation to a cocktail party given in his honour at one of the leading hotels. When introduced to Cesareo it was obvious that he liked me because he immediately offered to make me into a film star for his company. Since I was married and with a child I wasn't really interested as I thought the price I might have to pay would have been too high bearing in mind my experience with TV Tupi.

Life was very hectic. Lyana was attending kindergarten which she loved as she had done when we were in Vigo. Dona Maria the proprietor and director did not believe in punishment of any class but one day Lyana returned home with blood coming out from just under her eye. One of the other little girls, also a foreigner, had bitten her. Lyana was in such pain that I had to call the doctor who recommended I kept her from school. I decided to go and see Dona Maria and find out what had happened. She made very little of it saying it was children at play. "Children have to learn not to act like animals. Lyana is suffering and she could have lost her eye because of this other student. She must be punished!" I said. "But Mrs Armstrong, you know that this is not that kind of school, we do not give punishment!" "Very well, I shall wait here until the girl comes out!" "Mrs Armstrong, what are you going to do?" she asked me rather worriedly. "Dona Maria, I am going to bite that girl on her arm so that she knows what pain she has caused my daughter!" She was aghast! The girl's mother who turned out to be American was told and she gave me no time to get to her daughter. She took it upon herself to punish her there and then in front of me in such a way that my bite would have hurt less. Presumably she was frightened I might sue her as they do in the United States!

Since Jack and I got married he had had a different job at each and every one of the stations we had been sent to. He trained as a telegraph operator and that is what he was doing all the time in Salisbury, Southern Rhodesia. He was inside an office all the time he was on duty and seeing only his colleagues. When he was transferred to Nairobi, Kenya, he was sent to the Ngong Receiving Station where he was a technical watchkeeper. Again he never saw any public. In Vigo he spent his time in the office re-organizing it and now for the first time he was out and about meeting people and enjoying it. He loved his new position and turned out to be very good at it too. He spoke quite good Portuguese and his written commercial Portuguese was also very good. He had taken and passed his language exam very successfully so all in all he felt very happy about life. He met a lot of people, some became our friends which was rather nice as we did not have to depend on the Company staff. In fact we had always tended to keep our social life completely apart from Company life. Sometimes we would meet downtown for lunch and other times we met after he finished his work to go to the cinema or meet friends for drinks before returning home. We were all delighted with life in Brazil and looking forward to a successful long stay.

Carnival in Rio was absolutely incredible. The poor people from the favelas all supported their local samba school which prepared a float and paraded through the main streets of downtown Rio and competed for prestige and cash. They saved all year round every cent they could get in order to buy themselves the costumes they would wear. These would usually be quite flamboyant and probably represented their dreams and aspirations in life. The drums never stopped beating as they practiced day in day out in order to be at their very best. The floats were colourful and generally carried half naked well known actresses or dancers who performed with grace in spite of the somewhat unstable transport. The atmosphere was electrifying but hardly the place to take such a young child as Lyana because of the crowds of people pushing and hustling. The music and tempo was irresistible and you found yourself unconsciously dancing as you walked.

The Teatro Municipal held various balls where people in their masquerade competed against each other for the best costume. The main one that attracted most public was the one where the participants competing were generally older women, who, in their fine costumes costing thousands of dollars, specially designed and made for them and heavily embroidered with semi precious stones, aspired to find themselves a new 'boyfriend', a much younger man they would keep, if lucky, for a year. Then they had the Transvestite Ball where these young men also in magnificent costumes competed against each other.

Sometimes it was very difficult to believe your eyes; they were so beautiful and so feminine!

The first year we made arrangements to go with our American friends Shorty and his wife Benilda, Benny as we all called her, to go to this fabulous Ball. We dressed up in rather demure fancy dresses and joined the rest of the people who were not competing but there to dance and enjoy themselves. Semi nudity was what prevailed as far as the women's costumes were concerned. Those that looked more covered actually were not wearing any underwear. The great hall was packed to full capacity, people danced on top of chairs, tables and on the balcony's edge where they could stand up. I was dancing with Jack when the heat of so many bodies rubbing together made me faint. o one was aware of this until the music stopped and then only because I did not respond to Jack's questions. I was being held upright by the people around me. Anything was acceptable for those that wanted it. Many even enjoyed a certain sexual excitement as passion was aroused while they danced and gyrated. No one seemed to notice and if they did no one said anything!

The following years we did as most of our friends did and either went to a hotel or joined them in their country homes. When on our own we liked to go to Novo Friburgo where we had bought a small plot to eventually build ourselves a weekend hideaway. This area was well known as the Brazilian Switzerland. The weather was fresher and purer and we could enjoy a more moderate carnival season. Ruth had a very beautiful home with swimming pool in the scenic holiday town of Petropolis or we would go to another's home in the 'in' town of Teresopolis where we could still dance and celebrate without excesses.

My sisters all had increased their family too. Clementina had a little girl Vandra and they were now living in Hong Kong. My third sister Lottie had a little boy James and my younger sister Lena a girl Marisa. These two sisters still lived in Gibraltar. We had changed Lyana to the British School and she was growing up and participating in dance and elocution shows as well as enjoying her piano lessons very much. She was a little sweetheart but with a temperament of her own. She was very inquisitive always asking questions and trying to find out how things worked. Why did the doll's eyes open and close; how did their legs move; she would investigate so thoroughly that the toy would break. She would then bring things to me and very imperiously say "Fix it mummy." She loved to unscrew anything she could find with her own little fingers, whenever there was too much silence and peace we knew she was up to something. One day she discovered my makeup bag and she painted not only her face but everything else she could find. Another day I returned from shopping to find that her bed had been placed in the very middle of her room with all her toys spread around it. When I asked Olimpia what had happened she seriously said "Senorita ordered me to put things like that!" Senorita was only four. I remember turning to Olimpia and asking "And if Senorita tells you to jump out of the window you will do it too?" Lyana got into the habit of telling our friends that she had been at our wedding and when corrected she would nod her head up and down and very gravely say "I remember, mummy!" Since morality was the way it was in Brazil no doubt many believed her. I managed to quieten her by promising that when and if we made it to our silver anniversary we would get married again and she could come as a bridesmaid. Lyana would get very upset if she found any female visitor greeting her dad with a kiss. She would run to them and push herself between them to separate the woman from her dad and exclaim "No, he is MY daddy and my mummy's, go!" Jack too adored his little girl. He would spend hours just looking at her and saying how beautiful she was. She was a sturdy little miss with solemn big eyes with tremendously long eye lashes that curled to almost below her eyebrows, a cute little nose and cheeky smile. She looked very much like her dad who had taken after his own father. The colouring and flair for fun plus mischievousness she inherited from me.

It was only natural that by now my image had changed. Rio was a woman's paradise, very few women looked old. There was a great number of beauty salons, masseuses, sauna baths etc., everything and anything for the embellishment of feminine charms, and of course a very appreciative audience, the Brazilian male! It is impossible not to feel alive and wonderful with all the 'piropos' – compliments – describing all your beauty and charm given you by the men. The Brazilian man is taught from childhood to really appreciate female charms, you were never too thin, too fat, too young or too old, he always found a good point about your appearance, intelligence or 'simpatia'. I revelled in all this and I soon began to lose some inhibitions and enjoy the admiration. My physical appearance had also undergone a radical change. I had had my hair cut short and sexily styled, I wore fashionable and tighter clothes that showed my shape to its best advantage all in bright colours and I learned to use my make up to better bring out all I had good and hide the little problem areas. I had beautiful shoes made to order with heels that complimented my legs, in fact there was very little left of the old girl my mother and sisters had laughed at on my return from Rhodesia and called me a missionary!

The only location that I had not worked was at Vigo since it took me so long to recover fully from my ectopic operation. Head Office had also warned us that we would only remain for about a year which was the time they allocated Jack to do the job of reorganising the office. Now, although I kept myself busy it was not really how I liked to spend my time. I went out with Benny, Ruth, Phyllis and Gwen my closest friends, Gwen who was practically alone all the time enjoyed going to the bridge and canasta parties at the club. I went several times with her but I found the women rather cattish and two faced. One moment they would be greeting each other as the best of friends and no sooner out of hearing they would exclaim "Cow!" or "Bitch!" I got to the point that once seated I did not dare move for fear of what they would say about me. Practically everyone there had lovers, some even two of them, the more lovers they had the more powerful and beautiful they felt. The funny part was that they were actually introduced as 'Mrs Smith the mistress of the president' or 'Mrs Gouveia the mistress of General so and so or the mistress of the Ambassador of such and such a place!' I felt so plain and unexciting when introduced as simply Mrs Armstrong. I even asked Jack if there was anything wrong with me as I had not at any moment felt or thought of having anything to do with any other man! Ruth loved to shop. I did not mind going now and then but I could not afford to buy in the expensive boutiques she frequented and there was no fun for me. Phyllis enjoyed walking around talking and pointing out interesting things. I found her relaxing and kind. Benny being South American and with a teenage daughter was the one I much preferred to be with. She took the part of elder sister and was always trying to help and teach me. Jack and I often went to play canasta at their home and on Sundays went with them in their car to the lovely club to which she belonged and where she often played golf. On the whole although my life was pleasant I was soon bored and felt I should be doing something more energetic and perhaps profitable too.

About three months after my TV experience and when I was feeling particularly bored with the tediousness of life, I was contacted by the well known Brazilian empresario Walter Pinto for one of his famous shows at the Teatro Recreo in Praca Tiradentes. Having seen me on TV he wanted me for his 'guest dancer, doing a Spanish dance' I was thrilled as I would not have to rehearse like the others almost every afternoon. My experiences in this theatre were good fun. I lived, for the first time in my life, among honest to goodness professionals having to work hard for recognition in the theatre world. I had become a professional and successful dancer by chance, without any of the hardships and difficulties that usually go with it.

Unfortunately the contracted choreographer had to cancel due to sickness and the new one was an Englishman who could not speak a word of Portuguese or Spanish. Delf, the theatre manager asked me to go and interpret for them. Unfortunately there would now be no need for a Spanish dancer, but they insisted that I complete my contract and remain as the leading dancer. My relationship with the cast, mostly Argentinean girls with plenty of experience, was rather peculiar. They would never use foul language in front of me and always insisted on calling me 'senora'. The male dancers proved themselves very kind hearted and great friends, helpful and sympathetic. For some unknown reason everyone of the cast thought that Jack and I were not really married, but living together and with a child. All were extremely friendly and kind to me, although among themselves they would bicker and quarrel; and when they thought I was not within ear's reach, they would revert to foul language and the most uncouth behaviour. I was fascinated. All of them however did their best to protect me.

I found the choreographer's routine all very new and different to me: a mixture of jazz and modern ballet, which although I had studied and got through the exams satisfactorily to teach up to first year (which I never did as I always taught what I really knew, Spanish dance) I was really quite terrible and self conscious, and needless to say my poor body was in constant pain from muscles I had never used before. Apart from that practically none of the male dancers was very happy with me. I could not be lifted as I was frightened to do so and they would pant and puff trying to elevate me from the floor. When I had to do a pirouette and gracefully sit on my partner's hip I nearly threw him down into the orchestra pit. I was a disaster so I went to Delf and resigned. "No, no, you cannot leave" said a panic stricken Delf. I realised it was not my dancing but the translation I did for them was now all they really wanted. I agreed to think about it and stay on a few days more, and then I saw the clothing I would be expected to wear! First the shoes, they had extremely high stiletto heels to which I had never become accustomed and therefore when I walked I did so with knees bent so as to keep my balance but I was not exactly a sensational sight. The dresses, what there was of them, were too modern for me, low cut, so tight fitting that you could not breathe and showing more than I cared to do so. Without saying a word I just did not turn up any more. Delf came several times for me but I blatantly refused. Jack always said I would have been a great hit as the comedy star! His sense of humour. He actually used to come to all the rehearsals where he enjoyed laughing at my unsuccessful efforts with the strange movements. I decided to forget about dancing publicly. Jack was always very understanding and clever with me. He always left me to find out for myself what would not really work. He never stopped me from wanting to dance or anything else, perhaps realising that, 'Taurus – like' I would not have accepted his or anyone's advice once I happened to be set on doing something. I have always needed to feel free to decide what I wanted to do even if I made mistakes. I have always needed my own space. We did of course go on opening night to the show, but only as spectators!

Chapter 14

A NEW CAREER

After the disastrous dancing experiences I had, I decided that perhaps the time had come for me to find myself a secretarial job. Since I could read and write in English, Spanish and Portuguese and had basic clerical knowledge I soon found a position as assistant to the executive secretary of Paul J. Havas, the Managing Director of the Henry J Kaiser Company in Brazil. This company was a heavy engineering firm concerned with construction of dams, steel plant and so forth and I found this job very interesting.

Bertha, a much older person than I, was the Executive Secretary who had quite a lot of problems as she was involved with a married man, and, who in spite of all her many trips to San Antonio Church (St. Anthony is Patron Saint of the impossible) as well as dabbling in witchcraft, did not seem to have much success. She was often late, bad tempered or absent. I found myself doing more and more of her work. Eventually under Mr Havas' advice I went for shorthand lessons during my lunch hour and soon found myself taking dictation from him. Eventually I took over her job and had a young Brazilian girl Cleia come to work as my assistant. Nelio was the office boy. Both Cleia and Nelio were typical Brazilians with very good sense of humour and always ready to joke and smile. Nelio could turn a box of matches into a musical instrument and kept us amused when the going got too hard. Mr Havas was a very exacting person who demanded a lot from everyone. He reminded me of my father in build, and had the same laughing eyes Dad had. Unfortunately his temperament was not like Dad's. Whereas I was usually at the office before 9.00a.m., he arrived an hour later and invariably was suffering from hangovers, as most of his work and contracts were achieved through contacts at social gatherings. He would need an Alka-Seltzer before anything else. He would then read his mail which I had prepared in order of importance together with the appropriate files for follow up. No earlier than 10.00 o'clock I was called in for consultation. Between 1.00 p.m. and 3.00 p.m. he would leave for a business lunch and would start dictating when he returned, usually at 4.00 p.m. if I was lucky. He expected me to have all the letters typed and ready for signing before I left at 5.00 p.m. It was practically impossible so occasionally I was forced to stay late to keep up to date. In spite of this I enjoyed my work and I was really learning the hard way how to be a good secretary.

I had thought that being downtown like Jack and so close to his office that we would have been able to get together for lunch on the odd occasion and perhaps take the same bus home together even though he finished half an hour before me. But that was not to be. I found out something that I had not realised before I started working. Jack had been taking rather longer than time required to get back home. When he had been a little later than usual I took it for granted that his work had kept him busy. Now I was leaving at 5.00 p.m. while he finished at 4.30 p. m and yet inevitably I returned much earlier than he did!. I never have found out why! Only that he has insisted always that he was waiting in the bus queue?!

Socially we were having a lovely time. The group of 'friends' was being enlarged all the time. Through Mr Havas and his wife Leigh we met a lot of American and local government officials who invited us and we naturally reciprocated. It was amazing the differences between the nationalities. The English expatriates (and I am generalizing) were the worst. They were always stiff and full of protocol trying to be what they wanted to make believe they were and never just themselves. The food was usually not so good and not much of it yet the drinks were poured in abundance. I have never understood why it seems that the English need to drink excessively in order to show that they are having a good time! The Americans were always very casual and jovial. They preferred the buffet dinner parties and informal barbeques rather than those seated at dinner tables. They enjoyed drinking beer and having good conversation. The Brazilians, ah, the Brazilians enjoyed everything! If you had the luck of being invited to a 'feijoada completa' where the black beans had every kind of meat and chorizos imaginable as well as numerous side dishes that went together, your luncheon could last as much as six hours! But, like with everything else the attitude was to go slowly, chew every morsel, taste and enjoy every bit and wash it down with 'Caipirinhas' their own drink made of 'cachaca' something similar to vodka, lemon, plenty of ice and a some sugar which they reckoned helped your digestion!! In between there would also be the dancing and talking! I myself preferred sitting down dinners to everything else. I felt I could get to know my guests better and learn from their conversation and beliefs. Second best were the buffet dinners but I hated tea parties which I felt damaged your luncheon digestion and spoilt your dinner. Cocktail parties I abhorred. Since I was the one who cooked for the home entertainment I hated to have to make all those little bits and pieces!

Mr Havas had acquired a lovely sailing boat, Jorge, an Argentinean sailor was in charge and teaching them how to sail. Mr Havas was too impatient and by now everybody at the Yacht Club realized he was a danger so when they saw him going to his boat with guests but without Jorge they would quickly get out of his way. He had had a motor installed but once started the boat instead of going out to sea would do a complete circle and end up where he had started from. Club Members would cheer and clap. Mr Havas took it as a personal challenge and from then onwards spend as much time as he could at the sailing sessions. One day Mr. George Havas, my boss' brother and President of the Henry J Kaiser organization telephoned from the USA wanting to speak to him. I went to his office to find that the bird had flown his nest through the back door. I had to apologize and say my boss was in a very important conference and would phone him later, was there anything I could do? Fortunately I had all the files and was more or less able to deal with the situation there and then. After this happening I locked the back door, kept the key and Mr Havas had to leave a contact number in case of emergency.

Mr Havas could not stand my calling him always Mr Havas. "Call me Paul" he would say. "No, I cannot, you are on the other side of this desk and I must respect you" I would reply. At the end we came to an agreement. In the office he would be Mr. Havas but otherwise he would be our friend and I would, like Jack did, call him Paul!

One day the buzzer to call me shrilled in such a tremendous way that it was as if his finger had got stuck on it, followed by screams of agony. All of us rushed to his office to find him half seated in his chair grabbing the desk and with a dreadful look of agony! "Sunshine, don't leave me Sunshine" he really looked in bad pain, his face was deathly white and there were dark circles under his eyes. Turning to Nelio I asked him to fetch Mr Paulding next door who was Mr Havas' friend. When Mr Paulding arrived he took a look and said "I am calling for the private hospital ambulance, he will have to go to hospital, and this looks really serious!" Poor Mr Havas was like a child in tears, in pain and absolutely terrified. He would not let go of my hand and kept on repeating "Don't leave me". "It's OK, I'll stay with you until Leigh gets to your side, come on, don't worry, all will be fine!" But I too was preoccupied. Cleia was sent to phone Leigh at her residence and if she wasn't there to ask the maid where she could be contacted. "Phone everywhere you can think of and if you cannot find her leave messages and send Nelio by taxi to the yacht club where she can be paged and told". Fortunately all turned out satisfactorily but Mr Havas would have to cut down all or most of his entertainment, he had gallstones and his liver was being affected.

Jack continued to amaze me. Differences in character, background and customs became more obvious as time went on. Out of the blue Jack came telling me how we already had membership of the nudist camps. Astonished, I asked "What camp, you haven't said anything about getting membership. I am not going to show myself in the nude to strangers!" He not only had membership but the contacts of those involved. When I saw he really meant it and it was not one of his many jokes I did not seem to understand. I cried. Jack could not love me if he was prepared to show me to other men. I know what my father would have said. It was not because I had a bad figure; on the contrary, I was very proud of it! Eventually he confronted me and said that if I did not want to go he would go with Lyana! Faced with this, knowing what women were like and remembering Fr.Mondejar's words I agreed to accompany him to a dressed meeting of the club's members. The people I met all seemed quite normal and of different ages and sexes.

All of a sudden Jack started to speak about Dona Isabella a sixty year old woman. Where or when he had met her I don't know but one day he brought her home on the way to some place he was taking her. Dona Isabella did not look her age at all. Petite, hair cut in wisps, lovely dimples and the brightest smallest eyes that I had ever seen, eyes that bored holes into you. It was quite obvious that she was rather tickled by Jack. 'How could I be jealous of a sixty year old for goodness sake' I kept on thinking to myself, but jealous I was. It turned out that she was one of the assiduous members of the nudist club! Her poor husband, who we met later on, was only a couple of years older than her but he looked really ancient. As it turned out I was quite lucky for I did not have to put up with Isabella for long at all. Her daughter, seeing how ill her dad looked took them both to live with her in Sao Paulo! 'Good riddance' I thought. Before I knew what had happened we were meeting Merka and Gerardo who owned the boat scheduled to take us to some little island across the bay. Fortunately when we eventually went and boarded the ship everyone was wearing their bathing costumes.

My swimsuits compared to those of the local ladies on the beaches were very antiquated. In fact most women walked around in their very brief two piece swimsuits with a light see-through blouse over their shoulders both on the streets and in the neighbouring shops. Since I am a great believer in 'when in Rome do what the Romans do' I had invested in a couple of rather striking ones though not so brief. I still had some way to go before I integrated completely into their society!

We all lay on the boat deck. The movement of the boat, the slapping of the waves, and the sun all over me made me very relaxed and sleepy. With eyes closed I was enjoying the moment when I heard a man's voice say in Portuguese "Excuse me." I opened my eyes and right above my head there hung a dong that horrified me. Up to now the only man I had seen naked was Jack. This huge, dark thing was something else. I did not know what to do but believe me I was not too happy. Surprised I noticed everyone including Jack and Lyana were now in the nude. I became self conscious and uncomfortable, especially when everyone seemed to be staring at me. When we arrived at the island and I saw all these nude bodies getting into the small rowing boat to reach the beach I declined the ride preferring to swim to the shore only to be helped out of the sea by another naked man! I could have murdered Jack. He however was enjoying himself even though he did not like the sun or go swimming. Eventually I took courage and while in the sea I took off my top. What a difference it made to feel the water caressing my breasts! When I realised no one was bothering I took the bottom piece off as well and though apprehensive I began to enjoy the freedom of being like the day when I was born. It was rather intriguing that with a group of naked people no one showed signs of excitement and believe me it would have been very obvious, but when left alone we could not take our hands off each other. I even checked Jack when one of the young ladies was putting sun lotion on his back, the little angel did not stir, perhaps because Jack knew I was watching and he would have hell to pay at home where I always kept a gigantic pair of scissors just in case! It was the first of many enjoyable outings.

During one of these trips we met through Merka and Gerardo another couple in a luxurious yacht. Fafa was a short fat and round as a ball little man, dark skinned and quite ugly. He was of Italian descent a second generation Brazilian and he was a very clever architect and a millionaire. In his fifties he was, however, very simpatico and had a fabulous sense of humour being able to laugh at himself when no one else was daring to do so. His wife Elsa was in her late twenties like me, a quiet young woman totally dedicated to him, or so it seemed. When we first met them we felt sorry for Fafa. It was rather obvious to see that his young wife with all her luxuries was more interested in him as a provider than anything else. He turned out to be quite a selfish and egoistic man all out to enjoy himself and getting his own way regardless of anyone else. He was very generous as long as he got his way but nasty if upset. He had been paying out for everything in his life and he thought he would be able to buy friendship as well. He was in fact a sad, poor rich man.

Fafa's stories when in one of his excellent moods were really frightfully funny and he had a very appreciative audience, which he relished, whenever recounting his tales. He told us how he had sent to the USA for some kind of rubberised underwear garments that were supposed to hold his pounds of flesh together in such a way that his appearance would improve totally and he would seem to be a much slimmer man. He started to put on his knee length underpants pulling up energetically but his fat did not compress and instead bulged higher and higher until he found breathing very difficult "To hell with being slim, I'll take this contraption off" he whispered. Unfortunately the rubber had stuck to his skin and he was unable to remove the garment. The more he pulled the worse he could breathe; he was feeling faint and had to call for the maid. When the poor girl arrived in his room she found him in shock. She too tried to take the underpants off but nothing doing. At the end the girl had to rush for a pair of scissors to cut him free thus leaving an exhausted and deflated poor old man! Since he laughed at remembering, we all enjoyed hearing of his disastrous result to appear more seductive. Naturally he always told his stories with appropriate actions which made them even funnier.

His stories were at times unbelievable. He said that once he had met a very beautiful young woman for whom he had developed a great desire. He apparently approached her with expensive gifts which she returned, or with flowers and chocolates which she kept. She was married but he did not know her husband, (not that that would have mattered knowing Fafa). The woman was not having anything to do with him but nevertheless he pursued her until at the end she succumbed. He apparently took her to one of those private hotels used for this purpose where he knew the madame very well. They were both naked and in bed and the girl was enjoying sex so much that she was in a state of ecstasy when there was a knock at the door. It was the madame to inform him that the woman's husband was there demanding to check the rooms. The madame had brought with her a maid and they tried to separate the ecstatic woman from Fafa but apparently without success, maybe the fear or the magnificent orgasm she had had according to Fafa (who liked to think of himself as a well endowed bull) made her go into a contraction. They finally had to pull her apart when the girl fainted, having little time left they put her unconscious out onto the balcony while the maid got into bed with Fafa which is what the enraged husband saw and was satisfied his wife was not there. He even apologized! Can you imagine how the poor unconscious woman must have felt when she recovered? I thought it a terrific story to deter anyone from fooling with someone other than their mate.

We discovered Fafa's real marital situation in a rather amusing, yet unfortunate way. Our friend, Gwen, very much in café society, was giving a big dinner party where several ambassadors and politicians were invited and she thought millionaire Fafa and his wife Elsa would be a welcome change to the group. She looked up the telephone directory for his number and phoned. A lady answered, "I would like to speak to Mrs Estrada please" "This is Mrs Estrada speaking" "Hello, Elsa?" "I am sorry, I am Mrs Estrada – Isabella, Fafa's wife!" Very embarrassed my friend Gwen apologized and rang off. Gwen could not wait to tell me the scandal and reprimanded me for putting her in what could have been a compromising position.

Later Merka told me that it was the habit for rich men to take young girls as concubines. This was done with the full consent of the girl's family who worked out some kind of financial contract for themselves and their daughter to cover any circumstance and assure their welfare. Usually these liaisons were not long lasting as the lover generally tired and eventually exchanged her for a much younger model! This had been Elsa's case. Her family, honest, working class and paying with difficulty for their daughter's studies as a biologist had been approached by Fafa. They made what they had thought was a secured business transaction that would better their daughter's future as well as theirs for one section of the arrangement forced Fafa to buy them a home in the suburbs. Merka also explained that while Elsa lived with Fafa his official wife, Isabella, would be considered 'retired' but well looked after by her estranged husband who would still visit her. He would continue to take his laundry to her and would need her to accompany him to official functions! If by any chance any children were born out of the relationship they would be given the father's name and taken care of and if Fafa decided to take a younger girl he would then 'retire' Elsa, go and live with the new girl and make his real wife Isabella act as his illegitimate children's grandmother! All very civilized.

When Fafa and Elsa invited us for a day in their country house he suddenly remembered that he had left the keys for the house in his office in Copacabana. There and then he made a U-turn in his flamboyant Cadillac on the busy Avenida Atlantica in front of a traffic policeman. We expected the policeman to fine him and instead he was given a salute and big smile and all other traffic was stopped until he completed his manoeuvre. Later, as he speeded along the highway with one arm around Elsa's shoulder, the other arm suddenly appeared out of the window to cool down or so he said. We screamed when we realized both his hands were off the steering wheel, he was driving the car with his big fat stomach pressed against the wheel.

The fact that Fafa and Elsa were not married did not bother us. In any case we kept our business entertainment life apart from our private one. We had become quite fond of Elsa and enjoyed her eagerness to learn and please. Eventually a certain kind of friendship developed and we often went in their yacht as Lyana had Elsa's nephew, Kiko, slightly older than her, to play with. It was Kiko who taught Lyana how to swim and dive from the yacht. As Elsa did not have the exotic kind of brief bikinis which Jack now brought for me from Frederick's in Los Angeles, I gave one to her which she only wore when out with us. Fafa seeing Jack also wearing bikini shortened the legs of his own swim trunks to modernize his look. One day as he dived bending as close to the sea as possible we were shocked to see his entire 'privates' slipping out half way down his short legs, but most of it was his scrotum. Both Jack and I must have looked petrified and disgusted for we had never seen Elsa having such a good laugh. 'How on earth could she have sex with him' we wondered.

We loved going out sailing. From the sea the exciting panorama had a magical effect which somewhat mesmerised me and made me feel peacefully relaxed. The rows of majestic buildings along Copacabana beach seemed like extended fingers to the infinite heavens. After sunset thousands of lights twinkled like bright stars and the magnificence of the Sugar Loaf guarded Urca and its golden Praia Vermelha. The skies during the day were a beautiful cloudless blue yet so mysterious at nights.

Jack enjoyed Fafa's roué attitude to life. He laughed at all the different tales of conquest this funny little man told. One evening at home while eating I felt a foot on mine, looking I saw one of Fafa's shoeless feet 'caressing' mine and the other Elsa's. When I told Jack instead of getting annoyed he was amused and just said "The bugger". One day I had been detained at the office until quite late as Mr. Havas was going away on business so he offered to give me a ride home. When I arrived there Fafa was downstairs talking with Jack. After greeting me he made some stupid remarks about if I were his wife he would investigate what was going on with my boss! I was livid and waited for Jack's reaction to defend my honour, nothing happened. I left crying with Jack behind me wondering why the emotional behaviour. In a similar position my father, or any of my old male friends in Gibraltar, would have knocked Fafa down if he had suggested this about their womenfolk. Jack explained that he knew it was not true so why hit the poor old man! Jack reckoned I was imagining things just because of Fafa's reputation.

While shopping on my own in Copacabana I casually met with Fafa who was enjoying refreshment "Where are you going Ly?" he asked "I am catching a bus to go home, why?" "I am going to get Elsa now, come with me and we shall drive you home" Fafa finished his drink and together we started walking to where Elsa supposedly was waiting. Arriving at an apartment building he said he would go up. "OK I shall wait for you down here" I said "No, perhaps it is better to come up, you know what Elsa is like and she might not be ready!" When we reached the apartment door he rang the bell and proceeded to open it with his own key. "Come in, come in" he said pulling me in. He called Elsa several times and then I noticed he had locked the front door and he was trying to undress himself panting and puffing. "Are you alright?" I asked with concern. He lunged towards me and tried to grab hold of me. For a moment I was startled and even scared and then I looked at him, pants half down, huge tummy overflowing, hair all over showing a huge balding head and God help me I started to laugh but laugh with such mirth that he stopped his amorous advances and looking sadly at me said "You are mean, Lydia!" He opened the door and I left still laughing at him. He really made a sad yet very comical figure. I could not wait to tell Jack, but he still could not believe that Fafa had meant to rape me or whatever!

After this happening we did however see them occasionally. One day when Brazil was playing England in Maracana Stadium he phoned Jack to see if he wanted to go with him and Elsa to see the football match. Since Jack was going to be at the stadium anyway as he was providing services for the newspaper people he suggested that he took me instead. Although I did not know much about this game I accepted the invitation. They picked me up and Fafa's behaviour was as if he had not tried anything with me. Since the majority of the people there were local I felt I had to cheer the English team. The audience around me thinking I was local and cheering the wrong team complained. At half time he gave Elsa and me money to buy some ice cream. We went looking for a vendor but did not find any, there were just some flag sellers and so I bought an England flag with his ice cream money instead. On our return and without looking he asked "Where is my ice cream?" "There was none. look what I bought instead!" Fafa's face was a picture, he was aghast. The Brazilians around us started to swear. Just then Pele made a goal after some beautiful passes like a ballet dancer. Fafa turning towards me all proud and excited said "You see, you see WE are the best!" Before I could think what I was doing I hit him on the head with my England flag!! "I bring you to the game, I don't get my ice cream, you buy a foreign flag and then you hit me on the head with it!" I had to admit I had not been too sporting but he deserved it for his continuous bragging with reference to Brazil and the detrimental remarks about the English!

News from home was not good. My grandmother who had loved life and enjoyed it to the full had gone to bed and passed away in her sleep. I was devastated; she had been so much fun and so very good to us all. She always told us "When I die, I don't want you to go mourning and crying. I don't want any of you to wear black or stay at home because of my having died. What I want you to do is to show your love for me while I am alive and give me the best of everything, the biggest apple, the best peach etc, take me out, share fun with me, then when I am gone you need not mourn, you have done all you could for me to enjoy while I was alive." We all loved spoiling her and I adored taking her with me on my holidays as she had always been grand company, modern and a lot of fun! Now crying as I was I put on a red dress and went to the office. Mr Havas seeing me with red swollen eyes was very concerned and asked me what had happened. When I told him he looked aghast and said "You are wearing a red dress!" "Yes." I replied, "It's what she wanted!" He sent me home.

Jack was beginning to get home from the office later and later, and his temper was becoming shorter and shorter, I just could not understand how knowing that he was hurting me so much he continued to maintain that he was waiting for the bus from leaving the office at 4.30 p.m and arriving home as late as 7.30 p.m. He who loved me so much or so he said, who made sure to accompany me when going to rehearsals, who had taken such tender care of me when I miscarried, why was he behaving in this manner and treating me as if I was a stupid child? He was distant. He did not make love and when asked he would reply that he was overworking and not feeling too good. I couldn't stand the thought of him being with another woman and then to come to bed with me. It felt dirty and disgusting. I told him I had enough and I would leave. Of course he would complain that I did not understand, although I did too well. It is amazing how men don't seem to realise the repercussions of such behaviour. I did not deserve it. I was always there helping him in every way. Men found me very attractive and desirable and had I wanted would have had not one but many lovers, was he so sure of me that he felt he could carry on like this? Did he not realize that women do not forget such experiences? If he really wanted me why did he not change and behave himself? When was he going to grow up and face the consequences? Did he really think I would still feel the same for him after this? I loved Jack. He had always been a good husband and father and had taken great care of me when I was sick with polio. He had given me the greatest gift of all, a lovely daughter, but with all his latest behaviour I was beginning to dislike him and I feared that although I loved him I was no longer in love with him. Enough was enough!

I had seen so many love affairs going wrong, friends who had blossomed with a new man to look disastrous a few months later when the affair ended. I had been happy and content with what I had and what I knew, why change, why try something new if I had all I wanted at home? One day when I was most desperate I decided to do something about Jack's behaviour. I made arrangements to meet my confidential friend Benny, who was I must admit, unaware of my problem. We met after office hours, had tea, went to a cinema, and I was reluctant to return home. My friend Benny who knew me very well and knew that I always got home to be with my daughter and Jack could not understand my behaviour. "Lydia, I know you too well. What are you up to?" she asked. She would not believe me when I said nothing was wrong so finally I confessed. She promised she would never say anything unless needed. She left me at the corner of my street and I walked home. It was 9.30 p.m. I found Olimpia my maid waiting downstairs to warn me all worried and scared for what might happen. The Master was very upset, she said, and had on several occasions indicated he would call the police station and hospital in case I had had an accident. I sent her home and I went upstairs. I opened the front door and said "Hello darling." "Where the hell have you been, you know what time it is?" an infuriated Jack asked me. Lyana on seeing me, came running and saying "Mummy. I'm hungry." "My goodness Jack, haven't you eaten? Why did you not feed Lyana?" "Well, are you going to tell me where you have been?" "But of course darling" said I, "don't be so upset, nothing has happened. You see, I have been in the same bus queue that you go to and delays your coming back home every day"   I did not feel as brave as I sounded, my knees trembled with nerves and fear but I had done what I had set out to do. Did Jack ask me any more questions? No, he did not. But he stopped coming home late; and started being friendly and considerate once again but perhaps it was a little too late.

Chapter 15

THE COLONEL

It was during this period that Colonel Arthur walked into my life. For the first time since I had married, I was really affected by a man. He was magnetic and very manly. One day I had left the office tired and looking forward to getting home. I stood as always in the queue when suddenly this very attractive man elegantly dressed in a fine alpaca suit stopped; faced me, gave a charming smile and then lifted up the end of his top lip in a sort of a snarling action. I looked behind me to see who had received such admiration. I was the last one in the queue. I remember I smiled and why not admit it, I felt good, it was the booster I needed. The following day, and for the remainder of the week the same thing happened. Then, when I was looking forward to seeing him, he did not appear again for a few days. Then there he was once more and this time seemingly waiting for my arrival. I joined the queue and he stood behind me but never said a word. I got into the bus and he followed suit but did not sit next to me. Since I was in the front seat I did not look back but I was very conscious of his being there. I got out of the bus and started walking home. I heard footsteps so I accelerated and the steps quickened too. I did not dare look behind me. I was scared and started to run, and then I heard behind me someone running too. With someone holding me by the arm and very concernedly asking "Are you alright?" it was the man. "Good Lord, you frightened me!" "You are a very beautiful woman" he said "I would very much like to accompany you!" "You must be crazy, I am a married woman" I said "So what, I am a married man too. But, didn't you know that chicken every night is tiring and boring?" I laughed at his cheek but asked him to leave me alone which he did. He was however always hanging about the bus stop whenever I went home.

Another day as I came out of the office for lunch to walk to Mesbla (a fashionable big store like Harrods) where I usually had lunch and shopped, the man was there. Surprised, I smiled as if seeing a friend. He smiled back but then went away. A couple of days later just as I started to eat my usual ice cream sundae someone came to me and said "That is not good for you!" I looked back and there he was again. This time he stayed by my side and introduced himself, asking permission to sit but sat before I could answer him. I asked him how he knew I was there. To my surprise he said that one day as he was passing by a building near the bus stop he had seen me coming out and he had imagined that that would be where I worked. Another day he had stood guard at the lunch hour and had followed me to Mesbla. I must admit I was most gratified, here I was a grown up woman enjoying some form of flirtation with a handsome man who liked to talk to me and made me laugh. Arthur was tall, had a lovely smart appearance, beautiful mouth and teeth and sparkling black eyes, and was well built with a lovely muscular appearance. A real man in his mid forties and courting me! It was not as if I was dating, we just met casually and walked to the bus stop or met for lunch during office hours. As far as I was concerned I was not doing anything wrong, and I was enjoying the adulation. It was a friendship like I had with JP years earlier in Gibraltar. I could talk to him, discuss things, speak my mind and laugh together with him without him thinking me a nitwit or a silly fool. Additionally the fact that I was fully aware of the physical attraction between us which after all the time when I was unwanted by Jack made me feel extremely good and desirable, I enjoyed that very much.

After eighteen months Jack was transferred, from the downtown office to be in charge of the Copacabana office on the Avenida Atlantica right by Copacabana beach. Since all the embassies were situated in that area he was responsible for their communications and we began our new social life which became even more hectic. We were often asked to embassies where we met some very interesting people. Gwen, who had a splendid home, gave fantastic parties. She was quite wild for those days. She collected people from many backgrounds, ambassadors and their ladies, poets, writers, artists etc. Everyone who was invited had 'to pay for what they ate' by a performance. Guests told jokes, recited, sang, or did magic tricks and I usually did one of my Spanish dances. You never knew how to expect Gwen to be dressed. She was so much fun, so sophisticated and always could get away with her craziest of gear. Her favourite mode of dressing was leotards and tights worn with very high heel shoes and beads galore. More often than not she would also wear either flowers or a turban on her head. It was in Gwen's house that I had the occasion of dancing with a Mr. Khan. He was the charge d'affairs at the Pakistan Embassy. We started to dance a lively Brazilian tune and he mistook me for a carioca (local) girl. By now I had taken to Brazil like a duck to water. I had gained a lovely caramel coloured skin and dressed smartly and fashionably like the local ladies, so it was not his fault that he mistook me for a Brazilian girl. I always seemed to integrate well and was delighted.

My partner was an extremely charming, tall, very handsome and polite gentleman. He started to make small talk in his best Portuguese. I, trying to make things easier for him, said that he could, if he liked speak in English with me. "Oh! Where did you learn it?" He asked. Still dancing and very much in tune with the music, I answered "In Gibraltar, you see I am a British subject and extremely proud of it." This must have been a super charged reply. For no sooner had I said those magical words than I was left standing in the middle of the dance floor without a partner though not for long. This happened at the time when Pakistan came under martial law and was suspended from the Commonwealth therefore relations between Britain and Pakistan were at their lowest ebb. But what did that have to do with me?

I asked Gwen what happened to elderly women in Brazil. Gwen was from Jamaica and a long time resident in Rio. She herself was around forty-five and yet had the appearance of someone at least ten years younger. She explained to me that at the age of thirty five or forty, most women started to take hormones. Around forty-five, plastic surgery took care of everything at a reasonable cost. The face, neck, eyes, bosom etc., were all reshaped, re-done, or lifted by expert surgeons. She told me that she had had plastic surgery on her private parts so as to be like a virgin once again. She had been tucked in to give and feel more sexual pleasure. I did not know whether to take her seriously but years later she went into hospital for a 'tonsilitis operation' and returned looking younger than me!

Gwen was an amazing and wonderful woman. I loved her, her company and hearing her tell me tales. Her husband, according to her, was a man well endowed by nature but 'it is not a good tool that does an excellent job, but the method and technique in the using of such a tool!' her statements always left me fascinated and dumbstruck. That was not all. She frankly told me of her love affairs, and how she had two current lovers. But, she did it for a good cause, to help her husband have wonderful sex. He apparently always performed one hundred per cent better if he knew she had someone else wanting and desiring her! She 'sacrificed' herself so that her husband would know more passion.

In spite of all these extracurricular activities, Gwen was an assiduous churchgoer and a regular person in the confessional and at weekly Holy Communion. I just could not for my life understand how she had the courage and the daring for all this free-for-all love, yet confessing her affairs time after time, week after week, to the priest. I could not help myself asking her if she confessed her sins and her adultery every week knowing that she had not repented and was going to keep on doing it. "Confess", she said, "but why should I, they are not sins. You must remember, Ly, God said people must go out into the world and love each other, and this is precisely what I am doing!" I was flabbergasted at her optimistic and amusing way of interpreting God's words of love.

Jack had just returned from his office and was having a quick shower before we sat down for dinner when the doorbell rung. Olimpia came to me looking worried with an envelope in her hand. "What is it Olimpia, are you alright?" "Ah. Senora, it is a telegram!" she said handing it to me. In those days receiving a telegram could only mean bad news. Apprehensively I checked it and confirmed it was for us. I walked into the bathroom and said "Jack, there is a telegram for you!" "Who is it addressed to?" "Armstrong" I said. "Well, open it up. What are you waiting for?" I opened the envelope and read. It was from Mum Armstrong; Dad had had a heart attack and had passed away." Well?" Jack inquired. "You better come out and read it for yourself" I replied. The shower curtain opened, I handed Jack the towel and very softly he asked "Mum?" I gave him the envelope. "Oh, my God, Dad!" and there Jack stood tears streaming down his cheeks as he came to my arms and sobbed! It was the first time ever I had seen Jack cry. It made me feel really sad as I held him tightly. Lyana came rushing in and when she saw her Daddy and by then her Mummy crying too she said "Don't cry Mummy, don't cry Daddy, Nana good, Nana good!" "Yes darling, I know you are good. It's Daddy who hurt himself!" "I love you Mummy, I love you Daddy, don't cry". Jack wanted to go to the funeral but it was just not possible at that time.

Our friends all rallied round and soon life was back to normal. Ruth invited us to her beautiful home with quite a number of family friends. We were all seated and enjoying a lovely spread when the music started playing as usual in their home and everyone got up from the table waving arms held up above their heads and marching in time to the carnival music! "Come and join us, let's all dance!" We both got up and joined them and although to start with we felt quite silly we soon too enjoyed the abandonment to this contagious rhythm. It was good to let your hair down and bring joy to the heart. We looked forward to these gatherings where Lyana also came as Ruth had two boys who although older took great care of her sometimes teasing her for her Portuguese accent. One day the ladies were asked to go to Ruth's bedroom where we were to be entertained with educational films. What an education, what an eye opener! It was a porno film. Neither Jack nor I had ever seen anything like this before. It wasn't that we were prudish, we made love and experimented. (Fr. Mondejar always used to say that anything that went on behind the bedroom door between husband and wife was permissible as long as both were in agreement) But watching such a private matter on film was disgusting. I felt embarrassed, uncomfortable and dirty. Love making should be beautiful; this was cheap and nasty without joy or enjoyment. When the film finished the ladies left in order to let the men see the show! At least they had shown a little consideration by keeping men and women guests apart. When the men came down I could not look at their faces, not even Jack's. When the following day Phyllis asked what we had thought of the show my answer came prompt and direct. "We enjoy making love and not looking at people behaving like animals!" She had the grace of apologising for her sister. In Rio the sex act did not appear to have anything to do with love, it was just a physical necessity. Their attitude was, and I finally realised it when Cleia in the office said "If you have a headache you take an aspirin, if you have a toothache you go to the dentist, if you want sex you get a man, it doesn't matter who!"

No doubt my Loreto Convent education, belonging to the Legion of Mary as well as being a Daughter of Mary and belonging to the church choir had a lot to do with my attitude towards sex. You just did not go with a man unless you were married to him. You did not have lovers. You would bring shame on yourself and family and go to hell, (this last I thought was far fetched since people did worse things and were forgiven). I did not criticise anyone for doing otherwise but I would not be so generous if I caught Jack with more than the suspicions I had of his behaviour. The thought of having another man at the same time as my husband was unthinkable, I could only love one person at a time and if I found someone else I would not hesitate to leave Jack.

Cleia got married to Laudemar from Paulding Deltec's office. We were all invited to the wedding and I was so surprised to find that Cleia's divorced parents were there with their respective partners and family. They sat at the same table and were having a good time. I thought this was so civilized. I had never known my Grandad Emilio because he and Granny Elena had separated (divorce was not legal in Spain) and those separated were never on friendly terms with their ex-partners and the children had to make a choice with whom they wanted to keep in touch. To take Cleia's place in the office I engaged a very nice young woman, Andrea. Fortunately we all got on very well together so although we missed Cleia and her sense of humour plus her enjoyment in trying to teach me the many love positions – it was her favourite subject –at least in the office all was well.

One day Benny came home all aghast at what had happened to some American friends of theirs. Although none of us foreigners believed or wanted to know anything about Macumba it seemed Macumba can come to us when least expected. Apparently her friends owned a factory just on the outskirts of Rio city. The husband got sick and weaker and weaker, and as no doctor had been able to diagnose his illness in Rio the wife decided to take him to the USA to a famous tropical disease research centre for investigation. The doctors there tried everything without luck and the man was practically at death's door. One of the specialists on hearing that the patient had been living in Brazil quickly suggested the wife returned there and consult a witch doctor. The wife, who did not believe in such things, was horrified but the American doctor was emphatic. At their hospital they could not do anything to help her husband so why not try what he suggested as there was nothing to lose and everything to gain! The doctor would accompany her and the patient back to Rio.

One of the American couple's servants suggested the name of a renowned Macumbeira who on being called promptly told the wife and the doctor that the man had had the evil eye cast upon him. Questions were asked and the man had sacked some worker, "Is there any article of clothing missing?" The wife checked but thought all was correct. Then a maid remembered that they had given their unwanted clothing to the workers in the factory to share out between them. Knowing this the 'macumbeira' – witch doctor, went around their garden chanting some peculiar incantation. She finally stopped and told the people following her, amongst whom was the doctor as a witness (taking notes, as well as the patient's wife in his bedroom) to dig. Apparently it was proven later that as the digging ended with the appearance of the patient's old suit the man sat up in his bed and said "I am hungry, give me something to eat!" Benny followed up by saying that her friends were putting up their business for sale and would be leaving Brazil straight away. She also warned me that if I ever gave any of my clothing away

I was to wash it several times before doing so in order that none of my body odours remained!

What with all the sex, infidelity and macumba, life was becoming too ugly and I wanted desperately a change of environment and life style. I had felt so happy when we arrived and it seemed as if everything was going to be wonderful in Brazil and yet nothing had really turned out like that. The only positive thing was my professional life. It made me feel very happy that I had progressed in less than ten years from being so ignorant that I didn't even know what a 'records clerk' meant in Salisbury, Southern Rhodesia. I was now an executive secretary and for a firm where both presidents I had met, Mr. George Havas and Sam Ruvkun, had promised me they would be only too pleased to offer me employment wherever there was one of their offices.

I had always loved my birthdays and celebrating them. Now I was thirty, I was having a party but just felt lonely, sad and old. Before I knew what was happening I was crying my heart out. Lyana saw me and asked "Are you alright Mummy? Have you hurt yourself?" I put my arms around her and kissed her "No, Nana, I haven't hurt myself, I just feel old!" She pulled herself away from me, looked at my face and then said "No, Mummy, you are not old. You are only a little bit used up!" I could not help laughing and she was so happy too.

My friends gathered around me that night including Luciana who had somehow become a friend without my remembering how I had even met her. Luciana was my age, very rich, divorced, very pretty and with blond hair. She had a lovely Jaguar sports car, a sailing boat and lived in a beautiful house in one of the richest neighbourhoods. She was very spoilt too. She had invited me a couple of times to sail with her but I had stopped doing so when I noticed she deliberately kept me from returning home at the time I was supposed to. I told Jack. She would take me to the yacht clubhouse and there meet with a young crowd among whom was this silly 'mother's boy' who kept on flirting with me. I could not stand him or his stupid ways.

That night Luciana arrived radiant as always, all the male friends doting on her and showering her with attention. I was busy entertaining my guests and enjoying myself. Then I realised I had not seen Jack and went looking for him to find him having a tete a tete with Luciana very close together and whispering. I stopped by the door, frozen, then without saying a word, returned to my guests. I had had enough. I was confused, bewildered, fed up and very very angry. I was being made a fool in my own home on my thirtieth birthday! Luciana left and I never saw or heard from her again and when I eventually asked Jack what had happened to her he said that as she did not want to upset me. Having seen the look on my face she thought it best to end my friendship. How did Jack know that?

Meanwhile I had Arthur's friendship; he at least made me feel good and happy and I now looked forward to seeing him whenever I did. I arrived as usual at Mesbla and was going to the bar where I used to sit when he approached me. "Don't bother to sit down, today we are going to a little churasqueria (barbeque place) nearby" "I haven't got time for a big meal, you go, I shall stay here!" He pleaded so much that I relented when he promised I would be back in the office on time. We just sat down and started to eat, and then he said "You know we have known one another for a long time. We are both adults and both know what we want. Don't you think it is time to do something about it?" Startled I looked at him "What do you mean?" "Come off it, I have waited a long time, you know I desire you like I think you desire me!" I found him attractive, I enjoyed his company, felt good at his flattering, I liked him a lot but I was not in love with him. I did not want to enter into any clandestine arrangement, for what? I must have looked peculiar and I started to shake as I realised what I had got myself into. Surprised he said "You mean to say you have never cheated on your husband?" When I shook my head saying no he said "I like you too well to hurt you, finish up and I shall accompany you to your office!" It was the last time I saw him.

At the office I was unable to concentrate on my work. I made mistakes and had to retype a lot of my work. I couldn't stop thinking. What had I done? Why hadn't I stopped the friendship before getting to this point? By the time I left the office it was too late to get the normal bus so subsequently I arrived home later than usual. On seeing me Jack came to me and held my hand and in an intense voice said "Oh Ly, my darling, whatever happens, whatever you do, don't ever leave me!" I was stunned. What had brought that up? Had he seen me at the restaurant that day? Well, I had not done anything. As my Aunt Lottie used to say "Having sex with a strange man for the first time was as difficult as taking out the first olive from the jar!" I was not ashamed of anything. I had not taken out the first olive!

Chapter 16

THE CHANGE

Jack's attitude had changed. At least I could now speak to him and when I asked why he had behaved so strangely, why he had been so distant with me, he put it down to my imagination. He had been off colour for a while and perhaps he was going through the 'change of life', some change at thirty two years of age! I thought it best to leave things alone as news came that our tour there was coming to an end and we would be leaving Rio during the next couple of months.

Andrea was a nice, capable young woman. She was slightly taller than Cleia with huge black eyes just like a doll's. Being of Spanish ancestry her appearance and ways were more Europeanised. One day she came and told me that her uncle was sending his chauffeur driven car for her and if I wanted she could give me a lift. Her uncle had asked her to pick up some work of art at an artist's workshop which was near where I lived. I could accompany her and then she would drop me at home.

The art shop belonged to Ilio, an Italian artist. He had wonderful paintings and ceramic works which I found most irresistible. All his paintings oozed out energy and strength, the colours were incredible and his technique unusual, he painted more often than not with his fingers and hands. Whilst there I was surprised when he refused to sell one of his paintings on show to an American buyer, in fact he had been rather rude in his dealing with him. My curiousity was aroused and I asked him if the paintings were not for sale. "Of course they are." "Then why did you not sell it? The man was willing to pay your price!" "I did not sell to him because I did not like him." I found him such a character that I could not resist telling Jack all about him and his behaviour. Jack laughed and expressed his wishes of meeting Ilio, take Lyana with us and see if he would do her portrait if he found the painter as good as I had described.

The visit proved quite extraordinary, we had heard of unmarried mothers but never of unmarried fathers and that was Ilio's position. He had been in love with an Italian girl during the 1940 War and just as he was about to be moved to the front, he found she was expecting his child. Without any hesitation, Ilio who was very much in love with the girl, suggested they should marry immediately. It was then that he found that she was already a married woman with her husband away fighting. She did not want anything to do with the child. With so little time left he arranged for his mother to look after the girl until the baby was born and then his mother and sisters would take care of the child until he returned from the war. A little boy, Marcos, was born and as arranged the mother went away leaving him with his grandmother. They never saw or heard from Marcos' mother again.

Soon after the war was over, Ilio, who was a lawyer by profession, but a true artist at heart, could not settle down to peaceful existence, and his bohemian life was more than the family could put up with. At length he decided to emigrate to Argentina where he felt sure he could make a name for himself as an artist. He left his son Marcos with his grandmother to attend school in Torino so that he could have a family life until such time as he could join his father wherever that might be. In Argentina, Ilio dedicated his time to painting and learning all about ceramics. He would paint the ceramics made by his friends and thus made a respectable living. Nevertheless, he felt his real love for painting was being unrealized, and soon decided to break away from his partners to dedicate all of his time to his paintings.

He moved to Rio where he lived in a very picturesque house in the district of Urca with a grandiose view of the Sugar Loaf, the bay and the great Cristo do Corcovado with arms outstretched as if in blessing, holding us all to his bosom and protection.

Ilio was not a very tall man, his looks were very similar to Franco Nero's. He was an extremely intense man, hyperactive and very excitable. After a short while he made you feel tired to the point of exhaustion. As a man I found him rather intolerable, as an artist he was fantastic. When he painted he would play beautiful classical music which obviously seemed to relax him and put him in a receptive mood. His paintings were so touching and beautiful that his attitude of not wanting to sell wasn't surprising.

After our first visit to his studio and making the necessary arrangements we sent Lyana over with Olimpia but after a few visits there we found out that she was restless so we decided we would wait until our return from leave when we would try taking her ourselves. Lyana was only six years old and did not appreciate posing for long time. Ilio was not accustomed to dealing with children!

Ilio would occasionally visit us and we got into the habit of going to see him if we were nearby. It amused us to see how very impractical he was and how he never bothered about his appearance or his home. He used to have a huge hamper where he would keep on putting all his dirty clothes; and then when he had run out of all his clean shirts etc. and had to go out somewhere unexpectedly, he would rummage through all the soiled laundry picking out the cleanest of the garments cast aside, for re-ironing without first laundering it! I just could not understand his behaviour. With the sale of only one of his paintings he earned more than Jack did for a month's work yet he lived in a proper mess. Sometimes he did not even have enough money to pay his rent. Eventually we discovered that whenever he did sell one of his works he would pay some of his debts but give a lot to his other artist friends. We both knew that he was aiming to bring his son Marcos over now that he was a teenager but if he went on like this he would not be very successful.

Although it had nothing to do with us I found that I could not stand what I considered to be shabby and careless behaviour and somehow found myself bullying him, if not for his sake, at least for his son's. Ilio would rave at me and say "You have no heart, no art in you! Money does not mean everything!" When Jack laughed and I shouted saying "And how are you going to eat and keep Marcos?" He would quieten down. Pity we did not have much time left for us in Rio but before we left he had become better organized to the extent that he had enough funds to cover his expenses. I advised him to put some of his earnings away as 'Marcos Funds.'

I handed in my resignation giving Mr Havas a month's notice. Our life certainly turned very busy with all our friends giving us farewell parties even though they all knew we would be returning. As was the rule we had to pack up all our belongings and send them for storage. The apartment had to be vacated in case someone else wanted to move into it so we gave our own farewell party inviting quite a huge crowd of very different people including all our good friends. Paul and Leigh Havas were naturally amongst those present. Paul came with a gift for me; a smallish box very beautifully wrapped up with a lovely big bow. "Sunshine" he said "This is the last lesson I shall be giving you. Hopefully you will learn never to trust anyone in your business life again!" Intrigued at what he said I unwrapped the present to find all the coffee spoons that I had missed from my collection! I was amazed to say the least but it was a lesson well learnt. Each time he had been to our home he had unobtrusively taken away a coffee spoon!

Olimpia was distressed at saying goodbye to her little girl but eventually forgot all about us by getting her own life sorted out. She was going to marry a Portuguese who in the three years he had been in Rio from being just a lorry driver now had his own business which included two lorries. Olimpia would not need to go out to work again. We promised we would see her on our return. Once packed and everything taken care of we went to stay in a Copacabana hotel awaiting the arrival of the ship that would be taking us home for about four months holiday.

Chapter 17

VACATION

We chose to travel to England on a Blue Star ship which promised at least twenty-four hours in Funchal, Madeira, but when we arrived at this enchanting island for what would have been my first visit there since leaving as a teenager, we found that we were not allowed to go ashore due to the bad weather. I was so very upset and could not stop the tears flowing freely.

As the lights shone like winking cat's eyes in the night, and the waves broke against the ship, I could barely make out the outline of the Hotel Savoy; but yes, there was our Villa Honolulu in the hotel grounds! The saltiness of my tears mingled with the sea spray: the weather and sea were very bad. 'So near and yet so far' it felt as if you could practically touch land and yet it was so far away. I was badly disappointed.

"Mrs Armstrong is wanted at the purser's office" came loud and clear over the loud speaker. What else was going to happen? Would I be allowed to go ashore after all I wondered?. Tear stained and unhappy, I made my way to the office where I was handed a princely bouquet of orchids, at least six dozen of them, and attached to it a jeweller's box containing a beautiful gold necklace! It was a gift from one of our family's very dear friends. The orchids must have been given with lots of love and good wishes for they lasted until we arrived in Gibraltar a few weeks later!

As was now the custom we went to stay at the Exiles Club in Twickenham before going up north. This time Mum Armstrong who was now alone was coming with us for what was going to be her very first trip out of the UK and by ship. Jack had his good days and others when he didn't cease complaining about just everything. We had gone to London for final arrangements with Head Office and he kept on and on like a broken record. We were in a bus and the moment it stopped I got hold of Lyana and promptly got off the bus. Startled Jack followed me still grumbling "Shut up for Pete's Sake. I have had enough. If you are missing anyone and want to return to Rio be my guest. Let me have some peace!" Shocked at my outburst in the middle of the street Jack kept by my side without saying a word. From then on I had the peace I so much needed and wanted.

Lyana was thrilled to visit Madame Tussauds' where she was too intrigued with the wax figures, often addressing them, much to our mirth. The Planetarium fascinated her and she incessantly asked questions. At the end it had been a lovely and happy outing.

Once Jack had finished with Head Office we went to the North. Mum had sold the family house and moved to a place where she was living on her own but under proper care with a daily home help. These houses had only one bedroom, a sitting/dining room, kitchenette and bathroom, all very modern and compact. The house was provided with panic buttons in case of any emergency and was constantly supervised so both Len and Jeff, Jack's brothers, could get on with their own lives. She was very happy there but she could not have us stay with her. Aunt Dora and Uncle George invited us to stay at their home for the few days we would be there getting Mum ready for the trip .She was so excited. We had chosen to travel on the Canberra, then one of the bigger ships, which usually travelled to Australia carrying English emigrants who were mainly subsidized by the Government.

The crossing was excellent and we were all enjoying our time together. It was wonderful to see Mum enjoying herself and even partaking of the odd glass of wine which had never been allowed before while Dad was alive. She blossomed out and was eager to learn and participate in all she could.   Normally, every time we arrived in Gibraltar I was always met by a congregation of family and friends, this time it was only Auntie Lottie and a very pregnant Lena who came on board. I had this horrible feeling of desperation of some horrible happening. I knew that there was definitely something wrong for knowing my parents they would have all been there giving my mother-in-law a warm welcome. When I inquired what was wrong my aunt said that Mum was not feeling too well and that Dad, my darling Daddy, was waiting for us all at the dock. As we approached the shores I could see him standing all alone and holding a huge bouquet of flowers, something that he would never have done before as it was not a man's thing to do. What a pleasurable surprise that was!

As he saw me he ran towards me saying "Hija, Hija" (daughter, daughter) I embraced him saying "La Mama, where is la Mama?" "It's OK Chamaca, it's OK, Mum is in hospital but she is doing fine and you can now go there and see for yourself!"   Some of the orchids, at least a couple of dozen, had survived and knowing how much Mum loved these flowers and that they came from Madeira I took them to the hospital. She looked frail but well. She had been anaemic and needed special care but soon she would be home with us.

Since Granny Elena was no longer with us, Granny Armstrong was allocated her room and all of a sudden she became everyone's Granny including Dad's who showered her with attention. Jack's Mum's popularity knew no end with all the young members of the family; they had gained someone to tell a story to or to go out with. Since we were going to be a long time on holiday Lyana had to go to school so she joined her cousins and attended the Loreto Convent where she was able to take her First Holy Communion at home with all the family.

I missed Granny Elena very much. Somehow I expected to see her any time. She had taken great joy with then her only great-grandchild and had insisted on having a photograph portraying the four generations. She had dressed up and worn flowers in her hair on that day as she 'wanted Lyana to remember her always like that!' Poor Granny, she had always been such a good friend and guardian angel, so modern in her thinking and always helping us out of trouble with our Dad. Granny had been a strong, courageous woman. She had suffered heartbreak and hardships but with dignity, never losing faith or love for life and living .She was not there physically but I carried her in my heart as I think all the grownups did and it was no wonder now that Mum Armstrong had symbolically filled her place.

It was incredible to see how Jack's mum fitted in. She loved the food, enjoyed the sunshine and had been thrilled to visit Spain and even see the Holy Week processions in Sevilla. I must have changed a lot as I seemed to go unrecognized amongst the local shopkeepers where I had shopped most of my life and who tended to speak to me now in either French or Italian. Even some friends did not recognize me. I had gone to Eastern Beach with Lyana and Jack. I was wearing my red bikini, Brazilian beach jacket and little straw hat over a red and white spotted scarf. I saw an old friend of mine with her children nearby so, thrilled to see her. I got up and walked towards her "Aidita, Aidita" I called out with joy. "I don't know you" she said recoiling as if she had seen the devil himself. "For Pete's sake Aida have a good look, just because I am wearing a bikini does not mean that you should not know me!" Later, I discovered that I was the first Gibraltarian woman to wear this piece of swim wear. There was only one other woman, a French woman married to an RAF officer, who dared to wear a bikini.

Lena had her baby son Dominique, named after Dad, and I was asked to be his godmother. It was such a very happy occasion for us all. Father Grech, who had married my mother and all the Danino sisters with the exception of Clementina who had married in Nairobi, was officiating. "Well Lydia, aren't you ashamed of yourself? All your sisters, including the youngest one now have two children and you only have one!" "Why Father, it isn't for lack of trying you know!" having said this and seen my poor old fashioned Dad's reaction and words of "nina, nina" (girl!) I realized it sounded a bit too forward for Gibraltar so I quickly followed it with "You know, I have had five miscarriages since I had my little girl" His reaction was great "Keep at it, keep at it!"

It was time to return to the UK and take Mum back to the North. Aunt Dora and Uncle George were delighted to have us back for a few days more and once again we stayed at their home. During our previous stay I had complained about the coldness in the toilet during my nightly visit. Uncle George was therefore eager for night time to come for me to see what he had done for my comfort. I was really intrigued. As night fell, I went in, put on the light and sat down. My goodness me, it felt as if my head was being cooked, the heat coming from above was unbearable. I looked up and Uncle George had installed some kind of heater which worked in conjunction with the light bulb. Coming out, there he was waiting "Well, pet, how you did like that?" "Uncle George, it isn't my head that needs the heat, it's my bum!" Whilst Aunt Dora roared with laughter Uncle's face was a riot!

Chapter 18

CARIOCAS

We returned to Brazil on another Blue Star ship. When we called at Salvador, Bahia, a colleague came to see us on board bearing a telegram. Suddenly we weren't too keen to open and read it as we thought it was perhaps the Company telling us that we were to stay there instead of proceeding to Rio. We never gave a thought to any of the family members as they were all left in excellent health. It was from the Company, the Rio office welcoming the Armstrongs back. We sighed with relief as at least we already knew what to expect in Rio. On our return we found that in the few months we had been away there had been some changes. Quite a number of friends had been transferred so once again we would have to make new friends. Olimpia was already expecting a child and we were to stay in the hotel for over a month while the Company was refurbishing our old flat as if we were new tenants. It meant new decorations, furniture, and soft furnishings!

Whilst in the hotel I was able to interview some girls sent by friends and I finally decided to engage Josefa. Also Portuguese, she was very serious and to start with rather surly. She was however an excellent worker, very honest and could cook like an angel. I found her rather irritating for every time I asked her to do something she would reply "Pois nao, Senhora" which literally translated meant 'but no, Madame.' Yet after a short while she had accomplished what I had asked. One day, I was obviously not in such an understanding mood and I said "Josefa, I am sorry but you will have to go" "Why, Madame? I shall not go, I am a good responsible worker and no one has ever told me to go!" "You see what I mean? Every time I ask you to do something you tell me no and then you do it and now I send you away and you won't go!" "Ah Madame, You don't understand Portuguese too well, when I say pois nao, it means 'but sure!" She started to laugh and then I thought what the heck, she works well, and she does not spend as much money as Olimpia had and the food was great. Josefa stayed with us for the rest of the time we were in Rio and Lyana eventually doted on her. Josefa spoilt her no end!

Mr Havas on finding out that we had returned asked me to resume at his office but I was reluctant to do so as he had too demanding a way and his hours were not convenient for me now that Lyana was growing up and had more activities. Ilio too came to visit us and this time with his son Marcos who turned out to be extremely sensible and more like a father to Ilio than a son.

Jack made arrangements for me to take Lyana for her sittings and by then there was only a couple more sessions to complete her portrait. Ilio had begun to shower me with compliments and I found the whole situation rather ridiculous. He found me so beautiful – ha – that he wanted me to pose for him. I was 'bela bellisima' and I felt too ridiculous for words. But Ilio, an artist, took a different view. I was his muse! Jack was a different man, he came home on time, and we went out together and were all very happy. It was just like it was at the beginning of our stay there.

I soon tired of being just a housewife and mother and felt that I should get myself something to do to stimulate my brain. I found a position as private secretary to Mr Sammy Cohn. He was the owner and president of a firm importing the very popular Vespa mopeds, but I did not have anything to do with that department of his various enterprises. Mr Cohn had purchased an enormous amount of land in the interior and ran a colonising company. He had divided this land into plots of different sizes for developing into farms for the Eastern European immigrants. He had worked out, in minute detail, what to plant; the number of cattle; what amount of fertilizer then available, what kind of factories to have nearby, so as to control all the aspects of marketing and farming, raising of crops etc. I had great admiration for him and loved his remarkably well trained mind and intelligence. He was a quick thinker, a great man who never lost his cool and was always calm and collected and he treated me with great respect.

When I started working for Mr Cohn a young man from the Vespa department called Beno was his right hand man as until I went to work for him he had had no secretary to look after the colonizing business. Every time I had to do or get anything pertaining to my new boss I had to go and ask Beno. At last I decided to tackle Beno. He proved to be a very nice person and totally understanding. In fact he was as keen to hand over all Mr. Cohn's personal documents as I was keen to set up the office properly. I was quite busy for a while reorganizing things to my liking and when I had accomplished my task I was thrilled and proud to see how Beno was no longer bothered by any staff member when work pertained to the colonizing company.

Mr Cohn travelled frequently and he always returned with a little memento of his trip for me. Unfortunately while he travelled I had very little to do at the office and I began to get bored. I also wanted to get more money but I felt that in reality I was being overpaid for the very little amount of work I was doing so I did not dare approach Mr Cohn about it. Meanwhile I had met a Mrs Sheehy, personnel officer at the American Embassy, who was very keen to get me to work there if I could meet the qualifications required; the offer seemed too good for me to let it pass. So I started proceedings for the position.

Applying for a job at the American Embassy is an experience not to be forgotten! I had to take shorthand dictation, type letters, timed for speed, checked for accuracy and so on which were normal procedures. Then I was interviewed by a number of people who spoke to me in Portuguese, English, Spanish and French firing questions at me like from a shot gun. I was successful through all these phases so I thought the job was mine, but I was wrong!! I suppose the embassy is right checking and double checking and double checking again, but when you know you have nothing to hide and you are an OK person you feel like throwing everything overboard, forgetting the prestige and better salary.

Finally academically, I was found to be fine, but by then I was also being 'investigated' naturally unknown to me until much later. I also had to fill in many forms regarding my political beliefs, my moral tendencies, my drinking habits and a thousand more questions. At last I thought I had finished when I was told that I had to go through a complete medical check-up with the Embassy's own doctors. I had X-Rays taken; blood analysed, and once again questions to answer, lots of them and rather indiscreet as well as distasteful too. The doctor was again asking me another question, "How many operations have you had, Mrs Armstrong?" "Appendix out when a child, and a caesarean not so long ago" I answered "Hum, I see, tell me, Mrs Armstrong, have you one or two incisions?" That was really the last straw! "Look here doctor; I wonder if we are both aware of the job I am applying for!" "What do you mean, Mrs Armstrong?" "Well, I want a job as a secretary, and not as a striptease dancer, so what difference would it make if I have one or two scars?" Rather startled he replied very seriously "If there is any catastrophe you can always be recognized by markings on your body!" After this I was not too sure whether I wanted the job or not!

When I was finally approved and given the job as secretary to Dr Martin E. Little, deputy chief of the Education Division, Point IV. I had to face Mr. Cohn and give in my notice. "You want to leave me Mrs Armstrong, but why?" "Mr Cohn, I wanted more money." "Well, why didn't you ask me?" "I couldn't, I did not think I had enough work to warrant an increase!" "Mrs Armstrong, it is not for you to make that decision, it is for me and I am willing to increase it. Have you not realized that you are worth what you think you are worth? Don't be so humble! I shall not let you go." When he saw the look on my face he added "not until you find me someone as good as yourself!" I had to remain a fortnight extra training Paula who had just returned from the kibbutz in Israel and was a fabulous girl who could also write splendid French! With everybody now happy I transferred to my new position.

With the new job I had transportation as my boss and a couple of other executives lived my way and I was picked up in the mornings and returned after work. This was a terrific asset as I would not have to wait in any queues for a bus. Dr Little was kindness itself although I had to put up with a lot of kidding because of my British accented English, although I was soon accepted by everyone.

We still saw Phyllis but not so frequently. Benny and Shorty were like family members. With them we often went to the Paissandu Club and to Joa to see our other mutual friends Lucia and Alan. Gwen was always there. She was such a lot of fun and there was so much learnt from her. Now that I returned home relatively early we often went out together. One day, as she had rather a bad stomach, Gwen asked me if I would accompany her to one of the so-called 'faith healers.' When we arrived at his office I was fascinated to see the acting that went on and I couldn't for my life understand how such a sophisticated woman could believe in such a rigmarole. He sat down facing her with knees touching knees, he grabbed hold of her hands and while fixedly looking straight into her eyes he moved the arms around, lifting, rotating backwards, forwards. At the end of this he prescribed her a diet of boiled potatoes and olive oil for a few days and nothing but water to drink! Gwen carried it out to the letter. One evening the maid brought in her dinner all beautifully set out on a silver tray, little flower vase with a few fresh flowers, best china, embroidered napkin, real style. She excused herself for having to eat before we went out, dabbing the corner of her mouth as if enjoying a succulent meal. Then suddenly she stopped eating, got up and said. "Do forgive me Lydia but I must go out to fart!" Well, I had no idea what the word meant at all but I soon found out as before she reached the doorway she let out the loudest noise I had ever heard or thought possible of such a refined person like her. "Oh, Oh" I said. "Well, I did warn you, old girl" and she left the room for the toilet. I don't know why but I found the word I had just learnt quite enjoyable and satisfying and no sooner had I returned home than I was telling Jack all about it.

We also went out with Merka and Gerardo in their boat which now was often at the nudist island of Luz del Fuego. Luz del Fuego was the black sheep of a very prominent family in Brazil, an extremely intelligent woman, a true naturist and one of the first known friends of the earth. The island she had bought was very big, clean but quite barren. We loved to go mussel picking and cooking them over some embers. They were juicy and still with the taste of the sea. Here we could run around without any fear since the island was recognized as an official nudist retreat. When naked everyone was equal and we really got to know people extremely well. Luz had been a well known and successful dancer and actress, one of her acts consisted of her dancing with snakes cavorting over her scantily dressed body. At the end she gave up her career sickened with the world's hypocrisy and lived a very hermit like existence in the sun.

We naturally saw a lot of John and Eva who by now had a little boy Mark. Eva was mad about keeping the face young and experimented with all sorts of natural recipes which she kept discovering in old books. She would always look at me with my suntanned face and reprimand "The sun will make you look old. Lots of moisturizer, lots of it! And don't forget the neck; the neck is part of your face!" I was keener on keeping my body slim and would tell her off for her weakness for cakes and all things sweet. We would compare food recipes as we both loved cooking. It was only natural for Eva to love the story I had to tell her about my visit to Vidal Sassoon's salon while staying in London on home leave. I had heard so much about him that I decided to go. While there I discovered that Max Factor had the adjoining salon and when the service was combined it would give you a new look. Since I had nothing to lose and a lot to gain I thought I would give myself a treat. I had my hair re-styled first and then moved to Max Factor's place. They worked on my face and I was not allowed to look at myself at all until my hair was combed out. "There you are Madame; you can now look at yourself!" I was so startled to see someone I did not know looking at me from the mirror. I looked like a new person, a most beautiful woman. My mouth did not seem so big, my upper lip did not look so short, my nose was not so Roman looking, where was I? Almost frightened with the radical change I had to touch myself to convince myself that it was really me. No wonder film stars are so beautiful! The funny part was when I left Vidal's place I passed by my husband's side.

He gave me a great admiring look without recognizing me, his wife, and it was only when I walked away and he was still looking at this woman that he recognized me from my behind! "My God, Ly, but you are beautiful! Come on we must buy a new outfit to go with the face and then we shall go out to dinner for everyone to see you!" When we arrived at Casa Pepe anyone would have thought that a film star had arrived with the fabulous reception we received from the owner himself! It was a marvellous experience but when I got to the Exiles Club and had a really good look at myself it seemed as if I had over an inch of thick make up. No doubt Max Factor people were real artists! Eva lapped it all up and promised she too would see what they could do for her.

Ilio and Marcos invited us over to their house one day so that 'I could see how organized everything was with no dirty clothing anywhere!' Suddenly he asked Jack if he would allow Lyana and me to pose for him. He had not been able to do any real artistic work as he had now found an 'easy' way of making good and regular money. It seemed that it was very fashionable in Rio to have an 'antique' painting and as they were not his own creation but copies he found he could sell as soon as he had finished them. He called it his transition period. We sat down on the floor in a mother and child pose. He started painting and then all of a sudden, something strange and unforgettable happened. His eyes opened like those of an owl, his face twitched with excitement and intensity of feelings. His short hair seemed to stand on end, he was enthralled – living a moment of his very own, unaware of time passing by and our very uncomfortable position. After a while Lyana started to whimper. Jack signed that we stayed in place. Ilio changed his brushes for his spatula; then the spatula did not satisfy him either. He then started using his fingers, his hands, throwing the paints in blobs, and with nervous almost spastic movements he went on and on. At last awareness, or was it awakening from his own spell, he stopped and stood there without saying a word admiring his creation. It was a lovely work of art which he entitled 'le soleil' and which made us cry when we saw it. It is now in Turin.

He loved sending me and leaving me notes wherever and whenever he could. He kept on calling me the 'ice and fire girl' which I thought was quite a joke. He also started calling me 'Annie' in a rather enthusiastic way. It was a name I had never been called and I wondered where he had got it from. "Well, Jack calls you Annie, it is special for him and I do the same!" "Ilio, Jack never calls me Annie so what are you talking about?" At that very moment Jack turned and said "Ly, honey, Lyana is tired, it is time to go home." Ilio's eyes glowed. "You see, Jack called you Annie!" How we laughed!

Ilio's failings and weakness were in terms of huge, wide white walls. If he ever saw one, his eyes would open unblinkingly like saucepans, giving him rather a crazy look, his nose would twitch like a hunting Dane, his hands move in nervous expectation and as if in a dream, or under the influence of sleep walking, his legs would take him towards the unadorned wall. There he would start working out in his mind what scheme he would use for a mural. I always reckoned that what stopped him from doing so was the lack of paint! And I was proved correct!

Once, during San Juan's feast day, our friends Lucia and Alan who lived in Joa asked us over for an evening barbeque. Their house had a huge patio with terrific walls around it all always perfectly whitewashed. Ilio had also been invited and before I could even introduce him to some of the guests, he stopped, looked at the walls in disbelief and like a zombie unable to control himself or rationalize he grabbed hold of a few pieces of charcoal and there and then with all the many other guests staring in wonderment he produced the most beautiful and erotic mural. Guests clapped at the sheer beauty of those bodies holding on to pillars, distributing flowers and fruit. For us it was a nightmare as we saw Lucia's face of disgust with tears that she could not control flowing down her face, repeating "My beautiful whitewashed walls!" and then as she really looked seeing Ilio's work of art properly and saw the finished reclining woman she gasped out "My goodness me, he has painted a bow – yes, a bow down THERE!" Her husband just patted her hand saying "Cosita, cosita it's only a wall and we will whitewash it tomorrow!" While our hostess was so upset Ilio did very good business with all the American guests there who promptly asked for his Studio address and bought his paintings. Fortunately Ilio, realizing how troubled Lucia was, next day presented himself with Marcos carrying a lovely bouquet of flowers, some chocolates and a lovely Madonna painting which made up for his behaviour.

At the American Embassy I was finding time going very slowly. When I first arrived and the telephone rang I would go to answer. Dr Little stopped me by saying there was a telephonist who would pass the call through if it was for him. When I went to file some letters that we received and answered I would once again be informed to leave them in the 'for filing' basket and someone would come and file them. In desperation I asked Dr Little to allow me, when not needed by him, to roam about to the other departments and see if I could be of use to any of them. Consequently Dr Little was asked to allow me to cover meetings and conferences they held with the Brazilian government as it appeared they preferred an unbiased secretary, me – neither American nor Brazilian. I also found myself doing translations and helping out interpreting at the American Consulate dealing with non English speaking people!! I then really began to enjoy my work.

After some of these meetings where my boss had also been present we would talk about the day's subject. I could not understand why, in spite of the American Government giving so much so freely to the Brazilians the latter disliked the USA so much. The locals were usually very demanding and arrogant asking for more and more, never satisfied and always critical. Dr Little once said that perhaps it was the human failing in us, no one wants to be the underdog always, always receiving and being placed in a position of forced gratitude. Once I asked "Have you no poor people in the USA?" "Yes, Mrs Armstrong, we do, like everywhere else in the world!" "Then Dr. Little, why don't you help your own people who might appreciate it more?" "It is the way to fight against communism taking over!"

Dr Little was a very kind, sad looking, tall, almost fragile man. I loved to talk with him and often became engrossed in current affairs. One day he discovered that regardless of my having travelled so much and having had good schooling my knowledge of geography was very elementary. He was upset about it and felt he should do something about it. I did not want to discourage him but Jack, who loved geography and even made up geography games, had given up in despair to impart any of his knowledge to me.

Dr Little brought me books, but although I retained everything about customs, crops, manufacturing etc., I still didn't know where any country was on the map. I really was not very interested in the subject but I did try my very best in order not to disappoint him. It made Dr Little happy and kept us both busy. The amazing part about my job was that one month I discovered that I had been overpaid so I went to see the personnel officer who explained that the extra money was to pay for my overtime. I said that I had not stayed behind any day so she sweetly said "Mrs Armstrong, it is for the extra work you did for a different department." This meant that every time I took the minutes of a meeting or went to the Consulate during my own office hours I was paid extra!

We had been told by Head Office that we would be remaining in Brazil for the next several years and as things were going so well for us we had plans made for a country home in Muri, near Novo Friburgo. We were very excited when we saw them in print and could visualise what our little home would be like. First though Jack reckoned we should get a car of our own to be able to come and go without having to worry about other means of transportation which could make it awkward. The Company had started a plan whereby you could buy the car which they would finance and they would deduct a said amount of money every month from Jack's salary. Whilst we were so happy planning for the future Benny came to visit me to tell me the terrible news about our good friend Lucia. Her husband, Alan, had come to the house and told her "Cosita, I am getting my case ready as I am going away!" "Oh, when will you be back?" she asked." No, you don't understand Cosita, I am going away to live with another woman!" Poor Lucia suffered a traumatic crisis and had to be taken to the hospital where he later explained to her that he had been having an affair with his secretary for the last two years. Having received an ultimatum from her he had made the choice. The secretary was older than Lucia and had a grown up daughter. Alan did take care of Lucia decently but it was a blow. Was Brazil where we wanted to stay and live and have our child grow up?

Then as if in answer to a silent prayer we heard the news that Jack was being transferred to San Juan, Puerto Rico. The Rio office was not too pleased about this and tried to get Head Office to assign someone else but without success. We were delighted to be going to a new place but at the same time we were very sad to be leaving all the very good friends we had made there. Lyana was eight and a half years old and she too had her own friends whom she would have to leave behind and this time she was old enough to realize what was happening. The political situation in Brazil was rather chaotic. President Kubitcheck terminated his period in office, and the newly elected President, Janio Quadros of the 'Broomstick,' so called because he had used a broom as his symbol in the election campaign to sweep Brazil clean, assumed office. As a State Governor, Quadros had indeed done a lot of cleaning up, but perhaps the pressure on him as President had become too much for him after the work his predecessor had accomplished, particularly in moving the capital to a completely new city, Brasilia. One day unable to cope with the situation he packed up his bags, and fled to Europe without leaving anyone in his place. Things became very critical. The Vice-president Joao Goulart was not in Brazil and this added to the uncertainty. Food was difficult to obtain, petrol was scarce and people's feelings were getting rather frayed and in a complete muddle. No one knew what to expect, or what their future would be like, so we lived from day to day.

It was during this turmoil that our visas came through from the USA. We had had to fill in mountains of papers ascertaining that none of the three in our family had made a living by prostitution, were communists or worked for the downfall of the American Government! There were more farewell parties, more tears, and more packing. Josefa cried all the time but at the end when we told her that the colleagues replacing Jack had two little girls and as soon as they arrived they would be employing her, she felt better about going away and having a rest before starting work again. We remained in the same Copacabana hotel as before awaiting the ship that was going to take us away.

Japanese and Indonesian embassy wives. Rio de Janeiro

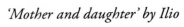

Ilio Burruni

'Mother and daughter' by Ilio

Portrait of Ana Lydia by Ilio

Sir John and Lady MacPherson in San Juan.

Colegio Villa Maria dancers at the feria del Pacifico, Lima

Lyana's graduation

DA CABEÇA

AOS PÉS

·GEORGE G.

Nome: ANA LYDIA ARMSTRONG. Nasceu em Gibraltar, portanto (... mas não sou a pontua- sendo uma britânica...), é mulher de boa altura, 1,67, com 59 lidade em pessoa...), e cabelos castanhos e que por tantas aven- qui..., olhos ..., não seria difícil escrever um livro rela- ...passou, não ... momentos vividos... ...ejando com perfeição, inglês, espanhol, fran- ...é um idioma falado entre os pretos em ...Uganda...). Sobre o nosso português ...os seus dois anos e meio de Bra... ...al...). Como acompanha de mark... ...ele é elemento graduado e uma ...fica...). Ana Lydia é uma minúci... ...cendo, em suas... Portu... ...Itália, França Suíça ...a meta será Suíça

TIMES
OF BRAZIL
FRIDAY, NOVEMBER 27, 1959

Mr. and Mrs. J. G. Armstrong entertained a number of friends at their home in Leblon last Saturday. Cocktails were served and an excellent buffet was enjoyed. Guests were delighted to have the opportunity of seeing Hostess Lydia dancing some special numbers. Earlier in the week this "simpatica" couple celebrated their tenth wedding anniversary. This suc- cessful party continued until the small hours.

...shburn, Mr. and Mrs. ... Russell, and Mr. and Dave Corner.

...and Mrs. Jack Arms- ...g were hosts at a buffet- ...her party at their apart- ...nt in Leblon on Thursday ...ning. After dinner, dan- ...g was led by hostess Lydia. ...e party was very gay and ...veryone stayed until a late ...our dancing. Among those present were: the Chargé d' Affaires of Turkey Mr. Ekrem Goksin, the Indian Embassy First Secretary and Mrs. Hus- sain, Mrs. Helen E. Sheehy (second Secretary U.S. Em- bassy), Mr. and Mrs. Arel. First Secretary of the Indone- sian Embassy and Mrs. Ad- nan Dipodiputro, Mr. and Mrs. Achmad Rusli, Mr. and Mrs. W. Hardiman, Mr. and Mrs. Duncan, Mr. and Mrs. Charles Nehnevajsa, Mr. and Mrs. Rolf Steiner, Mr. and Mrs. Ewen and many others.

Lyana Armstrong celebra- ed her eight birthday on Sa- turday, with a party for 18 of her friends of Rio's In- ternational colony.
They all had a lovely time and enjoyed the Cinema show after tea. Later in the even- ing, Lyana's parents, Lydia and Jack celebrated the oc- casion with a small party for a group of friends among whom were Mr. and Mrs. El-

0 000 Vespas fabricadas no Brasil — Em 1962 será 100% nacional

TIMES OF BRAZIL
PUBLISHED WEEKLY IN SÃO PAULO
Friday, September 16, 1960

Lydia and Jack Armstrong have returned from home leave and are staying in the Luxor Hotel, Copacabana, until their apartment is vacated. They had a wonderful time in England, Gibraltar (visiting Lydia's parents) and touring Spain.

No flagrante o sr. Fagim, subgerente da PANAUTO S.A. entrega ao sr. Sami Cohn, diretor-superintendente da VESPA, a 10.000.a Vespa fabricada no brasil.

CONTINENTAL FINISHING SCHOOL
FOR
POISE AND CHARM

Takes pleasure in inviting you to participate
courses that will start on _____

BOARD

Mrs. Lieschen Cuetara   M₁
Mrs. Lydia Amstrong   Mr. Carlos Sam₁

CURRIC'''

're — Figure Imp
'are — Make-U
uction (diction,

AMB
PUERTO RICO

BALLET EXPERIMENTAL DE PUERTO RICO

Deseamos informar a todos los amantes del baile que
hemos formado una compañía de Ballet que será conocida
por el nombre de "BALLET EXPERIMENTAL DE P. R.",
anteriormente "Ballets Concertantes". Nuestro propósito
es tener una agrupación semi-profesional de alto nivel ar-
tístico para la presentación de Ballets Clásicos y Contem-
poráneos.

Para la primera temporada ya están en ensayo El
Lago de los Cisnes, Contrastes y Mosaicos Latinoamericanos.
En la segunda temporada presentaremos Coppelia — los
tres actos, con su coreografía profesional original.

Son los organizadores de esta Compañía Artística:
Sra. Lotti Tischer — Directora
Sra. Yolanda Fernández — Secretaria
Srta. Nana Hudo — Sub-Secretaria
Sra. Lydia Armstrong — Tesorera
...a Esteves — Sub-Tesorera
...cinelli — Administrador

del público puer-

Natural de Gibraltar
Profesora de Cultura Física
Elogia Mujer Puertorriqueñ₂

Por Alba Raquel Cabrera

La profesora de cultura física
y bailes, Lydia Armstrong, natural de Gibraltar y criada en
España, y quien ha tenido
oportunidad de enseñar a dife-
rentes países, dice o...
puertorriqueña, a ...
muy linda, ar...
que e...

mo de
cuando s...
de l...

ACOSTA, BLANQUITA ....
ALEMAN, HILDA ....
ARMSTRONG, ANA LYDIA ....
...

ONE, TWO, THREE—Santa Teresita Academy in Santurce is one of the schools in Puerto Rico that has
initiated a physical culture program in accordance with the President's Physical Council requirements.
Practicing the Swedish rhythmic exercises, directed by Mrs. Lydia Armstrong, far right, are junior high
school girls. (STAR Photo by Eddie Crespo)

Fitness, Etiquette Taught At Santurce Private School

By ...RIEMIL RODRIGUEZ

One, two, three. . . one, two,
three. . . The aqua blue clad figures, followed in unison the routine
of the Swedish rhythmic exercises.
The music of the song Never On
Sunday and the crisp voice of the
physical fitness instructor could be
heard in the background.

"Many children have no idea of
how to hold themselves. How the
muscles can control the body and
vice-versa. They don't realize the
importance of good breathing."
said Mrs. Lydia Amstrong, physical culture instructor at Santa Te-

resita Academy in Santurce.
The tall and slender Gibraltan
has been teaching at the school
since August. She gives an etiquette and personal hygiene course to
ninth grade boys and girls and physical culture to the junior high
school girls.

The perseverant instructor, who
was once a victim of Infantile Pa-
ralysis, is a member of the International Federation of Physical
Culture. The ... she offers a...
Santa Tere... ...us the or...
mapped ou... ...eside...
Kennedy

program,
Bright and early in the morning
Mrs. Armstrong faces her ninth
grade stud...nts for an etiquette lesson. The ... young pupils practice the ...s of making in-
vitatio... ...ons, among
each ...

...strong

Academia Santa Teresita

Presents

OKLAHOMA

Director ....

Choral and Music Director .... Sr. PAUL JOSEPH

Choreographer .... Sr. THERESE MARY

.... Mrs. ANA LYDIA ARMSTRONG, I.F.P.C.

LA ASOCIACION DE MAESTRO₂

DE BAILE DE PUERTO RICO

Part Four

Tropicana 1961 - 1967

Chapter 19

NORTHWARDS

The ship Del Sur of the Delta Line arrived on the same day that Janio Quadros fled the country and so did not dock. The port was closed and no visitors were allowed into the area. The farewell cocktail party that we had arranged to give on board was cancelled. We had accumulated quite a lot of luggage, no less than sixteen packing cases and twelve suitcases, which were virtually dumped into the tender, (it was a miracle that nothing was broken or went astray) as the usual workers were not allowed into the docks. Like fugitives in the night, we were rushed and pushed onto the same tender.

On board we discovered we were indeed going to travel extra special first class as we had been allocated a super deluxe suite with all the trimmings it entailed. We were going to arrive in New Orleans in great style. Life on board this ship was luxurious compared to all the previous ones we had travelled on. To start with there was much more entertainment and everything was done to perfection. Occasionally we wondered what to expect once we had arrived at our final destination San Juan. New Orleans was only going to be a stopover for about ten days while Jack got acquainted with the American associate company with which from now onward he would have to liaise. The foreign friends in Brazil did not seem to think much of our new destination while the Americans we had asked seemed to have had a very poor opinion of the Puerto Ricans who went to live in the States. This they had obtained mainly from experiences in New York.

On the ship Lyana would go to an earlier dinner and either Jack or I would accompany her to see that she ate and did the correct thing. One evening she was hungry after a hectic day and went ahead of me, there she was with practically a whole chicken in her hands, completely immersed and enjoying herself "My goodness Nana, what do you think you are doing eating like that?" "Mummy, John (the steward) says that it is permissible to eat chicken with your fingers!" "I am sure Nana honey that John must have meant that you could eat the chicken with your fingers after you have cut off the big pieces of flesh from the bones. Why, the chicken you are eating is almost as big as you!" With this she started to laugh, carved some meat off the chicken and proceeded to eat.

It is funny how you remember places by the food you remember eating for the first time. In England I had encountered the yorkshire pudding which I enjoyed and the pease pudding which I didn't. And when I am served these I always remember my first experience. In Rhodesia it was the hot dogs and hamburgers. Who had ever heard of meat balls squashed up and put in between two pieces of bread, as my mother used to describe hamburgers. We also had corn on the cob for the first time there. In Kenya we had the flying fish and all the beautiful tropical fruit, the bread fruit similar to the custard apple but so much more sour. What delicious ice cream I used to make with it, so refreshing too! In Galicia there were the famous empanadas, yet when you think of Spain generally it is the paella that comes to mind. Brazil's feijoada was something we learnt to enjoy and to make myself and now on board this ship I came across my first piece of the most delicious dessert, pecan pie with vanilla ice-cream. I could have eaten it all night! It was so very mouth watering that I asked John if he could get me the recipe from the cook. He obliged. To our amusement and surprise and judging from the amounts quoted he must have given us the recipe for what he normally cooked for all the passengers and crew.

I had often dreamt of visiting the USA where the buildings are as tall as giants. As the ship approached New Orleans on the Mississippi River I thought the Captain must have made a mistake. From the docks I could not detect even one skyscraper, but then New Orleans is a place of its own, with its very interesting marked individual characteristics and historical values. I simply fell in love with this city and its charming people; perhaps because of the absence of skyscrapers, super highways and the rush rush of activity. It was such a relaxed and wonderful new feeling. Once we had docked we joined the other passengers on deck waiting for the gangway to be put down so as to disembark. There on the docks was a man very well dressed looking up at the people and making what was considered a very rude gesture in Brazil as he pointed to different people and then crossing the other arm touched the one that was pointing. Everyone was commenting when suddenly Jack said I bet the poor bugger is looking for us and he is gesturing what he believes to be a 'strong arm'. It was indeed our host!

Coming from a foreign land all luggage had to be inspected and many questions asked regarding what we had inside. As we had been forewarned we had written everything in great detail and knowing their fear of any grass, flowers, fruit or such items being brought in and with them germs of different types we made sure that no straw had been used in our packing cases. We had to remain at the docks for quite a long time feeling very tired but grateful that at the end only one case was opened and examined. Everyone was extremely polite and kind. We were then taken to a charming old fashioned hotel in the French Quarter where we relaxed and had a long cool drink before going in for our luncheon. Normally when in transit I do not bother to unpack completely but our American friend was very persuasive as he had made arrangements for us to be very busy during our stay there and we would need to dress up.

American hospitality is unique in the world. It was so lovely and interesting to discover that the Americans (like all of us Europeans) had similar problems to us; they worried about their mortgages, children's education and income tax like everyone else. Most of the Americans we had come across in the business circles overseas all seemed to have bulging wallets and endless funds for entertaining and so forth. Percy lived with his wife Laura and two children in a very attractive detached house in Metairie suburb which we visited a few days after our arrival there. We were sitting on their closed verandah when suddenly there was pandemonium, "A bug, a bug," they all screamed and rushed to get a flit gun and fly swat. We looked at them amazed wondering what sort of creature they were hunting with such desperation. Finally they all stared at the ground and said "It's dead." We approached and looked "My God, but it is only a house fly" both Jack and I chorused out simultaneously. Turning to our host and hostess I said "You should have seen those huge black cockroaches we had in Rio, they were only controlled a couple of years ago when the Cubans came and set up an exterminating firm to do so!" Making horrible faces they covered their faces and shivered with disgust. We just looked and laughed.

Percy, our host, took his responsibility to show Jack the ropes (as to the American way of selling the communication services) very seriously. He had a working schedule for Jack and a recreative one for Lyana and me. Katie, his secretary, would take Lyana and me around sightseeing and shopping and then to one of the well known and famous restaurants. Since in the evening Percy and Laura again took us to excellent and renowned restaurants I found my stomach could not cope with so much rich food, sweets etc. I had seen the bellboys from the hotel during their lunch hour eating outside in the street various delicious looking bread rolls filled with everything anyone could imagine. That day when Katie arrived and asked me what I wanted to do I suggested we took it easy and go to a park where Lyana could rest and then I wanted to try one of those sandwiches I had seen. "You mean that you want a 'poor boy' Mrs Armstrong?" "If that is what you call those appetising filled rolls, yes Katie, I would like that with a cold beer!" She took us to the delicatessen store where they were made. Three long tables fully laden with every kind of bread, salads, sauces and cold cuts were beautifully displayed. Three men in their white uniforms and tall hats stood behind the tables cutting the chosen bread and filling it with all the things you fancied. It was the best lunch I had had since leaving the ship!

While shopping with Katie I found some postcards where instead of the usual tourist attraction or funny cartoon, they gave the recipes for special native foods of the Creoles in New Orleans. To my joy amongst the many I bought there were two very special ones, the lemon meringue pie, excellent to taste with creamy lemon interior and crispy meringue outside and the delicious unforgettable pecan pie! We also discovered delicious home made Madame See's chocolates.

We could not as tourists miss at least one trip through Bourbon Street and its 'dime's worth' of strip-tease joints. As we passed by these clubs there would be a doorman offering a peep, after seeing this I jokingly said "I wonder whether they would be interested in my act. I reckon no one has seen a Spanish dancer, castanets clapping and feet stamping while doing a strip-tease!" Percy, bless his soul, a bit startled but nevertheless game said "Would you like me to find out?" It seemed Americans took any business proposition very seriously even if said in jest.

These clubs were not what we had at first thought as there were some very famous honest to goodness strip-artists and the hotel recommended that we went to see Kalantan, the best of them all. Inside, the club was luxurious and well decorated. There were many dancers, all very beautiful young girls, doing their rather exotic and wild dancing before the star of the show, Kalantan, made her appearance. Just a couple of tables away from ours sat a 'cartoon type' couple, a very short, slight man with a tremendously huge lady. He was a really henpecked husband being reprimanded constantly by the wife. The little man, like most of the other men present was ecstatic with the antics and tricks of the trade of one of the girls but when Kalantan arrived on the scene, so beautiful, with a gorgeous figure and all alone rhythmically dancing in sensuous movements he was practically hypnotized. Then as if realizing how he was, Kalantan knelt down close to him, swaying sensuously and keeping everyone in the audience spellbound in this electrifying atmosphere. Then as she bent backwards she started rotating her breasts with the tassels she was wearing going in different directions, then stopping and going in the same direction, and finally with a mixture of movements that were absolutely fascinating. Suddenly in the midst of this great quietness, out boomed the lady's loud voice "Henry, let's go home,

HENRY, don't you hear me, HENRY, I said let's go home!" Laughter, first politely, and then uninhibited, broke out and there behind this great colossus of a wife, trailed rather reluctantly poor Henry, all red in the face, still looking at the dancing girl, but showing great confusion when, as he stopped for a final view, the audience clapped and cheered him. I am sure Henry somehow must have managed to return to the club later on but alone!

One of our greatest discoveries for really good coffee, (American is usually watery and not like the coffee we knew, particularly after living in Brazil), was at the 'Morning Call' nearby the docks where they served gourmet coffee and the most delicious crispy doughnuts more like our Spanish fritters 'churros' than the regular American doughnut. From then on we went every morning for breakfast even though big breakfasts were served at the hotel.

Soon it was time to leave for San Juan, Puerto Rico having had a marvellous and interesting and most appreciated break in New Orleans. The only available ships going to Puerto Rico were freighters carrying a maximum of ten passengers. Although I knew this, I had not anticipated this freighter, the Claiborne, being so small. Normally on arrival at the docks you would see your ship in front of you but we actually had to go looking for this ship which was in fact hidden by the dock wall, the only visible thing being the masts. No one had said the cargo boat was going to be so very small. There had been hurricane warnings which had also been one of the reasons why we had been delayed longer than anticipated in New Orleans. I stopped and refused to board the ship, it would surely be like a nut shell on the high seas. I was terrified and loudly refused to budge any further. Then a loud, husky voice came from somewhere down below saying "Of course you are coming onto my ship, it is a strong sturdy ship!" It was the Captain, so what could I do?!

The Captain was a strong man with very set ideas. We were five couples in all plus Lyana the only child on board. We were led to our sleeping quarters which although not elaborate were very good and spacious with as was now usual, our own private bathroom and toilet. But the food, oh my God the food, was very basic, terribly cooked and badly served! There was little to do except to read and go for walks around the very limited space open to us passengers. Poor Lyana was the worst off as she had to be constantly restrained and soon got bored at having nothing to do. But we all survived.

Promptly at 5.30 p.m. all of us would go to the Captain's quarters to have delicious banana daiquiris, his speciality, and then at 6.00 p.m off to the most inedible dinner. The galley was left open after dinner and at around 10.00 p.m. all the passengers would raid the fridge for fruit, milk and some delicious cold ham or meat which we promptly devoured with bread. This was the happiest event of the day for we would all get together to talk and have good laughs, sometimes even playing a game of canasta. We would comment on the stillness and calmness, sometimes almost eerie, around us. Since we kept on hearing about hurricane warnings we would put it down to the 'calm before the storm' syndrome, but the ship continued its course avoiding the dangerous areas at sea with a very capable captain in charge, and not once did we feel the slightest bit of rolling or pitching. In this uneventful and unchanging way we arrived in Puerto Rico.

Chapter 20

BORINQUEN

Dick, the engineer and Jack's colleague was awaiting us at the docks to take us to the well equipped and serviced transient apartment in Santurce where we would be staying until we found a home to our liking. Once we had left our luggage and refreshed ourselves he very kindly took us to his home in Baldrich. Lyana was feeling rather sorry for herself but once at Dick and his wife Maria's house she rallied round and thoroughly enjoyed herself playing with their four daughters. Jane and Mary, both in their teens were older than Lyana, Sheila was only slightly older and Helen was slightly younger. All of a sudden she, as we did, found ourselves with friends for life. I lost Lyana to them or gained four more daughters at times. I decided there and then that I would like to live as close to the Keene family as possible and I never regretted this decision,

While in the temporary accommodation I proceeded to do my shopping, and to try my skill as a cook in my little kitchenette so that we would all be able to enjoy some home cooking again. I remember the thrill and satisfaction of being able to buy all those luxurious items unobtainable in Rio; all the marvellous foods, up to then, just trademarks and names to me, gathered from American magazines. In my excitement, I soon had my shopping trolley full to the top, when the meat price suddenly attracted my attention. $18.00 (eighteen dollars) for a joint of beef! Having converted this into 'cruzeiros', our Brazilian currency, I discovered it was more than I spent in a whole week on groceries in Rio. How on earth were we to live here, I wondered. I quickly and blushingly returned the goods to their shelves, hoping Maria would soon be able to tell me how we could live on 'the fat of the local land only!' Half way through this episode Jack arrived, and on seeing my activity, exclaimed, "What the heck are you doing, girl?" "We cannot afford to live here Jack, look at the prices." "Oh, you silly clot, here we are paid in DOLLARS and we shall have an adjustment in our cost of living quota, so go on honey, take what you want, I have been given an advance already so, go,go, that's my girl!"

With so many items I had not seen for so long we were inclined to be a little too extravagant at first but soon learnt what to buy, and what the staple foods from the country were. After a short while we were, for the first time in our lives, able to live on Jack's salary and even put away a few dollars every month, especially once we moved into our permanent home and had enough fridge and freezer capacity to buy in bulk when things were on special offer. We were delighted that Head Office had not changed their minds about Jack's transfer as had been the wish from Rio's office and also very pleased that Jack's work had been recognized and given the well earned promotion. He was now the commercial manager.

After a couple of weeks looking for a home we found a beautiful detached house only two blocks away from Maria and Dick. It was close to a shopping centre, church and school for Lyana to attend with the Keene children. The house belonged to the Mayor of Manati in Puerto Rico; it was well furnished and comfortable. The front gate opened to a garage that fitted three cars – we didn't have any as yet – and a small front garden with shrubs to the sides. The big garden and verandah was at the back. Downstairs the whole area was an open plan sitting-room/cum dining-room, bar and kitchen. Behind the kitchen there was another room with washing machine, dryer etc., and next to it by the bar area another room, Jack's office or den. The stairs which just seemed to hang in the air led to the bedrooms, four of them all with bathrooms ensuite, plus a huge closed verandah where later on I used to give my Spanish dancing classes. It was all very comfortable, big and Americanized. It was also in a filthy state.

To the right lived a doctor with his nurse wife and two children, a boy and a girl roughly Lyana's age, to the left a retired telephone company director and his wife and behind us three very sweet and gentle spinsters who loved birds.

I really fell in love with Puerto Rico and the Puerto Ricans, they were the most gentle and kind people I had come across in many years. They had a wonderful sense of humour and lived like the Gibraltarians in very close family units. They welcomed us generously and tried to help as much as they could from the first moment we got there. It was all so very different to Brazil. Since we arrived in November they were soon celebrating Thanksgiving Day, it was a celebration that we had never encountered before. We were invited to several homes of neighbours we didn't even know and finally opted to go next door to the doctor's house where Lyana could play with the children.

One day whilst at the cinema there was a short documentary about Borinquen, I was fascinated by its beauty and very seriously asked Jack if we could go there for a holiday. He turned round sharply and gave me the most surprised look "We are in Borinquen, it's the native name for Puerto Rico!"

Finally we took our heavy packing cases to the house to start organizing things. Before moving in we had found the place in a terrible state. The previous owner had left it in a hurry. After thirty years of married life the wife suddenly discovered that her husband had been unfaithful to her, even from the start, as he had several children by other women, some of them older than the legitimate children. I looked around for servants and found out that they were a precious and almost unobtainable commodity, and so although I had never done any house work in my life, I had to face the situation. But how? I could not move into the house in its unclean condition, and yet I had not the slightest clue as to where or how to start. It was then that a young Puerto Rican wife of one of Jack's English colleagues explained the simplicity of the procedure. All I had to do was "Get a good hose and hose down the place!" As I showed some surprise, she pointed to the floor, all neatly tiled, but with outlets in the very centre of the rooms to let the water out. I had a hose, so I would start work the following day.

I returned to the house after leaving Lyana at the school, all geared up for the hard work I knew lay before me. I proceeded to take the brand new hose I had bought inside the house. As I looked at the tremendous amount of dirt, I had a bright idea 'if I were to scatter soap-flakes, then the job would be better and more efficiently done'. I grabbed a box of Rinso and threw it all over the ground with drops of household ammonia. Somewhere someone had said that ammonia would clean the dirtiest of spots. I then started to hose down the place. Wanting to be even cleaner, I started to brush the floor with the broom. The soap suds started to rise. I put some more water and tried to push all the dirty water down the little drain. The floor was very slippery, I fell down, and there was so much soap that I couldn't even stand up. I started to cry, what to do? Walking, or rather crawling, with my bottom I managed to reach the phone and called Maria.

The moment I started telling Maria of my plight she started to laugh and the more she laughed the more desperate I got. Finally calmed she asked "Have you a squeegee?" I did not even know what it was supposed to be, but I knew I did not have anything but the broom and the hose and a few pieces of cloth and several sponges. Maria as always came to the rescue. Within ten minutes she had joined me together with a young man who was willing to help clean up having brought all the items needed to do the job. I was still seated on the floor but at the sight of them and Maria's laughter I too joined in.

Maria showed me how to clean and polish, and even how to hang the laundry for when it came to large items like sheets I made a real mess of it. I had my first fully automatic washing machine which I just loved to use even for a few handkerchiefs and underwear, never realising the cost of electricity and water. She taught me how to care for my plants and what to buy. There were no maids to be had only home helps at quite a price so I had to learn to cope. With pride I soon was able to show her what a capable housewife I had become.

My Spanish seemed to be misinterpreted by Puerto Ricans as they used words differently. In the house, half way up our open stair case there was a hat rack and console that once must have been a very beautiful piece of work made mainly with Roca crystal (cut glass beautifully assembled). Unfortunately all the back and skeleton of the furniture was of wood and this was full of woodworm which I thought made it dangerous as it could easily break. In Brazil we used the word 'bichinho' (for little worms) very often and I knew that 'bichitos' also existed in the Spanish vocabulary. I had forgotten the correct word but thought that by saying bichos (large worms) I would have been understood. When the house owner arrived at the house to see how and when I would finally move in, I showed him the furniture and asked him if he could take it away. "Take it away, Mrs Armstrong? Why, it is a beautiful piece of furniture. There are only two in Puerto Rico, this one and the other one is in the Governor's mansion." "That may be so, but it is full of bichos and I consider it dangerous particularly with children running about and the stairs having no banisters!" The visitor's reaction and behaviour to what I had said was most unnatural and curt "I am sending you my foreman, you talk to him!"

A couple of days later, when we already had moved into the house, the foreman, fat, with a cherub-like face arrived and politely asked me what the trouble was. Once again I explained my problem, and once again I had the same reaction from this man who was even more flustered than his boss. "Senora" he explained, "those things are called 'polillas' I shall see what I can do for you. But at present we have no storage place for it. However; I think you should go to your neighbour and ask her the meaning of the word you used so that you do not repeat it any more!"

No sooner had he left than I went to visit my next door neighbour, unfortunately during the time when her doctor husband was at home eating. Not knowing he was the very devil himself for his sense of humour, I asked in rather a hesitant way about 'bicho', when guffaws of laughter resounded all over the place. Apparently, 'bicho' in San

Juan referred to the most important part of the male anatomy, most unmentionable too. So much shock over a trifling thing! I am sure in Brazil the behaviour would have been very much different.

Every day I took Lyana to school for although it was near the house there was always quite a lot of traffic. I went the same way twice a day and soon a lady, Juanita, in a wheelchair started talking to me so I would have a chat and then return home to do the housework. Our retired couple from next door Mr and Mrs Medina visited a few weeks after we had moved in. "Dona Lydia, we have just bought a new car and I would like to offer you my old car. I can assure you it is in very good condition, that it knows its way home and if anything ever goes wrong it will happen in front of your house!" I had a good laugh and asked "What will such a jewel cost me Mr. Medina?" "For you $275.00, it is a good bargain as it is a relatively new model." Jack was there listening but not saying a word. "Well, Mr Medina I shall see what I can offer you" I said. Jack's look of surprise was quite a picture. I went upstairs and brought down an old sock where I had been saving every dollar I could since our arrival. I counted $230.00 and showed the money to Mr. Medina "It's far too little" he said rather sadly. "Please wait, I shall see if I can add some more." Shortly after, I returned with a $20.00 bill, offered him this, and said "That's really all I can spare" "You strike a good bargain, Dona Lydia, the car is yours for $250.00!"

Now the proud owner of a car I drove Lyana to school. Two or three days later a lady I did not know knocked at our door and enquired if everything was alright or if there was someone ill at home. Surprised I queried why she was asking that. Apparently the invalid lady, Juanita, had missed me, had waited patiently and then sent a relative to enquire! Once again how different the Puerto Ricans were from the Brazilians. The people here were really lovely, kind and perhaps rather naïve.

Lyana was unfortunately finding it difficult at school. After so many years in Brazil speaking Portuguese her spoken Spanish was not very good and she mixed it up very much, she could understand what people said and it took her some time to construct sentences. The teachers were thinking she was a little backward instead of realising the effort the poor child was making. I was forced to visit the Mother Superior and explain that although she might look Latin she was English and that we had just come from over five years in Brazil speaking a totally different language. Once this was clarified everyone started to help her and she was soon bringing home very good reports.

I was completely unaware of the effect I made upon my neighbours for I would, quite happily, walk to Maria's in the briefest of shorts or tight Brazilian style slacks. I had noticed people looking from behind their blinds but I did not realise the reputation I was attaining. I was to them the 'strange foreigner'. Things came to a head when I woke up from a siesta in the backyard where I was wearing my bikini to feel someone looking at me, yet I was unable to see anyone until on hearing my back door neighbours voice saying "Well, Juan, you seem to be enjoying the sights!" I looked up and saw the next door gardener sitting on top of the spinsters' garage roof! Jack's reaction on being told was "You should have cooled him down with the hose!"

Time hung on my hands and I became restless, as domestic work was not satisfying to me. I began to feel like an animal caged in without being able to express myself. I spent hours cooking, creating new dishes which were later on eaten in a few minutes, leaving a pile of dishes to wash. Both Jack and Lyana tried to help but there was something missing with my life here and I started to plan what to do next.

I heard that there was a dancing school in the same street, so I went to see the owner first to enrol Lyana for her ballet lessons and also to ask if she was interested in my teaching Spanish dance there. Although she was not she was able to put me in contact with Chely who owned another school in the neighbourhood. Chely was very kind and helpful and went to all the trouble of inviting her students' mothers to a demonstration class on keeping fit. If I was successful I could use her studio for my classes and give her a percentage of my takings as rental. I was soon teaching twice a week, morning and evening classes, and made a lot of happy and lasting friendships. After a while, I also gave the advanced Spanish dancing classes for her once a week which at least took up some of my time and gave me more stimulation and my own pocket money.

Maria one day called me to say that her friend Ushi who worked in the same office as her husband had told her that Valerie, a young divorcee, was apparently going after Jack. Since I had no intention of putting up with any nonsense any more, I dressed up to kill and presented myself in the office where Ushi took me round introducing me to all the staff. Finally I came to Valerie, "Oh yes, Valerie, my husband has told me all about you and how you are all the time trying to help him. He has a very good secretary you know so he really doesn't need you to bother about him!" A week later she resigned and left the office. From then on there was only peace and happiness. San Juan was definitely not like Brazil as far as women were concerned.

Jack and I had been brought up in a society where you did not owe people money, if you had any accounts; you paid them as soon as the bills came. We discovered that in the American society this was not so, there it seemed that you were worth much more every time you owed more and then your credit rating was higher. Most of our new friends loved to show us their many credit cards and a large percentage of their shopping and outings were financed through the credit card system. At home if you did not have the cash to buy a thing you did without it until you had saved enough!

Our first Christmas in San Juan was particularly wonderful and unforgettable. Maria's parents, even though they had a numerous family, still had room and love for more and they adopted us too. Everything that each of their children received as gifts we did too. We were asked to their home for Christmas Eve, the day they celebrated most, inherited no doubt from the Spaniards. They served us a typical meal of 'lechon y arroz con gandules' (roast suckling pig with rice and red beans). Maria's father was a genuine 'Jibarito' from Aibonito, a real darling.

He was a virile young man of eighty-five, a truly worthy person with a lovely well lived face. I recall his happy grin on his suntanned lined face, his bright (young, at times) old eyes, windows to the world mirroring all his successes, good and bad times, his loneliness, his wonderful sense of humour, his capricious airs of youth and always wearing with panache his wide rim cowboy hat.

Maria's mother was a very kind looking and placid person who no doubt had to adopt this attitude if only to survive her husband's gallant ways and roving eyes where females were concerned. She had a round sweet face and a beautiful smile. The generosity of the family, in spite of being retired, knew no limits. We were all presented with lovely hand woven baskets beautifully prepared full of fruit grown by the father in his little chakra. No matter what, I was never to forget Puerto Rico and its people.

On Christmas day, Mati, the doctor's wife, invited us to their family lunch, and then all the people living in our street, without exception, called on us – the foreigners – to take us to their homes, to welcome us into their midst. We had found real kind friends. It was lovely to hear the youngsters asking for the parents' blessings before leaving the homes and I was delighted to have Lyana growing up in this society.

I soon became well known in the neighbourhood. I had more friends than in any of the other places I had lived, people that really cared during both the good and the bad times. I gradually gained an excellent reputation as a physical education and dance teacher. Mother Superior of Lyana's convent school called me and offered me part- time work for three afternoons a week as the girl's P.E.Instructor.

With the old Hillman Minx we had bought from Agustin Medina we were able to visit all the island's beauty spots. There were picnics on lonely golden beaches where we could romp to our hearts desire, sometimes on our own and at other times with Maria, Dick and the girls.

Lyana was unsettled in spite of having the four girls to share her time with. In her short life she had known a number of friends that she had had to leave behind. Why could she not have a brother or sister who would then be there all the time even when she moved to other countries. She obviously discussed this with Jane, Mary, Sheila and Helen who always had each other to play with no matter where they went. Sheila was the one who always seemed to have an explanation and she told Lyana that perhaps if Jack and I got married again in the church we would then have another baby like when we had her! I patiently explained that you only really married once "But Mummy you promised me you would marry again if you got to your twenty-fifth wedding anniversary!" "Yes, Lyana honey, I know. We shall do that as we have promised you. Mummy and Daddy are trying to have more children but you don't always have what you want darling." "Mummy, Sheila says that it is because you don't do like Aunty Maria. You don't go to confession and Holy Communion every day. Promise me Mummy that you will!" Lyana cried in desperation. "OK, darling, I shall go to church every day and see what happens." Sheila on hearing this exclaimed "Hurrah, Lyana, Now that your mother will go to church she will become a good woman and God will give her brothers and sisters for you!"

When after a while I still hadn't produced any more offspring Lyana exclaimed "I am fed up Mummy, I have no brother, no sister, no dog, not even a cat!" It was because of this that when Pauline, the administration manager's wife, offered me a newly born kitten I accepted without even consulting Jack.

Ouiki was a tiny little fluff that could not yet see or drink out of a saucer. Jack's first attitude was to return the poor little tyke, who because he missed his mother, did nothing but cry all day long. I remembered someone once saying that when animals were this small and cried that the best thing to do was to wrap a clock in a towel and place it near the animal. Somehow it worked a treat. I used to feed Ouiki with a bottle and having him in my arms completely stole my heart. As he grew he seemed to realise that Jack was the boss and his staying in the house depended on him. He proceeded to show off with all sorts of tricks and made such a fuss that soon Jack forgot that he had insisted the cat could only remain downstairs in the laundry room or outside. He would play with both Jack and Lyana mostly but it was always that he turned to me if sick or wanted something as if he knew that I would protect him and never let him down.

Ouiki delighted Lyana. At long last she had her very own playmate who needed her love and looking after. He was so alive and full of mischief, yet so wonderful and patient with her. Lyana would take out her own baby clothing and with infinite tenderness and care, dress him up in full regalia, then place him in her dolls pram and take him out for walks. He would never stir nor object enjoying all the love and attention so lavishly given him. All this time since he first came home we checked to see what gender he was. There was nothing obvious to tell whether he was really a he.

One day Ouiki ran away. Lyana cried, Jack raved, blaming me for his disappearance, little realizing how upset I too was at his flight. By now Ouiki had become the family's pet and king of the house; he had the run of the whole place and my little students' attention when they now came for their weekly dancing lessons. By then I had also started classes at home. He used to join the class leaping in time with the music and lapping up all the admiration thrown his way. I was possibly the most affected by his absence, even though I could not give myself the luxury of even mentioning him. Both Lyana and Jack would start with the same complaint "You should have kept the door locked" as if it were possible to keep in a cat who wants to get out.

I was already thinking of phoning Pauline to see if I could get another cat for four days had gone by, when I heard loud miaows coming from the backyard. On opening the door, in walked proud Ouiki with very superior arrogant airs and behind him his lady friend. There was no doubt about his sex, he was very much a he man and by the way all the female cats came looking for him, quite a Casanova too!

This little episode was to cause Jack some embarrassment. I was so thrilled and happy upon Ouiki's return that I phoned Maria and in an excited and rather loud voice informed her of 'what the shameless little bastard had done, how worried I had been over his leaving home and his cheek of returning home with his paramour and expecting me to feed them both.' Apparently Cristina, Mati's servant, heard me and about a week later she approached me. "Good afternoon, Dona Lydia, and how is the American?" "American?" I asked "Which American?" "Your husband, Mr Jack." "Oh, he is not an American, he is English, and he is very well, thank you." "Has he gone away again lately?" she whispered more than asked, as if in conspiracy. "Gone away? But he has never been away from home." "Shame, you poor soul, on top of it all, you are even covering up for him!" Good Lord, I thought, she has misconstrued Ouiki's gallivanting for poor Jack. Fortunately Jack took it all as a great joke but there was no way of convincing Cristina that it was the cat we were talking about.

Cristina was a huge kind looking black woman who loved to talk whenever she saw me in the backyard. She was always asking questions as to where we had come from as we were so different from all the other Americans. She could not get into her head that just because we spoke English we were not from the USA. She used to make me laugh when I called Ouiki and he immediately responded and she would cry out "Valgame Dios si el gato habla ingles" (God bless my heart, the cat speaks English!)

Quiki was such a little dandy, if he was dirty he would go into the bathroom and walk on top of the bath crying until I would get hold of him and clean his paws, and tail or any part of his anatomy he had not been able to do himself. He would then lie down contentedly until I would make as if to submerge him in the bath, when the little blighter's spirit of self preservation would stir, and he would show his annoyance very quickly. After his wash, I would dry him, powder him and brush his coat until it shone; he really loved and enjoyed all the attention bestowed on him. Then he would languidly get up, stretch and go with his tail up and high, crying in a scarcely audible way towards his food dish, when he would be fed with a juicy morsel. He was quite a gourmet. He would put up his nose at most of the tinned cat food and relish the fish and chicken bits we gave him. He also loved peanuts, potato crisps and chocolate!

My sister Clementina, her husband Bill and the family had been transferred to Barbados, and it had been six years since I had last seen her, so we decided to go and visit her for a month, not knowing when we would be this near to her and her family again, particularly since we had not as yet met their children. Jack would be coming with me for a fortnight and Lyana and I remaining two weeks longer.

As Ouiki had become such an ardent playboy and kept on coming home somewhat damaged from his encounters with other tomcats, we decided that as he would have to stay at the veterinary kennels during our absence, the best thing would be for us to have him doctored at this time. Poor little soul, he soon seemed to realise that he would be away from home and us. His cries while being taken to the vet were so heartbreaking that I could not keep my tears away, and we almost changed our plans for this trip.

I also decided to hand in my notice at the school where the girls created more problems than anything else. They were not in the habit of doing any sort of exercising and the Spanish priest in charge of the school did not see it fit for girls to wear shorts and exercise while there were boys around! It was a losing battle. I also stopped the classes at home and asked the girls to join my other classes at Chely's. I had plans to do more things when I returned from Barbados.

We set sail towards Barbados feeling terribly excited. Six years had gone by and I worried in case Clem would not recognize me. Had I aged a lot? Had Brazil really made me so different? These thoughts never left me and afterwards when we got together we discovered that both of us had had the same thoughts. And yet when we saw each other, there was no hesitation. We just ran into each others arms and cried tears of happiness.

Clem and Bill had been posted to Hong Kong after their tour in Kenya and now they were in Barbados after a tour of one year in London. Clem had loved all her husband's previous postings but was not too happy in Barbados. She did not enjoy the sea too much. I on the other hand enjoyed myself tremendously, I loved the happy go-lucky ways of the island and its lovely beaches where I could, if allowed, stay all day long. I was usually only too happy as long as there was sunshine, beaches and let's not forget good ice-cream!

We visited all the beauty spots, saw the site for the film 'Island in the Sun' and I thoroughly enjoyed myself with the admiration shown by Clem's servant girl, Lilian, who thought I looked like a 'star woman'! Lilian was rather a character and had a peculiar rather catchy habit whenever she was asked anything. No matter if the answer was negative or positive she would say "No please – Yes please!" It amused me at first, but I was rather annoyed on finding out the habit had stuck to me while making fun of her and repeating the phrases!

My young niece Vandra was so much like I was at her age, although much more serious and sober than I, but, 'who was that little boy?' Clem was quite upset at my making believe I did not recognize her son. He was a really lovely chirpy young man full of freckles, a big grin on his face and eyes that sparkled and showed that he feared absolutely nothing. What a gorgeous cheeky little devil! He was running towards me and when he heard his mother telling me off he stopped suddenly. Then coming towards me very solemnly said "I don't love you, Aunty Lydia, I am going to run away and climb a 'twee'". I grabbed him in my arms and said "Martin, I shall climb the 'twee' with you because I do love you too, very much!" He laughed, did a couple of somersaults and then said "I love you three, Aunty" holding up his three fingers to emphasize his words. By the time I returned to San Juan, I was his favourite playmate and his love for me was from 'the top of the mountain down down to the bottom of the sea'.

Soon after our arrival in Barbados Clem gave a big party to welcome us and introduce us to all her friends. Jack who had been behaving himself so well since leaving Brazil and who I knew jolly well would not go looking for anything behaved rather differently if the female went hunting. He always excused himself saying "I am a gentleman, how can I say no and tell the woman to go away?" So he was always attentive and enjoyed a flirtation.

But sometimes women were the absolute end and would not leave things alone. This time there was a tiny little blonde without any breasts or bottom and not at all Jack's type but he was obviously hers as she made a bee line towards him and would not leave his side! She made him dance with her several times and then he saw me looking at him! Knowing what I meant by my killer look he excused himself, as he was coming towards me she 'accidentally' threw her drink over his trousers and then cheekily proceeded to wipe him?! "Jack, go and change your trousers" I said. I walked towards the bedroom and with the wardrobe door open I was getting him another pair when he entered. Just as I was going to bring out the trousers I heard him say "What the hell are you doing here, woman?" The blonde answered "I came to help you change your trousers!" I closed the wardrobe door and came out holding his trousers and sweetly saying "That won't be necessary my dear, I shall help him do so!" After this, knowing how the wind was blowing, Jack was very attentive to me but the woman never ceased to come in between the two of us! Later I found out that wherever we went she was also there and always after Jack who by now seemed quite prone to her admirations. Since I had learnt my lesson, the next party we went to I let a couple of males go a little further than usual, let them touch my behind, put their arms round me and hold me close saying the usual stupid things men say when they want or think they are going to get something! No sooner had this started and I had let it continue that Jack was by my side after telling the woman to get lost. Why is it men feel that what is good for the goose is definitely not for the gander?!

Jack flew back to San Juan while we left by ship two weeks later. After my experience while flying to Salisbury, Southern Rhodesia when first married, I did not want anything to do with planes! The trip back was most enjoyable and this time I did not see why I should not enjoy my admirers' attention! There was one poor fellow, a physicist, who found everybody on board, including Lyana, all bores and uninteresting, except apparently for me! He was a bit too much and at the end both Lyana and I had to be rude to him, which Lyana thought was rather fun!

Back home in San Juan, my first thought was for Ouiki. Poor, darling thing! He looked like a half dead rabbit, very nervous and on edge. Once inside the house he would hide under the bed appearing only for food, he was too nervy and on edge until he realised he was back where he belonged, to stay. I then made the decision not to send him to the kennels ever again.

Our second Christmas in Puerto Rico was rather a scream. I decided I would buy a turkey and make a Gibraltarian Christmas lunch and invite all our local friends. The turkey looked beautiful all wrapped up, cleaned etc and was the first we had bought in this condition. Usually the turkeys had come in need of further plucking and scorching plus the disagreeable task of cleaning the inside out. This one looked as if it had had a massage, the skin all lovely and smooth. I undid the legs that had been neatly put into the downstairs hole and lo and behold I found a little parcel. I took this out and found a piece of liver, the heart and various things I did not recognize. Then I looked inside the cavity and I could see a long, thick thing. I pulled and it would not come out. I pulled again without any success.

'No, it couldn't be the turkey's thingy in there, could it?' I placed the bird on a pan and calling Jack I showed him. He looked and pulled too but nothing happened. Just then I saw Cristina so I called her through the window and asked her if I could show her something. She waited. Jack came with me outside. I showed her the turkey and then making an exaggerated sign of the cross she exclaimed "Valgame Dios del Cielo, pues no quieren volver a la pava de dentro para fuera!" (My God in Heaven, but they are trying to turn the turkey inside out!) It was the turkey's neck that without cutting had been put doubled back into the cavity. I think the whole neighbourhood found out about this.

As soon as I returned I applied to go back to my studies, this time at the University of Rio Piedras. I went and made inquiries so as to be accepted as a credited student. It seemed that the easiest and quickest solution would be for me to take an entrance examination. So after more years than I wished to remember without studies I was going to sit for my exam within two weeks. I needed Spanish, English and mathematics. The first two I felt I should know enough but the last with things now being so different I needed coaching. One of my young pupils offered to help me. The day came and I felt really nervous, I was already nearly thirty two years of age and here I was with young kids in their late teens. My apprehension knew no end. When it seemed I had finished the first exam, English, far too quickly, even the teacher there advised me to re-read to see if I could do anything further. I had actually finished all my papers. Nevertheless I re-read everything and then not wanting to change or add anything I handed in the papers and left. When Jack came to pick me up he found me in quite a state, I was sure I had somehow blown it. I returned in the afternoon for my second subject, Spanish. I had a similar situation. This time I checked everything thoroughly and then handed in the papers and left quickly. All the other students looked sadly at me. What a failure I must be! I almost did not go for my maths exam. My confidence was at its lowest, but Jack firmly told me that since I had started it, it wasn't like me to give up; I must go and do my thing like a good girl. This paper took me longer, I read and re-read some questions that seemed so stupid that I felt there had to be a catch, at the end I did all the questions, handed in the papers and hoped for the best. What was to be would be, it was too late to do anything else about it.

Two weeks later I was asked to go to the university to see the dean of studies. I stood in front of him, fingers crossed, waiting to hear what he had to say. Imagine my surprise, delight and jubilation when he congratulated me and I found out that I had passed all my exams with such high grades that I was to be an honours student and could attend the university free. I couldn't wait to get home and tell Jack who in his phlegmatic way said "Gee, honey, if you had top marks, the others must have been real stupid!" Husbands!

I had just paid one visit to the university trying to see what credits I would get when one of the senior students started to talk to me and invited me to a cigarette, which I refused and then introducing some of his other friends he asked me if I wanted to join them all for a weekend. It seemed the age difference was not going to hamper me. On returning home, thrilled with my success as a student, and excited I told Jack all about it. He decided he too would join the university but he was not taking the entrance exam. He would search for all his school certificates and get in without any gruelling exams. Perhaps he did not want to join the others' ranking if he did not do as well as me! He wasn't going to take the chance. Kidding aside he was able to join me soon after and he even took the same credits as me. I did all the studying, made précis of the important things, and without much effort on his part he almost did as well as I did after my hours of swotting. But I loved it. I loved my renewed self and the wonderful stimulation. There was so much yet to learn. I was once again vibrantly alive. I had no idea Spanish literature could be so beautiful. Up to now all I had read was from English writers and poets. I was once again aware of the world and its problems, what a vegetable I had become!

We thoroughly enjoyed our university days. The young people accepted us freely and they did not seem to notice or care that we were so much older than them. If by any chance the professor did not turn up for class, unless we left the class room they stayed at their desks. Only when the English couple left would it be the correct thing to do!

The Spanish teacher was wonderful. Mrs Troche made me see for the first time in my life the beauty of Cervantes' language. Her lessons were terrific, absorbing. She was so full of enthusiasm that she assigned extra curriculum reading outside of regular classwork. I began to know significant Spanish writers and enjoy their works and essays which up to then I did not even know existed. My favourite ones were Ortega y Gasset and Miguel de Unamuno which I read and re-read and so enjoyed all the thoughts that they made me develop.

Although we only went to the university four days a week for three hours a day, we had undertaken a complete schedule of twelve credits. Mrs Mary de Piza was our English class teacher. She was a beautiful, gentle, grey haired lady, with a fantastic sense of humour and twinkle in her eyes yet strong willed and capable. We both enjoyed her talks and explanations and stimulating unscheduled philosophy of life from her. We often learned more from these unplanned lessons and unexpected examples of what a full happy life could teach. Mrs de Piza was to become our very good friend and counsellor. We didn't however appreciate it very much when she expected us to change our accent to the American. We used to laugh so much that at the end she realized she was never going to achieve this.

Since we had done part of this tour in Brazil we now had to go on home leave before our three years was up. It seemed we had been too short a time in San Juan perhaps because we had done so much and led such a healthy family life. We had our friends to consider since we would be away from between five to six months all told. First we asked to see if someone would take Ouiki temporarily while we were away but no one wanted to be bothered. The thought of putting him down was distasteful and horrifying. The spinsters who lived behind us said they would have him but it would have to be on a permanent basis.

Chapter 21

SOJOURN IN EUROPE

Now we were ready and actually looked forward to our vacation as we knew to our pleasure and happiness that we would definitely be returning. We left San Juan for England on a sunny day aboard the French Line ship, the Antilles. The trip was, as usual, full of activities and exciting surprises. We were wined and danced off our feet, being invited to the captain's, doctor's, and chief purser's tables practically every night. We had met with friends in some of the ports and it had been so wonderful that we were quite sorry to have arrived in England.

While in London we bought a Ford Anglia station wagon to use while on leave. As always we stayed at the Exiles Club, our home from home. Jack was at first seeing to all his Head Office arrangements and once this was over he started going to Hendon daily where he was taking a Company's course. During this time as I would be alone I decided to take an intensive course in beauty culture at the Christine Shaw College in Old Bond Street. I thought it would be beneficial to my business life and also stop me from investing money on products that were not compatible with my skin and eventually were thrown away. Once we made these decisions we arranged with Mum Armstrong to leave Lyana with her until both Jack and I had finished our courses. Once these were finished we too would come and join them for a while as well. Once back we stayed, as it had become the tradition, with Uncle George and Aunt Dora and often went out together. Sundays we generally went to a lovely pub for lunch where they were very well known by the owners. During one of these outings I looked around and realized I was the only foreigner there and exclaimed "My goodness, do you realize that I am the only foreigner amongst all of you natives?!" There was a deadly silence and then a couple of voices, amongst them Aunt Dora's, said "No, we are not natives!" I then replied "You are all English aren't you? This is your native land, England, isn't it? Therefore aren't you England's natives?" They were so very upset that I then realized that when the English in Gibraltar or any other country but theirs, called us 'natives', it was done in a derogatory manner, little realizing that everyone is a native of some place or other whether they like it or not! I think it took them a little while to digest what I said and hopefully they learnt the lesson. My father always used to say that people should always treat others with kindness and education and that those that did not, didn't know any better. We are all people with the same rights and aspirations regardless of the colour of our skins.

We left the UK in our overloaded Ford for France taking the ferry from Dover to Calais to begin a leisurely trip overland to Gibraltar. The poor car sighed and trembled as it climbed the steep winding roads from France to Belgium, Luxembourg and the French Riviera. In those days there were very few English registered cars and when we did see one another, we hooted and often stopped, even went for a drink together. It was a way to find out how roads were and gather information as to where to find good and reasonable accommodation and food. Travelling in those days was a lot of fun. On the French Riviera we made our way to Le Levandou and, of course, a visit to that famous nudist island, L'Ile du Levant.

This nudist colony, fully authorized by the government and perfectly legitimate and accepted by the public (all the other places though authorized had been in remote and almost hidden spots without any literature or motoring plans available except to the few members already 'in the know'), was quite an interesting experience. It was also the first of its kind we had ever visited.

The colony consisted of a fairly large island with plenty of hotel, pension and boarding-house accommodation, where it was permissible for you to take your meals, do your shopping and walk along the small narrow roads wearing only 'le minimum', something considerably less than a monokini, and equally by both sexes. The only place where complete nudity was insisted on was the beaches. On one beach we were sunning ourselves when a well built, muscular man arrived, flexed his muscles, oiled his body, getting admiring glances from several ladies. Then he stripped off his bathing trunks. A Frenchman beside us commented "He may be a bundle of dynamite but what a small fuse!"

Have you ever seen anyone doing their shopping with a big sun hat and string of beads around the necks, sunglasses, shoes and shopping basket? It is quite a sight, and one which made me giggle almost hysterically to Jack's admonition of keeping quiet and behaving myself. I think that what really shocked me was the fact that small boats that carried people to the island, with their fully clothed crew and passengers, came to the dock side to behold all this nudist glory. It was so very unexpected. Well, there is one thing for such people in their nudity; no one can impress the other by the quality, cost, or design of their garments, or display jewels and accessories. There you are worth what you really are even though some might need more ironing of their skin than others!

From Le Levandou we made our way to the Italian Riviera, Florence and Pisa, but before returning to the French Riviera we first called on our Brazil painter Ilio's eighty-year-old Mama in Turin. We then followed the coast on very poor roads eventually arriving in Gibraltar on July 13th, 1963.

Life in Gibraltar appeared not to have changed very much; all seemed the same, at least in its physical aspect. Once we had taken care of all the courtesies, calls and visits we decided we wanted to relax in a simple, open air camping style and off we went to La Chullera in Southern Spain and close to Gibraltar. We had a small tent, sleeping bags and all the necessary items for a relatively comfortable life. Did we have some fun! Our tent was not as expensive as that of our millionaire Brazilian friend Fafa with whom we had enjoyed the best, almost luxurious, camping weekends on the small island 'Adam and Eve' in the Guanabara Bay at Rio. Ours was slightly larger than the usual Boy Scout type, big enough to accommodate the three of us without cramping our style too much.

When we arrived at La Chullera, the wind was blowing rather hard and the sun was beginning to set. We therefore decided to put up the tent as quickly as possible to get all the hard work over. But this was easier said than done. Poor Jack, and poor me! I thought the wind was going to carry away the tent and us too. We discovered as I held on to the tent, pulling as hard as I could towards the ground, that the pegs that were supposed to hold the tent down were only wooden ones and not very good at that. No sooner were they in place, than out they came like champagne bottle tops. Our next door neighbours, some French people from Rabat on their way to France for their annual vacation, took pity on us and like good Samaritans came over to our help lending us some of their spare steel pegs until the following day when we were able to buy some for ourselves.

Will we ever forget that first night in the open, catering for ourselves in the good old primitive way? We had a small primus stove which just did not want to light up for Jack, who by now was not only swearing at it but also kicking it and pulling it to pieces in sheer desperation, as his stomach demanded nourishment. The stove was never lit, and the intended hot meal was off the menu. I ended up giving Lyana a tin of fruit with cream and some bread and butter, while for Jack and myself, I made some rough sandwiches with some tinned sardines. In the romantic light of the moon and with our hunger becoming steadily more acute, we had not been aware that the tin of sardines Jack had opened was not in a good state, it had blown. I soon began to feel certain discomfort and as my stomach started misbehaving I reckoned that a stiff dose of cognac would be the right remedial medicine to take. At home we are all great believers of the curing powers of the L'Eau de Vie. However, it seemed nothing would calm this uprising food poisoning. I have never been so sick. As I returned to the tent from the toilet facilities I saw the figure of a man barely able to walk as he crossed my path. I realised it was poor Jack who had also been stricken with the same ailment. I fail to remember the many times we crossed on our way back and forth, finally giving up and lying down on the ground, too exhausted and sick to return to our tent. We both felt the morning would see us dead and buried, but thank goodness when one is young a few hours sleep and rest soon had us on our feet again, the nightmare a thing of the past, filed and forgotten..

By late afternoon Jack had discovered the trick of how to make the primus stove work, plus the fact that the camping site also offered us limited restaurant facilities, and so we began to enjoy our open air holiday. Two days after this episode around 4.00 a m. we were startled by a lot of noise from some late, or was it early, arrivals. There seemed to be a lot of amusement and so unable to control our curiosity we got up. There, about 50 yards from us were two couples, obviously Germans by their speech, in their late seventies and in their birthday suits, actively and unhesistantly putting up their tent. It did look funny, and in a way, we were also jealous for they appeared to be in perfect physical fitness and full of pep at this infernal hour. About two hours later, they were at it again, this time frolicking in the water like little children.

My parents and complete family invaded the camp at the weekends. They all came carting mountain loads of delicious food which would last us for a few days. Like everyone else, we got as brown as berries, and when most of the original crowd started to leave for home or on their way to their ultimate goal, we too began to tire of the monotony of this life as the camp became extremely quiet and lonely during weekdays. After three weeks we returned home to the Rock and some exciting if less healthy recreation.

By chance we became friends with a fairly Bohemian crowd consisting mainly of English and Irish people, most of them prominent members of the Gibraltar society with high positions. It was interesting to discover that even Gibraltar had a 'Dolce Vita' of a kind, in spite of the narrow mindedness and critical bourgeoisie minds which often characterized our people. I wonder what they would have said had they seen their favourite and most efficient physician dancing 'por fandanguillos y soleares'? And what about those strip poker games we had also heard about? I loved going to these parties but unfortunately I have never been a night bird, come midnight I would be only too ready for bed and these parties only got really going in the earlier hours of the mornings. Going home so early really infuriated Jack!

A Gibraltarian lady who lived a little way from one of these particular groups, who were also writers and artists, one day phoned the police to complain about the atrocious behaviour of their neighbours who were indecent and an embarrassment to the neighbourhood. The police came to the house to see what this house owner was complaining about since she said that there was a lady posing playfully in the nude for the artist. The police then asked where the lady had seen such obscenity. She pointed outside, the policemen went and checked, they could not see anything, "We cannot see anything Madam" they said. "Yes, they are there. I saw them just before you turned up here." She went out and climbing over her garden hedge and then some rocks she stood up and said "There, can't you see?" The curiousity of this prude woman had made her climb over her own boundaries to see what was going on. It was she that got the reprimand for being a nosey parker!

In fact some people seemed to enjoy criticising others just for the heck of it. Jack and I, no matter how annoyed and upset we had been with one another, always had the habit of kissing each other whenever we left or met in the streets, we did this fairly regularly and it took away any asperity left over from misunderstandings. In any case, we enjoyed kissing. One of my Dad's neighbours, a young woman stopped me to complain about it. I looked at her in surprise as we had always behaved in this manner since we were married and had never given it a thought that it would be wrong or distasteful to anyone. I stared at her and then said "Carmen, I don't see why you should complain about seeing me kiss my husband, perhaps you should wait until you see me kissing yours!" The look on her face was so shocked that it was comical and I started laughing and then said "Can't you see I'm joking, anyway we are leaving shortly. Not to worry, but perhaps if you kissed your husband more often you wouldn't have time for criticism!"

This had been quite a long furlough and we were looking forward to our return back to Puerto Rico and get on with our studies and life. This time we returned overland via Madrid and Paris taking the shortest route and as soon as we got to England we sold the car and set sail.

Chapter 22

BACK TO SAN JUAN

Once in San Juan we had to go back to temporary accommodation until we found a new home for ourselves. By then Dick had been promoted to administration manager and he, Maria, and the family had moved to the manager's home in the Ocean Park area of Santurce. We wanted to be near them so that Lyana could go to the same school as her friends and not feel lonely once again. Within a week we found a beautiful bungalow on the sea front in Park Boulevard. By the second week we were already installed in our new home. So we decided to pay a visit to our neighbours in Baldrich and see how Ouiki was doing. When we saw the ladies we had left him with they were very upset as he had refused to stay with them from the very first day. Instead Mati, who had not wanted him in the first place as Luis was allergic to cats had been feeding him and the children played with him whenever they saw him. Naturally we were all very upset so decided to go looking for him in our old Hillman. We were just about to leave the street when we noticed Ouiki running like mad behind the car. We stopped, opened the door, and before we could get out he was inside with us, meowing, purring, and going from one to the other not knowing which one to choose to give more love. What a joyful reunion it was. Obviously he had missed us as much as we had missed him. The poor soul stayed inside the house for a few days and after this if he saw any luggage he would get all nervous thinking we would leave him again. Once he got accustomed to the new environment he spent a lot of time chasing the land crabs abounding in the garden and often coming off the worse for wear as he got too near sniffing them.

In Puerto Rico all our friends rallied round us and were extremely happy to have us back. Since our new house was so very near the sea, you just had to cross the road and the beach was there, we had open house every weekend that we were going to be at home. Friends popped in and stayed on until early evening and sometimes in a rota during the day. I would make a big pot of Puerto Rican hot beans, another one of rice and a salad and then as the friends arrived with their different offerings of sausage, steaks, hamburgers and the like went to the barbecue. They were lovely happy days full of clean fun.

It was so difficult to understand why the Puerto Ricans had such a bad reputation in the States. Everyone we had come across in San Juan was educated and so very kind, generous and helpful that it was unbelievable. One day I was invited to go with a social worker to visit La Perla and then I realised a little better the reason why a few were being judged for the majority. When you are very poor and live in substandard conditions where you don't know what a lavatory looks like it is very difficult to be transported to some dreadful district in the USA and expect people to know how to live and behave but that is the same for everyone. What about the hill-billies we came across years later in the California desert? Many of the immigrants to the States were of such an origin and although they were blessed with an inborn kindness and were quite polite they knew no better. The young people rebelled and things went from bad to worse. In La Perla the poverty had to be seen to be believed and yet we were offered drinks and people were very polite and appreciative for what the social worker was doing. Why they would leave Puerto Rico for the States is difficult to understand, at least in their homeland they had good weather, beautiful surroundings and warm friends.

We had lots of business friends we enjoyed being with and led a good social life in a very homly way. The Americans were in the habit of ending any party in the kitchen and when we were entertaining business people Jack made me very much aware that I needed to have the pantry full of the trade marks they represented. Lo and behold the problem if I made the wrong choice like having Coca Cola when it was the Pepsi Cola representative who was coming home! Jack's Company kept us all very well with lovely homes, children's education and so forth but moneywise we were always paid much less than our American counterparts so I had to learn from the very start how to make the dollar stretch to be able to reciprocate.

I gave our guests good tasty home cooking and I never had an invitation turned down. I think they particularly liked having home cooked meals. I was always very aware that it was Jack who was working for the Company and not I, not like some of the other senior staff wives that automatically proclaimed themselves in their husband's position. I had my own life, my own interests and my own means of making money and keeping myself should I need to. I helped Jack because he was my husband and it was my duty to do so. The relationship of business association often changed to that of being good friends and it was indeed through this friendship that Jack was able to keep all the business he did as unfortunately our Company was not in a position to give the kind of service the Americans did with their latest techniques and equipment.

Both Jack and I returned to the university for another year, a year which we thoroughly enjoyed and which totally enriched our lives. I started working at Lyana's new school Colegio Santa Teresita and introduced President Kennedy's Physical Fitness Programme. Unlike the previous school this one was totally committed and I set up the gym bringing in equipment for the children and I took over the physical education for all the schoolgirls while a male instructor continued to look after the boys. I also gave the health and etiquette class for both boys and girls which was greatly enjoyed by everyone participating.

All in all I loved this work which took only a certain amount of my morning time and gave me sufficient free time to continue with the grown-ups keep fit classes as well as to give and to take dance classes. The first school physical education show was featured in all the newspapers, on television and in cinemas and this coverage made the children want to do more. From then onwards we held a yearly show where eventually the boys also participated. Santa Teresita was the first school to offer such a physical education programme. While at school I also had to go to the dances held for the teenagers and I was often asked for a dance by the senior boys who somehow followed me around and always were willing to carry my books. I felt rather awkward as they would stick their faces next to mine and the nuns looked on beaming at us. I never felt so ridiculous especially as Lyana was not too happy at seeing me like this.

Jack belonged to the Commonwealth Society in San Juan, a social cultural club catering for the British community, and which I found rather boring. I was never particularly eager to go with him. However, this one time, for some reason or other, he insisted or rather demanded that I went with him. I was really annoyed and said "I shall go with you but I shall not enjoy it!" Funnily enough I had a lovely time as I met with Helga a German/American lady. She was married to a Scotsman, Gerry. Helga was interesting and as erudite as Gwen had been in Brazil but in a more sober way. We became excellent friends. We saw each other frequently after this encounter.

I was founder member of Ballet Concertantes de Puerto Rico with the well known Lottie Tischer as president. My dancing days were really interesting as now the Dance Teachers Association to which I also belonged brought States-side teachers for long seminars. I really loved these seminars and put my name down for all the courses. My ballet was absolutely atrocious and I regularly ended up as the 'model' for what a teacher should not allow their pupils to do. It always seemed as if my behind was never where it should have been and my plies never as low either. But my arabesques were an absolute delight. There was I thinking myself a Margot Fontaine when I caught myself in the mirror and Jumbo was more graceful than me. I enjoyed it very much and that was the main thing. I studied with such marvellous professors as Yurek Lasovsky, Thalia Mara, Goya and Mateo, and Halina Lutomski among others.

Our friend Loveday from Rhodesia came to visit for a fortnight and it was good to hear all the news. Unfortunately her sister Karenza had passed away very young leaving three children. Loveday had been taking care of them until her brother- in- law had remarried and she was now having time for herself. The news from Rhodesia was not so good and we were extremely happy that Jack had made the decision to return to the Company.

Ouiki flourished in his new home. He sometimes came with us to the beach and made a bee line towards the sea, the moment the cold water touched him he made a sort of somersault and then little jumps all hunched up that reminded you of a bull getting ready to charge. He loved Jack and horrors of horrors he would lick Jack's feet. He would purr no end and once the job finished would unceremoniously plonk himself on top of Jack's chest without getting any complaints! Ouiki grew rounder and fatter, spending most of his time sleeping, and hunting at nights when he would bring a collection of his trophies to leave them in front of the kitchen door for us to find in the mornings. There would be lizards, and perhaps a mouse or rat that seemed to thrive amongst the banana trees notwithstanding our constant fight against these marauders. Ouiki's dandified appearance was deceiving; he was not as soft nor as helpless as he looked. One night there was a terrific 'helluva' outside and we kept hearing Ouiki's little voice at its fullest as if asking for protection. Both Jack and I were wide awake and could not help feeling sorry so out we went to aid our pet. It was an impressive, comical and unbelievable sight. OUR Ouiki, the little spoilt pet in all his glory, courageous and defiant, sat with one paw holding a stranger cat down on the ground, while with the other he hit the poor opponent with the equivalent of a boxer's punch. Unperturbed at the screeching, and at our intrusion, he proceeded to enjoy each blow with a sadistic meow of victory. He was a proper little bully and so against our wishes, we had to end the fight by protecting the victim.

When I was cooking Ouiki would come to keep me company in the kitchen. All would be well until I brought out either meat or fish; then as he smelled his favourite food, his nose would twitch; his hairs go on end, until finally he emitted the softest of sounds opening his mouth to the maximum. He was patient and never stole anything even though I would purposely leave little bits on the kitchen counter to test him. He would never climb up or jump onto the table, yet he often sat on top of our tall fridge. He was quite a cat!

Ouiki objected to us having any guests for dinner, and would insist on sitting on his special chair. It was our fault for often when we ate, he would sit in 'his place', and wait for me to dish out his 'portion' too and take it to the laundry room. He would then jump down from the chair, thank us by going round our legs and then walk tail up to eat his food. If we ignored him, he would get down to the floor, complain loudly and then pat first Jack, and then me on the legs. This would go on until we served him too. If by any chance any guest gave him a titbit he would ignore it until it was placed down on the ground when very delicately he would stretch his leg and gather the food with his paw.

He knew our car and would recognize its sound before I could even hear it. Then he would rush to the door and wait for the key in the lock, or for one of us to open it, when he would jump up in fervent greetings. Sometimes Lyana would play hide and seek and if he didn't hear anything for more than a minute he would stalk carefully to see what was happening, curiousity being stronger than anything else.

Ouiki fitted the family to perfection, and did odd, unexpected things like getting a dog for his best friend. He loved a little Daschund that lived close by and often went there to visit. At first Fritz objected to this attention from a cat, but after a while both animals became very attached to each other and when Fritz passed our house on his daily walk with his mistress, he would bark and whine until Ouiki left whatever he was doing and went out. If Ouiki was inside the house, he would then come and look for us to show us to the door, which he would then scratch in order to get out to his friend.

His fights with the land crabs were terrific, exciting and amazing. He would lie down perfectly still as if dead. The only thing that moved was his nostrils and eyes, while his long moustache would stand on end as if stretched, and gently tremble; then all of a sudden, the crab would look out of its hole, hesitating as if unsure of its safety, when bang! There would be Ouiki on top of it. But, Mr Crab was no ninny; he would come back at Ouiki who would then run away mystified at this brute who dared return his attack. This game went on until finding that he was not achieving anything but a few bites or scratches from the crab, Ouiki would give up and haughtily walk away.

Housework was a lot of fun in this house. I had the lovely beach with its lonely coconut tree right by my door so I spent time in a rather peculiar, to my neighbours, way. I would start my housework usually in bathing costume. As soon as it got too hot and I started perspiring I would rush out of the gates, cross the road, jump down to the beach and enjoy a swim. I am sure everyone thought I was raving mad, particularly when later on my husband bought me an eight by four foot paddling pool and where to everyone's amusement I would spend most of my time soaking away while doing my studies for the university. When these finished I had to do something else so I thought of opening a slimming salon in a little house in the back garden once intended for domestic help. To equip it as I desired was impossible with the cash I had saved, so I decided to go to Sears and ask how I could do business with them on a hire purchase basis. It was the first time in my life that I was not making cash payment but credit was refused me as I had no credit rating because I didn't owe anybody anything. Maria's sister who had a boutique backed me, but then I changed my mind and did not invest in anything. Instead Jack obtained the Diners Club, American Express, Swiss Chalet and other cards. We enjoyed the most sumptuous outings and delicious meals, usually at the end of the month as by then we were broke and used the cards instead. We had learned to live the American way.

We loved to go to the Spanish Club where we could enjoy real paella and read all the Spanish magazines in a wonderful atmosphere and amongst very congenial people. Life was really good and peaceful. I was thrilled to find that I was once again pregnant but did not want to tell Lyana after all the miscarriages I had had by then. One day I was talking to the Mother Superior at the school when for no reason I started to cry. Hours later I had miscarried. Somehow it always happened like this. I was entering my third month, was rushed to the hospital for a D & C. where the gynaecologist reckoned I had endometriosis and that was why I couldn't carry my babies. I was put on treatment but nothing happened.

The Caparra Country Club asked me if I would run a summer holiday camp for the members' children. It meant six weeks of my summer holiday working but the conditions and salary were too good for me to turn down particularly when I could have Lyana with me and with all her meals paid for too. The hours were quite good for it was from 9.00 a.m. till 3.00 p.m. only. Jack was not too thrilled but I was determined to have enough cash to put down for a house in England on our next leave and I took the job. Every cent went into a savings account I opened for this purpose and I did this work for the last two years we spent in San Juan. In any case it still left us enough time to go on vacation. It was at this time that we received an invitation to go to New York for the World Fair. The invitation came from one of the senior executives of a well known American company.

Chapter 23

THE BIG APPLE

I was terribly excited about going to New York. To me it promised all that meant life and excitement. I had heard about Manhattan, Brooklyn, Times Square, and so on from films, but I had never been there before, the real land of tall skyscrapers. I have never been so eager to visit a place. At long last I would be seeing the Statue of Liberty, the Empire State Building, and the many other sights that, not only I, but my mother had always dreamt of seeing.

We were to stay in one of the exclusive suburbs where all executives lived. This was another aspect of American life that was different from most of Europe where people, unless extremely rich, lived in any area. It was not the district or the address that you had that made them 'people,' the important factor in Europe was breeding, tradition and family names that made you important and 'in'.

In the States it seemed to me that the place you chose to live marked your social and of course, financial status, whether you had any education (and I don't mean the general school education) or not. It seemed that quite a number of people actually lived in a much higher bracket than they could really afford only to appear more important.

I visited a number of such homes, great beautiful places but lacking the elegance or good taste that should have been obvious. It was funny how the display of elegant expensive furniture, selected decorations, Persian carpets, and porcelains were destroyed by a monstrous print or painting which was not part of the professional interior design and decorator's prospectus.

Shopping was another aspect that began to lose its attraction for me in New York, unless you went into an expensive boutique or top departmental store, most of the sales-ladies were always in a hurry to get rid of you. Used to the wonderful personal attention always bestowed on me in the other countries I had lived I felt completely disappointed.

I did like the beautiful restaurants particularly the Four Seasons, the NY Athletic Club, and the Inn in the Park but whereas at these top eating places the service was absolutely wonderful often with a waiter for each customer, apart from the well known bistros, the rest lacked the kind of service we always received in South America. Although I enjoyed my short stay I discovered New York was too fast and at times too ruthless for me to wish to live there on a permanent basis. In fact I was rather disappointed perhaps because I had dreamt so much about it.

Our host and hostess gave us a magnificent American style welcome, and we thoroughly enjoyed their hospitality even though at times the peculiar behaviour of the hostess made us wonder as to the length of time we would be remaining there. The first surprise was when on our very first day we arrived, to find our hostess, completely starkers talking to her gardener. Later on we discovered that she rarely if ever wore panties and bras, and she took an immense pleasure in letting you discover this fact for yourself. Somehow her behaviour made me feel a little suspicious, not knowing what to expect next, yet apart from this, the couple's behaviour was most friendly and cordial at all times.

Apprehensively I spoke to Jack who thought that perhaps her attitude was due to the fact that she might have heard we were naturists. But naturists don't go exhibiting themselves as this beautiful woman did, flaunting her body by constantly uncovering herself in rather an exotic and sensuous way. I felt that our host and hostess were quite in error as to their concept of naturism and what they expected or anticipated from us. I was very reluctant to stay in their home and constantly begged Jack to cut our stay short. I had this terrible feeling that they misconstrued the idea of the nudism of the naturist to 'sex and orgies'. Jack, as always, said I was reading too much into this behaviour and that I was narrow minded,

The straw that broke the camel's back was the hostess appearing naked in my bedroom with Lyana still sleeping in her bed. I woke Lyana up and quickly went to the bathroom as I thought the behaviour most inappropriate and disgusting yet I could not say anything as nothing else had been said or done. As soon as we were out of the bathroom, I dressed myself and Lyana, then gathering my passport and what little money I had, walked out of this house and somehow found the house of an older couple who without my realizing it I was compromising, as Mary's husband was our host's deputy. As soon as she saw me come in with my daughter Mary remarked "Don't say she has been up to her tricks again!" What I heard from Mary was exactly what I had thought and told Jack that these people were in the habit of exchanging partners and I don't want to know what else. Jack had gone off with his host to visit the offices and on returning he discovered I had gone with Lyana and did not leave any note behind. I would not allow Mary or her husband to phone and let them know where I was as I insisted I wanted to return to San Juan. Eventually seeing how worried Mary's husband was particularly as it could affect his job; I relented and let him contact Jack. I refused to return to the house and blamed Jack for being so thick skinned and not listening to me in the first place. Jack had to return to their home to pack our things. He returned for Lyana and I to take us to a hotel for the night. I was in a really nasty temper and told Jack that if he wanted to be involved in these things he could count me out once and for all. I was even in no mood to continue with the scheduled itinerary but at the end I agreed to continue to Massachusetts. On Cape Cod we stayed at Yarmouth with other American friends, these with points of view that coincided with ours or mine at least!

Our visit to New England was wonderful. I really loved Boston and the whole surrounding area where we visited many historical sights at Lexington, where the Revolution began in 1775, and Concord of the famous Minute Men. There we also visited the house of Louisa May Alcott, the authoress of one of my favourite stories 'Little Women'. As Yarmouth is so near Hyannis we went to see where the Kennedy family lived (we were not invited in) on our way to the beach where on this occasion we were chased away from our picnic by swarms of the biggest and hungriest horse flies I've ever seen. On another day we spent time at Plymouth where we visited Plymouth Plantation and the Plymouth Rock, supposedly the point where the Pilgrim Fathers first stepped ashore in the New World. We ate many meals of delicious New England lobsters and other great sea food so we were very sorry to leave.

Chapter 24

FINAL DAYS

It was however, lovely to be back home in San Juan and to go to sleep with the faint murmurs of the waves as they broke quietly on to the beach by our own front door. It was the sweetest of music to our ears as it signalled the uninterrupted singing of the jovial 'coquis', the coquis are little frog like creatures particular to San Juan's beach front houses. They would spend their time actually calling coqui, coqui, coqui, therefore their name.

Not long after we returned Mum started writing about the many problems they were facing in Gibraltar with the Spanish Government's attitude concerning the Gibraltarians who were British and wanted to remain so. Franco's nationalist government wanted to convert us to being Spanish even against our will and our rights. First his government restricted Spanish workers from leaving Spain to work in Gibraltar, and then the holy wine for mass and oxygen for the hospital were not allowed to be sent over the border. The situation was so critical that the Spaniards were slowly closing the frontier therefore no one would be able to get in or out of the Rock

The tourism that existed, mainly French people residing in Morocco and travelling on the ferry 'Mons Calpe' between Tangiers and Gibraltar to obtain perfume and other tax-free goods cheaper than in France was hit. The Mons Calpe was the ship which was featured in the Alec Guinness film Captains Paradise - often the actual Captain was asked if it was a true story based on his life - I have no comment to make! The norm was for french to stay a couple of days, and then cross the border into Spain on their way to France. The Gibraltarians were at a loss, what to do in such a limited area that didn't produce anything? Housewives, for the first time, had to take care of their household chores as Spanish servants were no longer available. Many even helped by taking hotel jobs in order to continue to provide for at least the holiday maker and to try to keep the economy going. Women were driving buses and a new society with different roles developed for the betterment of women and their emancipation generally.

In San Juan I avoided buying anything Spanish thinking that it was the only thing I could do. At school the priest in charge of Santa Teresita, also a Spaniard, ironically named Father Franco started being obnoxious with me all the time making uncalled for comments about the Rock and its people. One day while at the office with Mother Superior he stopped in front of me and without any provocation said that he had an infallible way to stop all the problems between Spain and England because of a few Gibraltarians. Thinking he would be preaching the word of God I inquired what would he do about the problem and precarious situation. His answer shocked me to the very depth. Calmly looking at me, fixedly with his one glass eye and the remaining good one, he said "I would put an atom bomb on the top of the Rock and bang, the problem will be over!" He almost lost his good eye! The nuns had to come and take me away from him. Later on I discovered that with so much feeling for Spain he had in fact changed his nationality to American as he did not want to return to his homeland! And there was I thinking and believing that you did not change ever, either your religion or the nationality you were born with! What was really amazing was the fact that he had seen it perfectly okay to voluntarily change from being Spanish to American to suit his own circumstances to guarantee himself a good home and yet he could not understand that we had perfectly good homes and enjoyed happiness under the British flag and did not want anything different. Spain had not been good for him and he wanted it to be good and acceptable to us! What hypocrisy!

There was no love left between the two of us and I avoided him like the plague. Eventually when the time came for me to leave San Juan he had the grace to apologise for what he had said and to tell me how much the school was going to miss me for I was an excellent teacher 'in spite of being from Gibraltar'! I had been taught to respect the cloth that was worn by these ministers of the church and religion but with an example such as his it was no wonder that for a while I did not go to church!

Our tour in Puerto Rico was coming to an end and Jack wrote to Head Office to query our future movements. Already Maria, Dick and his family were packing up for their transfer. After many years in Puerto Rico they were leaving for good and Dick was going to St Lucia as the General Manager. It was still in the Caribbean and not too far from Puerto Rico so they were quite happy to be going. We had no idea who would be replacing him. In the middle of all this I discovered that I was once again pregnant and I hoped then that because of my pregnancy Head Office would allow us to remain in San Juan since I had to be under surveillance all the time.

A visitor from Head Office, the Company Chairman, a lovely dear gentle gentleman arrived with his good wife. Sir John McPherson was a most entertaining personality and somehow he appreciated my sense of humour as much as I did his. We met several times during their stay and reached quite a rapport. I became his 'nuisance girl' as he called me. He could have some fun and not worry too much about what he had to say! In fact we kept in touch all the time for many years but not all the Head Office visitors were as nice and charming as the Chairman.

Because of Dick's imminent transfer all the responsibility of entertaining fell on us. Shortly afterwards we gave a small and very select party for two other visiting VIPs. One was an extremely well educated and charming man directly in charge of Jack's head office department, the other was a thick set, obese man who rather fancied himself as the English version of Rodolfo Valentino with open neck shirt and silk cravat. He strutted

around as proud as a peacock but really as great as a peacock's behind!.
I hate this type of man. During the course of the evening a few people
went out to the verandah, it was a gorgeous full moon with the sky all
lit up by the million stars. As a good hostess I went from place to place
seeing all was going well and that plenty of refreshment was available.
I went out to the verandah and unfortunately he was the only person
there. I turned round to leave him alone when without any ceremony
I felt his hands grabbing my chest from the back trying to turn me
round so as to kiss me. A spitfire had nothing on me. He was such
a disgusting man who should have gone to the dentist before even
thinking of kissing any woman! An ageing, passé man being so utterly
ridiculous as he whispered hoarsely "You fascinating creature!" The
other gentleman, obviously knowing what this one was like, came to
my rescue. The casanova started behaving ridiculously with a couple of
other ladies who were not in the least interested in him and there and
then I announced that the party was over. The following day I received
a marvellous bouquet of flowers and a note from the nice gentleman
apologizing for his companion's behaviour. I don't know whether other
wives put up with these things to help their husbands get on in the
Company but I certainly was not one of them. Jack had enough merits
of his own to do well without that kind of help from me!

The new manager arrived and since Maria was not too well and there
was not going to be any official farewell or welcoming party we decided
to give a party so that the newcomers could meet some of our best
clients that were our good friends. Instead of being happy about this
we were questioned why the Governor or Mayor had not been invited.
It might have been the case on the small Caribbean Islands, which had
been or were still British colonies, that the manager of our Company
was no doubt very important, but this was Puerto Rico and American
territory and while our Company was quite a big one there were very
many more American companies that were much more important
to the Governor! As a matter of fact I had met the previous Mayor
Dona Felisa Gautier but not because of where my husband worked but
because of my own work at the school and she had recently retired.

During the last eighteen months in Puerto Rico we met a very nice couple our age at the Condado Club. They had recently arrived there and the wife Lili was a colonial like me, but from Malta. We moved in the same circles and had many things in common. Jack too got on extremely well with her husband David so we saw quite a lot of each other as both Lili and I loved sunning ourselves at the club. Lili was a very attractive woman and always impeccably dressed for whatever occasion, but there was one thing I could not understand, when in bathing suit she always made sure, and actually combed, her pubic hairs so that they could be seen on either side of her crotch. Men naturally looked at her and she relished the attention bestowed on her as she thought she was being very sexy.

Another couple that we met and were out of the ordinary was Chela, an Argentinean lady in her mid forties, and her German husband who was much older than her and was the director of a very well known pharmaceutical firm. I was at this very important reception when I heard some dreadful swearing in Spanish by a woman. Turning round I saw this gorgeous female, beautifully dressed, enjoying the situation. I could not believe that she had said the things she had. Then smiling she calmly told me in Spanish "They only speak English, they can't understand me but this is really bloody boring". We both laughed and from then on saw each other often. She gave me the first panty hose that I possessed as they had not yet become as popular as they are today. Chela and her husband invited us to one of the top hotel's restaurant. The maitre'd obviously knew them quite well. He recommended certain specialities and Chela ordered steak tartare. I looked with interest to see the maitre'd's preparation and then after a few final slaps he made a hamburger and placed it on her plate with a sprig of parsley. I looked at him and said "You forgot to cook it" Chela laughed, saying "You funny thing" but I felt really bad at my ignorance.

Soon afterwards they went to Argentina on holiday and Chela stayed longer. On her return she was a changed person. Apparently her husband suffered from diabetes and this illness, plus the fact that he was at least twenty years older, meant they did not have much of a sexual relationship. Chela hadn't missed it but then in Argentina she had met with an old boyfriend and rediscovered sex. I don't know whether it was this alone or that she was obviously menopausal but she started to go on her own to the Condado Hotel bar at nights to pick up men. Later when some other girl actually making a living out of this practice challenged her saying "You get the men because you give it for free" Chela started to walk the streets too. Finally the poor husband, a grand gentleman, was forced to put her in a clinic for treatment.

Bill, my sister Clem's husband, had now finished his tour in Barbados and they were on their way to the UK where they would now be staying permanently as their daughter Vandra was having a very bad time with asthma. They were coming to San Juan for a couple of weeks prior to their return home. Meanwhile my friends started to phone me to say that the new manager's wife had been calling them and saying "I am the Company manager's wife, will you come to dinner on such and such a day?" and they wanted to know if I was also going. I had also received an invitation but the days did not coincide. When the people she had invited realized that she had actually divided the group into two – the general managers, and the deputy/assistant managers or like Jack, commercial managers -- they did not like this and wanted to boycott the new arrivals, after all, they had been our friends for nearly six years.

When my sister and her family arrived I organized a big party with three musicians to play live music and I had not only our business friends but also the dance teachers, neighbours etc., I only invited one couple from the Company who had always been very nice to me. Although throughout the time I was there I was always left to find accommodation for the other members of the staff as well as school for their children etc both Maria, a natural Puerto Rican and I, the two senior members' wives were never totally accepted by the other expatriate staff because we were foreigners, even though I was British, I was not English! Naturally as expected the new manager's wife found out from many of my guests how much they had enjoyed our party until the early hours of the morning. Surprisingly enough she came to see me and admonish me that what I had done was not the correct thing .My reply was short and sweet. "I am sorry, this was my private party and I invite whomever I want. They were all my friends regardless of grade or position. In any case YOU started this!" I had no problems with her after this and in fact we got on very well and she turned out to be very nice and kind just that her husband's position had turned her head a little bit. Thank God I had my own interests where I could be as important as I wanted in my own right! I used to be such a nice person and now I had become as cattish as the best of them!

About a fortnight after my sister and family left and while at school I started to feel unwell and suddenly I discovered that I was once again miscarrying. I was taken to the hospital and my husband notified. I had never felt like this before because now not only had I lost another child but also the chance of staying in San Juan. The thought of leaving my beloved pupils was too much. I had really become extremely fond of them and all our lovely friends, locals and expatriates. It was then that the new manager's wife showed her kindness as she would come and make me snap out of my lethargy. She would also do things for Jack and Lyana, in fact everyone was very helpful.

The best medicine however was the fact that our very dear friends from Brazil, Shorty, Benny and their daughter Irene were coming to visit us for ten days. Suddenly I was busy preparing for their stay and organizing how best to entertain them and show them our beautiful island. Shorty had now retired and they were going back to the States for good. They intended settling down in Fort Lauderdale, Florida. Irene had grown up into a beautiful young woman and was most vivacious and good company. Lyana was thrilled too. They were still with us when Jack received news from Head Office letting us know that we definitely were not returning to San Juan and this time we had to pack up everything to take with us. There was a possibility that we would be staying in England for a home posting.

Our next worry was Ouiki, what were we going to do with him?. He was perky and lovely and the recommendation from some of the Company's wives to put him to sleep 'it being the kindest thing to do' was not for me. No one though wanted an 'old cat.' We were getting quite desperate when we heard who Jack's replacement would be. How very happy we were to know that John and Eva our very good friends would soon be arriving together with their two children Mark, whom we had seen in Brazil as a baby and Ruth his sister. I hoped Eva might take Ouiki over so waited patiently for their arrival keeping my fingers crossed.

When I asked Eva if she would take our cat she looked at Ouiki, he looked back at her with those big eyes of his and she said "Of course, Lydia, I shall take him; every time I look at him he will remind me of you. He has your eyes!" Thus our problem was solved. Eva did not wish to remain in our house. She did not fancy being so close to the sea as we did have a couple of hurricane warnings during our time there and in fact we had had to leave the house on one occasion. Instead she looked for a spacious apartment in the same area.

The remaining time proved to be very hectic with all the farewell parties and last minute packing. We knew when we should be leaving Puerto Rico but alas we could not find any ships to leave around the scheduled departure date. In the end, on December 13th 1966, we flew to St. Thomas, though only a short flight we weren't too happy about it. Our luggage had to follow on a cargo ship. In St Thomas we boarded a German ship to New York. On board the 'Europa' everything was so sterilised and clean that for the first time since travelling by sea, a lot of the passengers including us, were ill. It felt as if instead of being on a ship we were in a travelling hospital with the smell of disinfectant and what appeared to be carbolic soap. We were so very pleased to arrive at New York.

My mother's cousin Aida was waiting for us at the docks and then took us to the hotel which would be home while waiting for the 'Independence,' the ship that would be taking us back to Gibraltar. In the same hotel we found that Sir Joshua Hassan, Gibraltar's Chief Minister, (or Salvador Hassan as we knew him) was also staying together with Alfredo Gache, part of our extended family. Alfredo was the elder brother of Pepe, my first dancing partner in Madeira. Unfortunately when we had gone to say goodbye to Pepe the day before our wedding in 1949, he was in hospital suffering from tuberculosis, we did not know it would be the last time we would see him. Afterwards Pepe had gone with his mother to Ronda for treatment but when he did not improve at the sanatorium, in fact he got worse, he begged his mother to take him home. On the way back Gibraltar could be seen in the distance and his mother pointed this out. Pepe looked and sighed, said "Ah, home" and then died. His mother continued with her arm around her son and her face next to his holding him up and like this passed through the frontier saying to the guards when asked "He is asleep, my poor son". When they finally arrived at the hospital in Gibraltar and they pulled them apart, the mother had her son's face imprinted on hers. It was all very tragic and very sad. We did not learn this until many years later.

The other old friend there was Peter Isola, Leader of the Opposition, and we all met later at the Scottish Bar. What a reunion that was! It was great to hear first hand information about the situation at home and to enjoy all the gossip regarding mutual friends on the Rock. Salvador, Peter and Alfred were in New York for another United Nations meeting, to argue the case for the Rock's future. Knowing that we had been in Puerto Rico for the past six years both Salvador and Peter were very interested to hear first hand from us what were the advantages of the political system there. The Commonwealth of Puerto Rico was known in Spanish as 'El Estado Libre Asociado' (Associated Free State) and how perhaps the idea of free association could be the way forward for Gibraltar's relationship with Britain.

We embarked on the 'Independence' for home with the first snow of New York's winter to bid us farewell. Christmas day on board was one of the saddest we had ever spent without family or friends to share it with. The other travellers too were lonely people, husbands without their wives or wives without partners, people without families to share. People cried as they remembered sons fighting in Vietnam. It was really the most poignant time of our trip, perhaps of our lives.

This time the scheduled visit to the enchanting island of Madeira was going to come true. I returned to Funchal twenty years after I had left her to return home to Gibraltar and Dad in 1945. History was repeating itself but this time I had taken Mum's place and Lyana my own although at not quite the same age. The so much dreamt of moment had arrived as we met and embraced all those good friends who had been almost like family during the war years.

Everyone was kindness itself, courteous and polite, generous to the point of extravagance. We were showered with gifts and overwhelming attention. We enjoyed a champagne breakfast first thing in the morning with the scrumptious 'Bolo de Mel' their speciality at this time of the year, a beautiful rich cake I had not eaten for so long. When I had been a child there everything seemed so big and spacious. As children when we had to walk from the Hotel Savoy to town it seemed a terrific distance away and now everything seemed so close to each other and quite compact. We re-visited Villa Honolulu, the Savoy Hotel and all the places I had roamed about as a child. I also remembered the family as it had been and the members that we still greatly loved who were no longer with us.

The next stop was Casablanca and here I had rather a surprising experience. I walked into a shop with Jack and Lyana looking at all their lovely Moroccan goods when the salesman came and spoke to me in Arabic. I smiled at him and said I could not understand him. Amazingly he replied "You cannot lie to me, from your eyes I see you are one of us!" When I eventually got home and asked Dad if we had Arab blood he was most displeased saying "We are all Catholics, always have been". And that was one of the shortest conversations I ever had with Dad.

Chapter 25

CHANGE OF PLANS

At home we celebrated New Year's Eve together for the first time in twelve years! How thrilling and so touching when I walked into the hotel for the event and Johnny Osborne and the band started playing "Llevame donde naci" (Take me to where I was born) a song which was almost the national anthem of all those Gibraltarians living abroad. Johnny had always come to play at my birthday parties when I was still a single girl! It was impossible to hold back the tears slowly coming down my cheeks.

Gibraltar normally so conservative had had a face lift. Although at first the change was hardly perceptible it became, after a few days, increasingly noticeable. Not only were there new buildings for homes, a rare commodity in Gibraltar, but completely new suburbs had sprung up like mushrooms in the most unexpected places. New hotels with swimming pools, a miniature golf course, clubs, and a most marvellous modern casino, supposedly one of the best in Europe, with fabulous sophisticated shows featuring international artists, had been built.

We stayed in Gibraltar for two months but expecting to stay in England for some time we looked forward to buying our own house. My parents as well were overjoyed at the thought of our being closer to Gibraltar as we would be seeing each other more frequently.

Buying a house in England was not such an easy thing. We booked with an estate agent in Twickenham since that was where my sister had her lovely spacious house and if we were going to live there we wanted to be as near as possible to each other. After a couple of days going out viewing houses we did find a semidetached house two roads away from hers. We thought it was quite nice and would go the following day to arrange things with them. When we did go we discovered that someone had gone to view it after us and there and then given a deposit so the house was no longer available. Having lived in such beautiful and big houses abroad it was very hard to find a place that could compare to them with the amount we could afford. The type of homes we were accustomed to were to be found at Esher in Surrey and such places far above our means so it was really a question of having to make do with the best we could get in an area where our way of living, dressing and thinking would not be too noticeable. In fact when I suggested viewing a house in the Teddington area the estate agent said quite emphatically "That place is not for you!" although the house looked attractive enough.

We then booked with another agent in Hampton. He showed us some places that we didn't even bother to get out of the car to see. Finally when we were all getting quite tired and fed up with the whole rigmarole he said two houses had come on to the market and we had first viewing. One of these houses was in Staines Road opposite the Common. It was a corner house, very spacious and in tiptop condition and only slightly more than we intended spending but still within our means. I told him I would go for my sister to view it and she too liked it very much. So we made arrangements to go the following day to settle up. That night I could hardly sleep. I kept on hearing someone calling for help, screams and that call going on and on. In the morning when we woke up I told Jack that I had changed my mind and did not want the house, to my amazement he agreed without any argument and then proceeded to tell me that he had hardly been able to sleep and that he felt there was something wrong with the house. Going down to breakfast we broke our news to my sister and she came to me, put her arms around me, and once again said "Ly, I am glad, there is something wrong with the house, we will find another". We did not buy it and later we discovered that the owner's teenage daughter had been raped and killed on the Common. It might be a coincidence but it is what happened. The estate agent would not say anything.

We then went to the second house, smallish but detached, in Cardinal's Walk, Hampton, opposite Bushy Park and near the River Thames. Just from outside, without even going in, I fell in love with it. It was a happy house. I felt I really wanted it in spite of it being yet much more expensive than the previous one in Staines Road. Inside we found it had a reasonably sized lounge/dining room leading into the most beautiful garden I had ever seen. There were climbing roses, fruit trees and flowers of every kind, the garden alone enchanted me. The kitchen was a fair size and had a big pantry. Off the hall there was a toilet and under the stairs plenty of cupboard space. The upstairs had three bedrooms and a full large size bathroom. Time was of the essence as the people had to be out by the time our heavy luggage arrived in England as we did not want it to go into storage. We also wanted to be organized for the date when Jack would be starting work at Head office. It was all agreed and the necessary papers were signed.

Our heavy luggage arrived safely except for Lyana's precious piano which was damaged beyond repair. It was something that none of us will ever forget. The previous owners departed as pre-arranged. We had, at last, our very own home! We inherited the old dining room furniture for which we were very grateful. There was no carpeting, other than in the entrance hall and on the stairs leading to the top floor so that carpets were our first priority. Once we had accomplished this, the house looked alive and welcoming. Next were the beds – at long last we were going to have our very own new beds, beds on which nobody else had slept before and this meant a lot to us all. We had been married in 1949 and here it was 1967. Eighteen years living in other people's homes and with other people's furniture and now we had our own house with brand new beds! We felt so luxurious and we were determined to have the very best we could buy even if we had to go short on other things.

The shopkeepers must have thought us mad! We would lie down on the beds, sit on them, lie down again as we checked them, until at last we found what we really wanted. What a great thrill and adventure it was. In the kitchen we had been left the old gas cooker which would do for a while since we needed to buy a fridge as well. Then even without any other furniture we moved into our home. We had where to sleep and where to eat. Whilst Jack was busy opening the first trunk and getting out the crockery and kitchen utensils etc., Lyana and I went shopping for curtains and to the furniture shop for an inexpensive settee and coffee table. We were very lucky that one of the shops had quite a decent settee that had been repossessed and so was going much cheaper than normal. Once this was delivered we felt like children with a new toy.

Once all of the packing cases were opened I knew it would be a lovely warm house to come to after a long day at work. With posies of garden flowers in every vase I could find to fill it was already a pleasure to be there. The house was very near the railway station so Jack would not have to waste much time as I would be driving him there whenever possible and the lawyer was trying to get Lyana a place in the Lady Eleanor Hollis School in Twickenham where she would be able to continue her studies. We were all set and very happy and then came the telephone call! Head Office wanted Jack to go to London as plans had changed again!

When Jack returned from Head Office I knew straight away that something was very wrong. We were going to be leaving for Lima, Peru. We had nothing against this country except that while in Head Office he discovered that the general manager in Peru was someone who would bring nothing but trouble to us all. While in Rio, this man, Thomas married to an Anglo Argentinean, Carole, had apparently used me to make his wife jealous making her believe that there was something going on between us. He should have picked someone else. I had no idea that this was going on. One day when in Rio I invited them for dinner, they lived across the bay in Niteroi whilst we were in Leblon. Carole excused herself by saying she was ill. The following evening we were invited to a party in Niteroi and she was there. When

I mentioned this to a friend she looked at me and said "But don't you know? She hates your guts. Thomas uses you to make her jealous!" As with everything I do, I did not think twice and I marched up to her and there and then, in front of everybody, I said "Carole, I don't know why you worry about your husband and me; I don't like him at all. In fact if he were the only man left in the world and I was panting for sex I would still say no!" When Jack was asked in Head Office to give a reason why he did not want to go to Lima he found it too embarrassing to tell the truth so kept quiet and accepted the post.

We had just unpacked and now we had to repack everything. Our beds were going to be left for others to use while still brand new as we decided we would rent our house out for the period of time our contract would last and return there for our holiday. We decided to name our house 'Cocapu' after the three most frequently swear words used by Luis, our doctor neighbour in San Juan. They were 'Cono, carajo, puneta' these words mean the woman's sex, the man's sex and what they both did when happy.

When a neighbour asked what the name meant I promptly answered that it was the name of a Brazilian bird. The neighbour replied "Oh, it sounds exotic; I would love to see what it looks like!" So would we, I thought!

Part Five

Land Of The Incas 1967 - 1970

Chapter 26

TOWARDS LIMA

When Sir John and his good wife, Lady McPherson found out that we were leaving England and going to Peru they very kindly invited us to dinner at their London apartment together with Mr & Mrs Walters who were on leave before going to Gibraltar where he was to be manager. There was another middle aged gentleman present. He was very tall, very slim, wore glasses and looked very kind and friendly. I was seated on Sir John's left side and this gentleman was on my left. I was told to call him Enery and we both had a terrific time together. He told me how he had restored some stables and made a beautiful home and how his wife had left him. I felt sad for him and put my arm round his shoulder and commiserated with him. Suddenly I asked "Where do you work?" "Oh, I work for (and he mentioned our Company)" "Really" said I, surprised "How long have you been working for them?" "A couple of years" said Enery. Laughingly, I shoved him with my hand and said "Just you wait until you have been as long as us!" Sir John hearing all this came close to me and whispered "Careful, nuisance girl, he is the Managing Director!" I nearly freaked out. Enery, noticing my confusion, put his arm round me and said "Never mind, it has been great talking to you" and he continued being nice and friendly to me until we left with everyone wishing us good luck in the new posting. Jack later told me his name was Sir Henry but he had not objected to my calling him Enery!

Head Office sent us a circular regarding what to expect in our future place of residence. The funniest thing was that they recommended ladies to take a crinoline and carry a parasol! When we finally arrived there we found that nothing in the circular was correct or up to date. You could buy practically everything you needed and wanted. The weather was indeed very hot in the summer and the humidity 90% the whole year round. It never rained. In winter there was a very fine drizzle which would make you wet but no one used umbrellas. In summer with the heat the foul smell of fish meal was to penetrate the last corner of your home and since the farm animals (except the odd farm we learned about from locals) were fed with fish meal. EVERYTHING from eggs, to fowl, to bacon and pork tasted of fish. It was disgusting.

The first contretemps came with news that Lyana would not be able to accompany us as the manager's wife had not been able to find a school for her in Lima. Lyana did not want to go to boarding school so Head Office accepted that she should accompany us. If we definitely did not find a school, they would pay for Lyana and I to return to the UK so that she could find a suitable place there. We decided to travel to Peru via San Juan, Puerto Rico where I could go and see my old school and friends. It was great seeing Dick and Maria who were visiting family before continuing on their way to St. Lucia, as well as Eva and John now settled down in their apartment.

When we visited their home Ouiki received us with calculated coldness and disdain. He lay there bothering with no one, too intent on his daily ablutions to even bother to look. It was very obvious to see that this time he had found himself in a good home and although we had been a much shorter period of time away from him than when we had left Baldrich his circumstances had improved no end. He was now more handsome than ever, fat and round as a ball, the apparent king of the house. I was naturally very happy to see how well looked after he was in his new home, but I could have murdered the little bastard, to think of all I had done for him, all my love and worries over him, yet now I was no longer needed and therefore why should he bother with me!

Eva was worried about Ouiki as she felt that where they lived it did not offer facilities for Ouiki to have much of a social life. There was neither garden nor verandah, so the poor fellow had to remain indoors all day and night. Ouiki did nothing but eat and sleep during the day but at nights he had taken to waking up the household and all the neighbours with his midnight wails and moans. Eva was now trying to get him a new place in the countryside but up to then he still lorded it over everyone in their home.

We only remained three days in San Juan but had plenty of time to go and visit my school children who were delighted to see me and paradoxically sad when they discovered I was not there to stay. Sister Regina Maris was so pleased to see me too. It was well worth our visit for upon telling her about Lyana's school predicament in Peru, she said she could help by giving me a letter of introduction to the best Peruvian school and which was run by the same order of nuns. So it was with a much lighter heart that we set forth for Lima. Sister Regina also promised to follow up and write to Colegio Villa Maria's Mother Superior herself and make sure all worked out well.

When we finally arrived in Lima we were met by a good friend from our pre marriage days. I had met Basil shortly after Jack in 1945 and we had all become very good friends. He took us to the transient apartment the Company had rented for us. He had no idea what they were like but our bad time in the new posting was definitely starting with a vengeance. The place was filthy. Even the bed linen and towels were soiled. A little chicken had been squeezed inside an iced refrigerator that had not been defrosted in years and had it not been for Basil's kindness and his desire to help I would have returned home to England there and then. Basil took us out for lunch after we all complained to the manager of the apartment building and on our return things were slightly better.

The odyssey had only just started. When it was realized that not only was Lyana with us but that I had also found one of the best schools for her to attend and Head Office was informed it did me no further good. How popular could I get?!! Every time we thought we had found a house that met with all the Company's requirements the General Manager turned it down. Everyone in the office became aware of the miserable treatment we were receiving, so much so, that during a brief absence of the General Manager, his deputy who was in charge immediately gave us permission to rent a house. By the time Thomas returned we were living in a beautiful home in San Isidro a very exclusive residential area.

The house was beautifully furnished and very tastefully decorated. It was never meant to have been a rented home. The owner, Dona Clara, had to travel to Italy to look after her sick mother and had decided at the last moment to rent if she found the right tenants. As luck would have it Basil knew someone who knew Clara's family. We met and signed a contract for a year's lease. The whole block of three houses belonged to Clara and her two daughters, Olga and Betty. The houses had been built so as to share one huge garden in the centre while each house also had its own private garden. We found ourselves not only with a gorgeous luxurious home for everything had been left intact as when Clara lived there, but also with two new friends who introduced us to many lovely people.

The ground floor of the house consisted of a huge entrance hall. To the left there was a corridor leading to a bedroom which was going to be Lyana's and then at the end of the corridor another one, of fantastic size, which was to be ours and included an en- suite bathroom. There was a shower room directly opposite Lyana's room. To the right there was a very long wide corridor with plenty of cupboard space. A door to the left led to a wonderful big, bright room with glass doors facing the garden. This was the dining-room with lovely furniture and a beautiful chandelier. Then further down the corridor there was a huge kitchen and at the very end a spacious garage for two cars beyond which were the servants' quarters. The dining-room also led to the hall just one step above the magnificent sitting room with Louis Quinze furniture, chandeliers and lovely antique pieces. Gorgeous carpets were everywhere over polished parquet flooring. Upstairs there was a hall leading to a small den and bathroom and on to an extremely spacious room with a bar at one end. Dona Clara gave bridge and canasta parties for all the society ladies in this room.

Fortified by Sister Regina's letter, I visited the college to find that Lyana was immediately accepted. She was however placed in the mathematics class when in reality she would have preferred being in literature. I returned to the college to see Mother Superior and asked her to change Lyana from one stream to the other. She was very nice with me but she had received Sister Regina's letter which told her of my being a PE Teacher and all I had done for the department in San Juan. So she had a proposition to make, she would change Lyana's classes if I took the position of physical education and dance workshop teacher as Miss Marich the actual PE teacher was returning to the States. Having gone through so much in San Juan when leaving my lovely children there I did not want to be involved any more to avoid the pain that leaving these would bring. I had already converted the bar room upstairs in my house into a studio and was doing extremely well giving my exercise classes only a couple of hours three times a week. But I had to give in.

We had arrived in Lima when the weather was dull and grey. This sort of climate lasts for nine months of the year due to the Humboldt Current which makes it very depressing for you if you are not accustomed. There would be a lot of thunder and lightning but no rain and all the expatriates were given time off to go elsewhere for a change as a health precaution.

Betty and Olga asked their servants, who were all related, to see if they could find a girl for me. Alicia, their cousin from the country would be available so I accepted interviewing her. Alicia was a frail looking little negro girl with a huge smile but very sad eyes. She appeared to be very nice though I doubted whether she would be strong enough to do housework. I was however willing to give her a chance. The first thing I noticed was that when Alicia started to sweep the stairs instead of starting from the top she did the reverse, there and then I realised that she did not have much experience of housework. I went to her and explained that she would have to start at the top from the bar room, to the hall and down the stairs. She started to cry. I felt really bad as I had not been mean about it but she was embarrassed that she had not known. Somehow this endeared her to me. I had to teach her how to clean the toilet and everything else. I was later on informed by Betty that the servants had neither toilet nor bathroom where they lived in the countryside and that in fact their home was built straight on to the earth. Although our house had plenty of room for her to sleep at nights neither she nor I wanted a sleeping in maid, not after all the freedom we had enjoyed in San Juan. In fact Alicia only worked weekdays unless I was to be entertaining then she would come to wash up and tidy things and would go to either of her cousins next door to sleep.

When meal time came and I served her her meal I noticed when I went into the kitchen that she had only eaten about half of her portion so I asked her "Alicia, did you not like the food?" "Yes, Senora, but this is for tomorrow!" "Oh Alicia, you don't have to keep food for tomorrow for I shall be giving you some more!" "Then Senora, may I be allowed to take this home with me?" I knew then that for as long as we were in Lima Alicia would be staying with us! The poverty there was astounding, it was the same as it had been in Rio but in general people were not so happy.

It is awful when you see people; human beings like yourself, rummaging in the dustbin looking for food and if lucky enough to find an old meat bone see how they would pull and eat whatever morsel they could pick from it. The native Amer- Indians, or the Cholitos as the locals called them, all looked so well and healthy when they lived up in the mountains and you wondered why they bothered to come into town to such misery amongst people they did not know.

At first Jack was having a very hard time at the office where Thomas was playing as many dirty tricks as he could think of. Jack found difficulties wherever he turned, he couldn't even entertain a client without asking first for dear Thomas's permission, which made his business work very difficult. He could not write directly to Head Office as every letter had to go through the general manager, so it was a losing battle.

Chapter 27

AT SCHOOL

The day eventually came when I had to start at Villa Maria. I had already made my working plans in accordance with the Government physical education requirements, and I had received all the students' names etc. I walked up to the modern gymnasium further up from the college's main building beautifully set on the very top of the mountain range. The girls were all in rather defiant positions looking at me arrogantly as I came in. I stopped brusquely and stared back at the girls, thinking 'I don't want to be here and I am not going to put up with any nonsense, I don't need the job and this kind of attitude is definitely not for me.' They looked at each other smirking and then at me, still in a depreciative way. I walked towards each little group without saying a word, looked at them from top to bottom and then slowly turning round with a last look at them I walked out of the gym. Suddenly there was plenty of action as they followed me out of the gym calling "Mrs Armstrong, Mrs Armstrong, where are you going?" "Home. I think there has been a mistake. I was told I was going to teach society girls in this school and all I find is bad manners and no education or respect!" "My mother is the Minister of Education" said one of the girls. "So then you should know better how to treat a teacher!" I replied. "My dad is the Mayor" said another one. "I really would not have thought so by your behaviour. Girls, I really feel sorry for all your parents." I answered back. In a chorus they all said "Please Mrs Armstrong, we are very sorry!" So I walked back with them. It was the worst class I had ever had to face. The news went quickly around the school that I was not putting up with any nonsense. I lived where they did, I did not need the job, and what was more I could not be bothered! Eventually I discovered that they had been under the impression that it was because of my arrival that Miss Marich was leaving the College. The funny part was that Toni Marich did not leave; she kept only the graduating class as her PE students but took over the gymnastic groups and the typing and shorthand classes. We became firm friends both at school and outside socially. Eventually I began to enjoy the girls and the girls behaved with respect. I was then asked to take the comprehensive English class and by then the girls liked me so much that they wanted to speak 'real' English like me which was not always how Oxford English sounds (my accent still is different) and not American English which is what they were used to.

I suppose that since the ladies in our social bracket in Peru did not go out to work, it must have appeared rather mystifying to them why I had taken a teaching job at a school. It was fine to have your own business like classes at home, but to be a teacher when they were paid such meagre salaries? The teaching profession in Peru was very badly remunerated and most teachers that lived from their teaching salaries generally needed at least two jobs to exist unless married or living with their families. In fact I couldn't even buy one dress with what I received as my monthly salary, but stay I did.

The dance workshop did extremely well and for the years I was at the college we won first place and first grade diplomas and in 1969 the college was the overall winner of the annual schools' music and dance competition sponsored by the Ministry of Education for the whole of Peru. A group of my girls also performed that year at La Feria del Pacifico and appeared on television.

Socially I became extremely friendly with Katita, a Hungarian/Chilean, married to an Anglo Argentinean expatriate in the Company. They were both most amusing and entertaining friends. It was the second marriage for both of them and you could see that both had been accustomed to a much better social class and lifestyle than the one they were now experiencing. Katita was at least twelve years older than me, with an inborn elegance and class that was admirable. She was a petite lady with bright eyes and wicked smile, so feminine, so dainty, and so well dressed and such a great friend and person. Gil, her husband, who had been an officer with the Ghurkhas during the Second World War, also had a wonderful sense of humour and both of them were able to turn grotesque stories into very amusing tales. Shopping with Katita was an experience, even when buying a handbag she would stand in front of the mirror and move to one side and another, make a pose, suck in her cheeks, and twirl around. She kept her hair very short and raven black and her figure was that of a teenager. I thoroughly enjoyed listening to her stories and most particularly as to how she had ended up meeting and marrying Gil.

In the early 1930's Katita and her parents, well to do Jewish business people left Hungary for Chile where they set up a prosperous business in Santiago. Katita met a young man in similar circumstances to her parents and they married. They had two sons and they lived a good social life together. One day Katita fell in love with an artist, Samuel, who gave her a lot of romance, poetry and time, something that her husband had not been able to do for quite a while, and since the boyfriend was single, she decided to ask for a divorce to go to live with her lover. The husband who really cared a lot for her tried to save their marriage by taking her on a super round the world trip but that only made her more homesick and hungering for her lover. On their return they parted their ways and she took over an apartment to live with Samuel. Samuel had a mother whom he said he could not leave alone so therefore he would be unable to share this apartment. He then told her he would also wait until the old lady died before he could marry Katita. The mother eventually passed away but Samuel, instead of keeping his promise, married someone else and actually went with his new wife to give Katita the 'good news.' As can well be imagined Katita was devastated. Her husband was willing to take her back but she would have nothing to do with him. She went to Vina del Mar, a seaside resort near Valparaiso, for a change of air and to relax and get away from all her problems.

Gil, a happily married man with two daughters, arrived home one day to find a letter from his wife telling him that she no longer cared and had gone off with a friend of the family. Gil also went to Vina del Mar where he saw Katita and was attracted to her even though he realized that she was much older than him. They started talking and spending time together, they had found shoulders to cry upon and thus commiserated with one another. One thing led to another and they married. Gil worked for the Company and was, like us, financially okay but not to the level Katita had been accustomed and certainly not to having bosses with less education and standards telling her what to do. But they were very happy together and Gil was mad about his Katita.

She adored him too and on his arrival from work gave him his slippers and pipe and prepared his favourite manhattans or pisco sour cocktails with a little tray of canapés to go with the drink while relaxing from a hard day's work.

Limenos, like Peru itself, have themselves well divided into three categories:-

There are the 'Cholos', usually the sierra, jungle, Amerindian people or anyone with dark skin. There were a great number of them in town, down from the sierra in search of prosperity, whereas all they found was extreme poverty and abuse from their fellow men. They lived like animals, generally by the river side in small shacks made of four mats; others used the open air rubbish dump as their residential area. They made their living from hunting in the trash, selecting and collecting whatever they could to sell or to use. The predicament of these poor people was worse than that of the 'favela' people in Rio. They are worse than miserably poor; they live in the most desolate almost inhuman way.

Then there are the 'Gente'. The self-styled elite, mainly of Spanish origin, although this group also includes those Peruvians born to emigrants from Italy, Germany and other west European nations. They rest on ancient Inca laurels of culture and greatness, yet show very little consideration for the 'Cholos' whom they treat with contempt. Naturally there are always exceptions to the rule. But, I'm writing about the people I have seen in big American cars, practically running over a street vendor for just being there and not giving them the right of way. It was almost as if those poor people had no right to walk, or ride, or even be on the streets. On the other hand many society ladies spent a great part of their life doing social work of great merit, at the expense of sometimes relegating their own children to the sole supervision of their Cholo servants. Then they wondered and commented at the lack of respect, bad manners, or vocabulary of these children. What else could they expect? If their servants had been in a position to educate these children properly they would not be working in a house receiving disdain and insults. They would be earning their living in a different capacity.

The third group in Lima was composed by people like us, the 'Gringos', neither here nor there, good for a laugh or a drink, unless you were lucky enough to find someone like we did with Olga, Betty and their good friend Agnes who were all really helpful and nice from the start. It took us a year before the 'Gente' received us into their homes although they had accepted our invitations by being clients of the Company. They had to study us well and digest our manners and behaviour before allowing us to enter their usually magnificent homes. We, the gringos, comprised the greater part of the higher middle class, as we had sufficient means to give our children a good education in their pricey and excellent schools, to dress and eat well, but we were not up to par with the very rich 'gente' and their café society and continuous club hobnobbing way of life. The Company made us members of a good social club, but these clubs cost a small fortune to cover the entrance fee, shares, and monthly dues. However, although these self styled very rich 'gente' were classified as such in Peru not many of them would have been able to afford a big house or servants in England. It was all rather relative.

Peru, according to many books, consists of beautiful countryside, interesting historical sites, quaint towns like Cuzco, Huancaya and Ayacucho. Everywhere you will find brochures saying that although the sun does not shine in the city of Lima, the sun is within one's reach only a short twenty minutes car ride away. That was quite true but then practically everyone who lived in the city would travel out of it, especially at weekends, in search of the sun and as there was only one road to the Sierra everywhere was terribly crowded. It was really unfortunate that Lima had no sun for eight to nine months of the year, where the continuous greyness, humidity and cold deprived you of your vitality and even your sense of humour. In the sun everything looked lovely and everyone felt good.

It is rather ironical that, if only Pizarro had chosen some other part of Peru for his city, we would think it the most beautiful place in the world, with its mixture of culture and its grandiose past. The city of Lima was very interesting, quaint and very picturesque. The old fine architecture was a pleasure to see as were the many museums loaded with precious works of art, gold figures and precious jewels. I had never enjoyed such fine workmanship as that seen in some of these museums where the Inca, Mochica, Chimu and Nazca artistry still remained, in their pottery, jewels, and fine clothes, including velvet, jersey and embroidery. Imagine, many of the exhibits were over 2000 years old, and yet their colours and fine texture still glowed in great splendour. That Lima had its fascinating traits there was no denying. The rest of Peru also spelled excitement and adventure to all the tourists. The people once they accepted you were very hospitable and friendly.

Our first year in our house in Alvarez Calderon was coming to an end and we wondered what would become of us as we knew Thomas would once again be the mean bastard that he was and make things difficult for us. Fortunately Dona Clara returned from Italy but only for a short stay as she felt that she should remain there to take care of her mother as long as this one lived. She also promised us that we could stay in her house until Jack's term in Peru finished as we were very good tenants. So at least we knew we would have decent quarters while there. Things would never improve as the only one time when we coincided with Thomas at a party when he started implying things with me, I there and then put a stop to all his nonsense in front of everyone. Both Jack and I decided to avoid going to wherever the Thomas's would be and always made quite sure of this.

Apart from Jack's problems caused by Thomas we had a good family life and enjoyed ourselves as much as possible. During our first year's local holiday, for us to enjoy a change of climate, Lyana and I decided to go to San Juan and visit our friends for a while. We then continued to St Lucia to visit Dick, Maria and the family and where Jack later met up with us. Jack and I then flew over to Guadeloupe for a short honeymoon away from everyone. In San Juan I found things had changed a lot and what once had had great appeal to me no longer held any fascination. Friends had moved away and those left behind had continued with their lifestyle and made new friends with whom to share their time. It was then that I learned that one should make the best of every day of your life and never look back on what you have left behind. In fact San Juan had given us a lot of love and happiness but culturally it did not have the treasures that Peru enjoyed. Every place has its charm and good things as well as bad ones.

St Lucia was a captivating, sunny and friendly place, a lovely island, and of course our very dear friends were there. It was the best part of our holiday as we played around on the golden sands and enjoyed the warm Caribbean sea again. Maria and Dick's home was perched precariously on one of the highest hills overlooking Castries, the capital town. It was nestled in abundant green foliage and was such a contrast to Lima's silent, barren hills where everything, even the cactus had to be planted. Somehow I returned to Peru a much better person appreciating more the efforts of the people there.

Chapter 28

VISITING BRAZIL

For our second year's local leave Lyana and I left first for Rio de Janeiro once again visiting all our old friends and where Jack caught up with us. Together the three of us flew to Buenos Aires, Argentina where we were to meet my mother's cousins, the children of the uncle who had gone there to serve on the railways and their families. We were the first family members that they were going to meet since emigrating to Argentina and none of us knew what to expect. The only photograph I had ever seen of them was of the two sisters embroidering a table cloth which was sent to my mother in 1928 for her wedding present. We descended from the plane and looked at the very many people there not knowing who was who, when suddenly we heard screams of "Lydia, Jack, Lyana". We looked up and saw a number of people waving with handkerchieves; it had to be our relatives! It was quite a reunion, everyone animatedly talking at the same time, wanting to know everything about the family. It was difficult to leave them for our hotel and we have never known such love and dedication as theirs during all our stay when towards the end they did not know where else to take us or what to do for us. It was an unforgettable experience to care for a family you had never seen before.

Over seven years had passed since we had left the 'Cidade Maravilhosa' (The marvellous city-Rio). It still held the same wonderful fascination but this was a better, more organized Rio. The changes we found were plentiful and all for the best. It even looked as if the Brazilians had finally learned how to drive and accept the rules of the highway code. Pedestrians finally had a right to walk on the streets; even the traffic policemen were obeyed. There were new wide highways and the progress in keeping Rio clean was most noticeable and welcome. The cockroaches ceased to be so 'baratas' (cheap) – there were hardly any to be seen.

Ipanema now made popular by the song 'Girl from Ipanema' also showed great improvement. The girls, all the 'brotinhos', (blooms) very much like Twiggy, adorned the golden sand beaches, wearing bikinis even more brief than during our stay there. Gone were the guitar shape figures, but the girls still retained that unmistakeable Brazilian stride like thoroughbred horses.

The boutiques and stores were still laden with the latest fashions and fads. Prices, compared to Lima, were ridiculously low, yet, thinking back to our 'Carioca' days, when we had lived in Rio, they had certainly increased. Restaurants with their exotic cuisine were on a par with Peruvian counterparts with regard to their exalted prices. What we now paid for one person usually used to cover the expense for the three of us before. But the restaurants had much atmosphere and charm and somehow one did not mind paying the extra.

Joa, where our friends Lucia and Alan had lived, then so countrified was almost unrecognizable. Where once had stood a solitary restaurant competing with rustic shacks serving delicious prawns on the spit, there were now rows of lovely, modern, open-air restaurants. Things had certainly changed. We saw Lucia now all alone. The lively happy person who had once taken her guitar to sing to us all was gone for ever. She looked older than her years and in her desperation to look appealing and young she had dyed her hair a copper colour that only made her look cheap and common. It was sad to think that after so many years working alongside her husband, saving and making sacrifices it was now the other woman who was benefitting from it all. My good friend Phyllis was now also alone as Frankie had passed away. Her sister Ruth was now a very matronly grandmother of two. So staid and serious that it was hard to believe she had been the same woman who had offered Jack a May West invitation of "If you are bored and don't know what to do come down and see me sometime!" She now entertained herself by making ceramic articles and hand painting them.

By far the greatest surprise was given us by Fafa and Elsa. They were finally living together as man and wife, the proud parents of a little girl. Now, his official wife was completely retired, Elsa was his present wife where he took his laundry and visited to see his daughter. But he now had a girl friend with whom to have sex and she was in her late teens only! How to keep young I presume! They were all very happy to see us and their hospitality knew no end. Unexpectedly I also saw Arthur, kind, gentle greying Arthur, trying so hard to be the same man of the world he was when we first met, practically at the beginning of our stay in Brazil. His face was now heavily lined, his eyes sadder and wiser, so deeply pleased to see me again. It is strange there was not the slightest tingling, just a few beautiful memories of a kind man who had been wise and respectful enough as well as manly enough to stop himself from ruining my life. It was good and satisfying to know he had retired with the rank of a general and that he enjoyed a prosperous retirement life.

Surprisingly enough when the time came to return to Lima we were all happy to be going 'home,' it was not after all such a bad place. We had just arrived back in Lima when we received the last bombshell. Thomas had contrived to get Jack transferred out of Peru with Lyana not quite a year left to graduate from Villa Maria. We were devastated and this time Jack insisted that his letter be sent to Head Office asking that he be allowed to remain in Lima at least until Lyana could graduate from college. It meant we would not complete a full three year tour but that did not worry us, all we wanted was for Lyana to finish her education and graduate with the girlfriends she had already made. Some fairy godmother in Head Office must have taken pity on us and approved for us to remain,

When I told Betty, Olga and Agnes they insisted I went to a witch woman who might be able to help solve our problem, this was before we received Head Office approval to stay. We made an appointment and arrived at the appropriate time. She was a Mulata woman, very colourful and very large. She was in a rather small shack and just above where she sat there was a coop full of chickens. She sat on a very big chair, like a throne, and was smoking a cigar. On her lower lip she had stuck what appeared to be cotton wool and as she smoked she spat out. My friends with me were all as astounded as I was and we all kept very close to each other and very quiet too. After she had asked who was the client she made me sit down. She took out the cigar she had been smoking and lit another one spitting out the end she had chewed, out also came whatever she had on her lip and a new piece was inserted. She started to smoke like mad, spitting and dashing the ashes in an envelope. In the meantime she asked me to think only on what I wanted to happen, which as far as I was concerned, was for Thomas to be made more reasonable and understanding. She finished smoking and what little was left of the cigar was laid on a huge stone on the floor and which had been in use for a long time as you could see how it had worn out in certain areas. She then solemnly said "Step on it, my child, step on it hard and you will be stepping on all your troubles" Did I step on the cigar end with gusto? So hard that there was absolutely nothing left. Then she shook the envelope and threw the ashes onto a dish. She began to tell me how I was soon going to travel, but not on the date when I thought I had to, but also not as late as I had anticipated. She forecast other things and in particular that we would not have any more problems only good tidings.

No sooner had I returned home than the telephone rang. It was Jack. "Ly, have you gone to that witch woman you told me about?" "Yes, why do you ask?" "My God, do you know what has happened?" "Jack, are you OK, what has gone wrong?" I wondered what more bad news he had to give me. "At what time were you with that woman?" When I told him, he said "Oh my God what have you done, guess what, Thomas was in the office corridor and without any warning he fell and has not been able to walk, he is in hospital now!" I had not wished him anything bad, at least not consciously, but these things didn't really work, did they? I wondered. I know what I will do. I'll go to church and pray for all to be well again. Just when I was going out the phone rang again. It was a Kenyan born girl, Heather, who was married to another Company employee. "Have you heard the news? My voodoo has got the bastard after all!" "What do you mean, Heather?" "I have been indulging in African witchcraft for a while and at long last it has happened!" I felt much better. It wasn't my doing after all. I had a couple more phone calls and everyone was thrilled at the office happening. How much hatred can a person invite?!

With the news that we were to remain in Lima until Lyana finished her year we were able to enjoy summer on the lovely beaches along the coast, lined with hundreds of undulating sand dunes, and the happiness that good weather always brings. We had been starved for the radiant heat of sunshine. Lima and its suburbs began to take on a new look as the great mass of dreary grey lifted. Although since our arrival we had suffered a couple of short earth tremors now we were to have a new experience. It was a Sunday morning and we had woken up late. I was cooking a brunch lunch and on seeing the bottle of Cinzano I gave myself a drink, suddenly the frying pan was moving like mad, the floor seemed to do so and there I stood thinking 'but I've only had a sip.' Then both Lyana and Jack were shouting "We are coming, we are coming, don't move" How the heck did they know what was happening to me? I wondered, as they came running and then stopped under the door archway and kept on calling for me to join them there All I could think of was turning off the gas and somehow I found it difficult, then as I finally got to their sides the whole house moved and a lot of the pots and pans fell from the cupboards along the long corridor. We had experienced a really bad earthquake! Once it was over we had our brunch and all was fine until the following day when for no apparent reason I fainted. Delayed reaction the doctor said!

For Lyana's fifteenth birthday we went to a lovely club in Chosica and as luck would have it I fell down and broke my arm – a double fracture and a long way from any hospital. Everyone at the Club rallied round since Jack had gone off with Lyana and her guests to take films. When Jack returned, he did not know what to do for me or what to say to console me. As always he was kindness itself as he was every time I needed him. He would patiently dress me, comb me, cut my meat etc. Once I had recuperated Jack decided that since we were on our last section of our stay we should start seeing more of Peru.

A safari up the Andes was arranged. We just packed up and without giving a thought to the 'seroche' (mountain illness) off we went, feeling, I am sure, like Ponce de Leon on his search for the 'Fountain of Youth'. How we loved the change! Nature is magnificent! As we climbed the Cordillera the whole atmosphere and colour of this country changed. The beauty was indeed inspiring. The climb was quite a struggle but it held us enthralled as we slowly passed hill after hill. There was such a variety of earth strata. Some hills looked very soft and held together precariously, balancing themselves, giving the impression of ready-to-collapse gigantic sand dunes. Cactus plants of different types grew like a patchwork carpet coloured by areas of beautiful wild flowers.

Other hills were of porous-like material that reminded one of huge sponges with their openings turning into gigantic caves. The climb, some 16,000 feet of it, was full of glorious surprises and passed in almost too short a time. The most impressive mountains had at least six strata of earth, each in a different colour and forming these beautiful mosaic designs that I am sure inspired the natives here in the weaving of their ponchos and other clothes. I am sure our eyes had never enjoyed such a spectacle of natural colour. There were so many shades of brown from vibrant copper to almost mauve; the sun's reflection only increased the beauty. We even passed the highest bodega in the world that of the Casapalca wine where we didn't dare to stop to taste the wine. The roads were unexpectedly good.

It is difficult to describe the wonder and excitement of Ticlio, supposedly the highest paved road in the world. It was like scenic Switzerland in front of our spellbound eyes as beautiful never ending entwining, almost sensual, high mountains in their ermine white cloaks stood with their humble subjects at their feet as the big rambling lakes paid homage to them. Beauty, real beauty, free for the entire world to see and enjoy. Then suddenly the severe headaches, ear aches and funny sensation of dryness caused by the height hit us but what a small fee to pay for such a delightful view.

The countryside was superb, at times we thought ourselves on the highest moors with the gorse bushes and wild lavender, this blending as on a painter's palette, into the green generous countryside of beautiful tranquil England; then once again it would change into gorges and valleys surrounded by tall, clean smelling eucalyptus trees.

Huancayo is just a small, not too clean country town, but how lovely, kind and generous those sierra people were. The women were femininely petite yet in build sort of squarish and strong, with lovely round healthy rosy cheeks, wearing their typical dresses with numerous underskirts bulging under fine embroidered 'pano de la tierra'; The men were slightly taller, as polite and courteous they all greeted us with a flip to their hats! The Sunday open-air market was a precious sight. The long straight dirt road oozed with so much magic, a glorious riot of colour, the exotic smell of fruits as they mingled with the prosaic everyday odours of open air cooking, flowers, dirt, and good old honest sweat.

The stalls displayed in a chaotic manner the greatest collection of art work, with contrasting colours combined in a most pleasing way. Unfortunately, but bringing back long forgotten Rhodesia days, we had not bothered to book in at a hotel so we were compelled to stay at a primitive rustic motel that was to enhance our short enjoyable visit The views, the food and the hospitality was way beyond our expectations.

Jack's health was beginning to show deterioration. Yet the doctors weren't able to diagnose anything, it was obvious that the conditions at the office were the cause of it all and there was nothing much to be done. For Lyana's sake we had to remain until she finished and graduated from college. Fortunately for us an old official acquaintance from Head Office was paying a visit to Lima. He was now a VIP. To my surprise he made a bee-line towards me and greeted me as if we were the best of friends, later on offering me, and not the General Manager's wife, his arm to go in for dinner. Miraculously Thomas stopped his nasty persecution of Jack.

Life is like a very busy road at weekends. You drive patiently behind the stream of traffic, gradually losing patience so you make an effort and overtake the car just in front of you to find that your effort was almost useless; there is another, and another, and yet another car to overtake. So having tried a few times, you resign yourself to circumstances and take things more complacently, every so often breaking the monotony by a sudden spurt and a leap over another obstacle. At times it might seem fruitless but, this is the way it is.

Lyana had discovered boys a few months before her fifteenth birthday and now she enjoyed going out mainly with a group of friends her age. There was a young man a couple of years older than her named Jorge but known to all his friends and family endearingly as Coquito (little coconut). He seemed to be a favourite and he was always hanging around inviting Lyana to go out horse riding, sailing or outings always in a chauffeur driven car. His father was a well known banker and they lived in a very luxurious home near us. Eventually we were introduced to the family who made rather a big fuss of us all. In fact it worried me that Jorge's mother most particularly was taking her son's relationship with our daughter too seriously. We were often asked to their dinner parties where butlers wearing their white gloves served at dinner and the food was cooked at home for them by the Hotel Bolivar's own chef. It was therefore rather fun when Chela, Jorge's mother visited me. If I was cooking she would come into the kitchen and enjoyed tasting whatever I was making! Edgar her husband was also a gentle man with a fantastic way of looking at life. He was a stickler for punctuality, something very rare amongst the Peruvians. If you gave a time and said 'English time' he would be pressing the doorbell at that particular time right on the dot.

Although our first Christmas there had been a quiet one, shared only with our friend Basil, our second Christmas was a charming change. We had asked Basil and another Company man on a special assignment from Gibraltar and on his own to join us for Christmas dinner for which

I had bought an eleven pound turkey and a tinned ham to provide us with the characteristic season's favourites.

On Christmas Eve we had an unexpected invitation to Chela and Edgar's home for a family dinner. They apparently also celebrated Christmas Eve like in Spain. We made arrangements to go first to Midnight Mass, then after the Mass and at that late time we enjoyed a festive dinner Peruvian style, the dinner did not finish until after 3.00 a.m. I, in turn, then asked them, their son Coquito and their daughter for the next day. Christmas Day brought us an unexpected call from a dear American friend and his wife on business there to join them at their hotel for lunch. It was only natural for them to join us later for dinner. So what had started as a dinner for five ended by being rather a nice party for eleven!

The New Year's celebration was once again spent with Chela and Edgar in their club. We received 1969 with music, laughter and much love. We danced all night and into the morning and at 7.00 a.m. we breakfasted on eggs and bacon, very English style. It was the very first time in our lives that we had stayed awake all through the night because of a celebration. It was crazy and I needed a few days to recuperate.

Chapter 29

DISCOVERY

Aware that we only had a year left in Peru and we didn't know when or if we would revisit one day we wanted to see as much as possible so our third local holiday was to be spent discovering the country. We decided to make use of the college mid-term recess to make our get away. This time we planned a grand itinerary to Cuzco and Machu Pichu. We set forth in our Peugeot 404 southward towards Arequipa, along the Pan-American Highway which joins Ecuador to Chile and runs the whole length of the Pacific coastal strip. How much, how great, how beautiful and interesting it was to be – a unique experience of discomfort, arguments, and magnificence as our trip unrolled, but each and every moment making us all the more human as we discovered and appreciated other ways of life, unbelievable, yet true. Realization hit us as we recognized how very lucky we were and how many blessings had been bestowed upon us.

Our first stop was Paracas, once upon a time an exclusive millionaires' holiday club some 180 miles from Lima. Then it offered a good, rather rustic, but modern hotel. We had been on this road several times during the summer but only as far as Pucusana, an overcrowded fishing village some 50 miles from Lima, as we visited different beaches every Sunday. We had been told that beyond Pucusana the trip would be across desolate desert so imagine our surprise when suddenly, after a sharp turn in the road, the banana plantations of Male appeared before us as if by magic. Our blood began to flow quicker at this unexpected pleasure and we were convinced that many more unusual sights would be ours in this contrasting land.

We were not to be disappointed. The appearance, at irregular intervals along the way, of minute oasis complete with a few customary date palms and an occasional aristocratic–looking, haughty llama grazing around them, delighted us. At one of these beauty spots we came across a little 'shepherd', a native boy of no more than seven or eight, just staring motionless through unseeing eyes, so young and yet so adult. We noticed his attitude of resignation and acceptance of his lot as one of the main characteristics of the Andean Indian as they sat or stood, head bowed, with eyes vacant as if in a trance.

Paracas did not reach expectations, the beautiful sandy beaches were condemned because of sting-rays and jelly fish; the proximity of a fish meal factory was not very pleasant either in spite of the landscaped gardens and walkways, surrounding the bungalows and two swimming pools provided for hotel guests. We spent the night there leaving immediately after breakfast for Chala, from where, legend has it, the Chesquia (messengers), running in relay form, carried fresh salt-water fish to their Inca Emperor at Macchu Picchu every day.

The mountain roads to this peaceful, lost and almost forgotten port, once the only escape from boredom for the personnel of the Marcona Mining Corporation, intrigued us as once more we came into contact with the many kinds of earth strata and structure. The land was completely barren but for an evergreen ridge where water from the melted mountain snow would drip down all day enabling thick moss and a few wild bushes to grow. Then a riot of funny shaped sand dunes looking like round African huts populated the way giving us the impression of some giant child having just made sand pies while whiling his hours away. We admired the shoreline across fierce looking rocks which dangerously hung over the cliffs, gently balancing on almost sculptured smaller bases as if in argument with the mighty waves. Up again across land prodigal in bush fertility, the scene then mellowed into the well patterned vineyards. Amazingly beautiful there was no time to relax for fear of missing an instant of all this free natural beauty.

From Chala to Arequipa we travelled partly at sea level crossing empty beaches and then slowly climbing over barren sections where big boulders often served as pillars and walls for humble homes, where people, poor miserable human beings, actually lived without comfort, heating or sanitation. Their only extravagance was a few dirty and peculiar faced pigs eating from the trash that surrounded these small areas. We wondered how they could exist at all without any apparent supply of drinking water or food.

When the monotony of the bare land began to tire us we would come across a hidden valley waiting to surprise us like a jack-in-the-box with mile after mile of heavenly perfumed orange groves such as those at Palpa. Eerie, misty narrow roads wound up and down across dead lands, suddenly as if to gladden our tired eyes there appeared an extensive olive grove to greet us.

Arequipa, at the foot of the Andes, guarded by 'El Misti' volcano, is one of the most important cities of Peru and founded twice over, once by the first Inca emperors with the name of 'are-que-pay' meaning 'you may stay here' and the second time by the Spaniards in 1540. This lovely 'ciudad blanca' – white city – so called because of its construction in white volcanic rock, typical of the area, and its ideal climate, enchanted us. Barely a few hours after our arrival and having left our car in a lock-up garage we boarded a train, our new means of locomotion to Cuzco as the dirt roads and the altitude through which we would have to travel did not stimulate our desire to drive all the way. On the train, with solicitous service, and cleanliness, in the sleeper coach – we travelled to Juliaca, about 12,000 feet above sea level – was most welcome, and misleading too, as we anticipated the same treatment throughout, but we were badly let down later, much to our despair.

We arrived in Juliaca at 5.00. a.m. to a most reviving coldness which however did not make up for the lack of oxygen. The station, even at this early hour, was flooded with humble vendors selling their beautiful art work for next to nothing. Perhaps they were there because they had nowhere else to go. It was such striking poverty, what a fight for such a miserable existence.

The usual comforts of a railway station were noticeable by their absence. We therefore decided to eat breakfast from our own picnic basket as we had been advised to take a few food stuffs with us. Sitting on a rough wooden bench under the glare of inquisitive staring eyes we ate our meagre food, perhaps to those eyes our meal appeared like a banquet. Having satisfied our complaining stomachs I made my way to the 'rest room' proudly announced as 'Ladies – 1st Class'. My goodness, what a revolting place! I was compelled to quickly run away – forgotten were all my necessities.

The train was scheduled to depart at 7.00 a.m. but here we were already two hours late and no one had any idea why the delay and least of all, the station master! When finally it appeared there was a mad rush as a group of quite rough people forced their way aboard, carrying a most interesting variety of luggage in baskets, woven mats, bags and boxes. Everyone seemed to be travelling first class – but one could hardly describe these tatty looking uncomfortable coaches as such! Suddenly the prospect of travelling under such conditions – if we ever found a seat that was – overcame me.

Finally my moans and complaints had their effect as we were given three seats which had been pointed out as occupied but which were in reality wanted by the one man who, following tradition, expected to use them for a sleep-in, and an un-burdened trip! Our fellow passengers charmed us after a while making me forget my bout of bad temper as interest quickened my sight. At times I just couldn't tear my eyes away from the family of four occupying eight seats – all wearing their Sunday best, with parcels galore and the biggest saucepans imaginable proudly arranged on top of the table next to massive chunks of bread and a piping hot beverage, all of which the mother efficiently distributed as we impatiently waited for the train to whistle away. We finally started – three and half hours late!

As soon as the train was in motion I made my way to the 'little room' only to be greeted by a similar sight to that which I had run away from at Juliaca station. The ticket collector, on seeing my predicament and realising I was a 'gringo' instructed me in painful but extremely polite English to follow him, 'please'. Obediently, and by this time desperately, I did so, to find paradise in the form of the 'buffet car' facilities. This coach was full of foreign passengers who had obviously been warned by their travel agents, and therefore knew – when in Peru, don't travel first class. Pay a dollar extra and reserve your place in the buffet car. Once we knew, we made our contribution and were able to change to civilization once again.

The trip to Cuzco was assuredly a very slow one; we found out that the one locomotive which usually pulled seven coaches was now burdened with double that number. Obviously it was too much and eventually, very suddenly, it came to a standstill in the middle of nowhere, on the 'altiplano'(high Andean plain) under the scorching rays of the sun and complete lack of oxygen. We were stuck halfway between Pucara, famous for its pottery, and Ayaviri

What commotion there was when an elderly German lady fainted and the poor concerned husband begged for an ambulance. Tragic though the situation was one could not help but smile at the 'faith' of this visitor who must have thought Peruvian towns to be on a par with those in Europe. He certainly had not realized that these little places were hardly comparable with a village; if you were not careful you were through the town without noticing it. Once the lady received oxygen administered by the Good Samaritan, 'my' ticket collector, the husband calmed down, while we all waited patiently for another locomotive to arrive and bring the spare parts required for us to proceed.

People became restless and hungry. The buffet car, not being big enough or sufficiently well stocked to cater for this emergency, was soon of no use. Passengers walked about the train to investigate and since we could understand the locals we went back to the first class compartment. Everyone of them had taken out their baskets and all kinds of food was brought out. The family of four opened up the big pans, and went almost berserk as they ravenously helped themselves with their fingers, unaware that some Japanese tourists were going crazy taking films of what was happening. I could not get near enough but the food looked like a 'couscous' of sorts, or whatever. It must have been delicious, although I did not find it appetising at all, they sucked their fingers and smacked their lips in great appreciation.

Once the repairs to the train were made we set off for the next town Ayaviri, where we were to have an unforgettably strange experience. It seemed as if the bush telegraph had been considerably busy for by the time the train bellowed to a jerky standstill at Ayaviri there were dozens of fat, rosy cheeked, little native women showing their goodies in varying styles and manners. Food of every description welcomed us, some placed on top of paper laid on the ground, and some on rickety tables. It seemed as if the end of the world was near the way the travellers thronged the stalls of their particular choice. Something that looked like potatoes drowned in a thick yellow sauce, with spit-roast goat and lamb, seemed to be the favourite dishes if one could judge by the way these tired hungry travellers revelled in their food. They tore the huge chunks of meat away from the bones which were left for the last to chew as well. The various stews and thick soups also had their followers.

The smell of the spit-meat was most inviting and it was a shame that the sensitivity of our stomachs and habits prevented us from having a meal. Another couple in our compartment, tourists and obviously city people, however, were unable to stand this temptation and so made their way to an old lady in her many coloured skirts and bright waistcoat who by the time they reached her was already selling her last piece of meat. They approached the vendor and we saw them making signals that they wanted food. To our surprise, consternation and delight – the old lady vendor opened up her waistcoat, lifted up her yellowish and dirty blouse from under which she proceeded to take two more pieces of lamb! We could hardly believe our eyes but then neither could we understand how the couple could make themselves buy and then ravenously gobble their share – to our ughs of disgust – the possible explanation for such hiding place must have been to keep the meat warm! When we thought of the lack of water and absence of personal hygiene – the meat must have had additional exotic flavour! We were fascinated by the sight. How we would have loved capturing this moment on film to relive and enjoy in future years – as I am sure the Japanese must be doing still.

Around this area Peru's unique natural pasture 'ichu', which is the diet for the vicunas, llamas, and alpacas, was most abundant, growing to considerable height and in great profusion. In texture very much like hay it is used by the natives for making little animals and dolls, and bags which they sold at every train stop. We seemed no nearer to arriving at our destination. The discomfort, heat and hunger, did not make us very compatible travellers particularly as we discovered a new and different 'fragrance'. Before the train broke down the ticket collector had bought complete raw sides of lamb which had been badly wrapped in pieces of plastic or some less suitable material. By now, with this unexpected delay, blood was seeping through and added another unpleasant smell to the already loaded atmosphere of dirt and human bodies. We were too nauseated to worry over the fact that we were over six hours behind scheduled time.

Eventually when we arrived in Cuzco, we discovered that our hotel rooms had been released to someone else and we had to make do with one small room for the three of us. Although it was the very best hotel then in Cuzco, there was no hot water that night, neither was there any during the days we remained there, problems with the electricity or so we were told. At least we had cold water showers which Jack hated and he moaned about it incessantly.

Breakfast time greeted us with the news, in the form of a telegram, that our house in Lima had been burgled – once we were able to contact our friend Basil and confirmed our losses we decided that since nothing would be achieved by returning immediately we would remain and enjoy the few days left of our visit. We engaged a taxi-driver with the exotic name of Teteychoquecheca 'but please call me Jose', as he explained in excellent English how it meant 'son of the river'. He was to be our good guide and friend showing us around the nearby ruins and other places of interest. He was always on time, courteous and reasonable. We visited the fortress of Sacseyhuaman made of enormous stones, really massive blocks of granite weighing several tons each and positioned with mathematical precision. Also on the outskirts of Cuzco we visited Kenko, an amphitheatre with its mysterious curved stones and what is believed to be an altar for some horrible cult. There was Tambomachay's 'bath of the Incas' where water still flows from its fountains. In Cuzco itself there are so many temples, palaces and residences of varying ages it was impossible to visit them all. Outstanding were the Church of La Compania, which in Inca days was the Cancha Amaru (a part of Huayna Capac's palace), the Church of Santo Domingo, built on the Inti Nuasi or Temple of the Sun in the days of the Inca, and the Cathedral built over the palace of Inca Viracocha. There is no doubt that Cuzco's boast to be the archaeological capital of the Americas is well merited – the fusion of Inca and Spanish colonial styles has made it so. The mind travelled through the ages giving one a chance to relive and enjoy the past.

Our trip to Macchu Picchu was quite an odyssey, through disorganization and mismanagement we were sold tickets for the autocar – single carriage diesel trains that normally made the journey from Cuzco to Macchu Picchu in two and a half hours, but these had all been reserved by two large groups of tourists so independent travellers like ourselves were shuttled onto a waiting train, of six carriages, which took nearly five hours to make the journey. This not being enough we had to wait for over an hour for one of the small buses that was to take us up the mountain to the ruins themselves. All this occurred at the hottest time of the day and to make it even more interesting I was stung by a bee! One thing we learned – never go to Macchu Picchu during the school vacation time!

Once at the top, the magnificence of Macchu Picchu made us forget all the discomfort and hard times as we made our way through the roads and houses of this famous citadel, the lost city, discovered by Hiram Bingham in 1911. Surrounded by steeply terraced gardens, its site on the cone of a high rocky peak, hundreds of feet up amongst dense vegetation, and guarded by the snake-like Urubamba River below, no wonder then that it remained undiscovered for so long, no wonder that Spaniards and modern Peruvians alike were unable to find this amazing city. It is thought that the Virgins of the Sun hid away here when the Spaniards reached Cuzco. This belief is supported by the fact that in the majority of the tombs remains of women have been found. From Cuzco to Puno on Lake Titicaca and back to Arequipa, this time in the buffet car all the way! It was a pleasure to travel in it, heavily guarded by the waiters who protected us from the 'other classes' thus giving us comfort and cleanliness but taking away the human touch and flavour of the many delightfully picturesque people. Their sadness and their battles were portrayed in the lost vacant eyes, bent heads and the whispering speech of those vendors that entered into the other carriages to sell their goods. I shall never forget the haggard, and miserably old-looking women with dry brown leather-like skin whose stench lingered hours after they had passed by, slowly pulling themselves along with the greatest of difficulty and sometimes carrying a child on their backs. Were these poor women really old or did they have more hardship than they could bear?

Puno is one of the most interesting places in Peru and is known as the Folklore Capital because of the many celebrations there. Although it is also one of the poorest districts of Peru, it was here that we enjoyed the best accommodation, with central heating and plenty of hot water and delicious food all at very reasonable cost. Puno is the port through which all travellers from Bolivia using the lake steamer must pass. Lake Titicaca is the highest navigable lake in the world and according to legend, Manco Capec and Mama Ocllo, founders of the Inca Empire, rose from its waves. On the waters of the lake are the unique 'floating islands', clusters of floating houses made of reeds and inhabited by the Uros Indians, a picturesque race that is dying out. The totora straw rafts of the natives add further charm.

How people exist like this is beyond comprehension, at a time when man has already been to the moon there are people still living in such conditions. It is almost inhuman even if colourful, but should one give colour to a country through the misery and sufferings of fellow beings? Children, adults and animals, all live together on the food extracted from the lake – there is an abundance of trout and other fish; and from the sale of little replicas of their totora boats. Their meagre finance was slightly augmented by the tips for posing in their unique surroundings for photographs for the tourists.

Back in our car we made our way from Arequipa along the same route, Jack making a short deviation and so delighted me by the unexpected appearance of a real big oasis among gigantic white sand dunes. It was Huacachina, a beautiful green medicinal lake, surrounded by many graceful palms and numerous hotels of all standards. It was while at lunch and listening to the twittering of the many caged birds that we realised that we had seen no birds during our entire trip. What happened to the birds in this part of Peru, we wondered, but no one we spoke to was able to give a satisfactory explanation.

It was great being back home where everything looked so grand and glamourous. Lyana had to get ready for the graduating class ball which was celebrated before the actual graduation. When she told me that her partner was going to be Augusto, a twenty-six year old young man and not Coquito with whom she had been going out for most of her time in Lima, I warned her that she was asking for trouble. She argued that all the other male partners were friends of Augusto and were older and did not know Coquito, so surely he would feel left out of place. Lyana looking beautiful like a young bride was escorted by Augusto. Although Coquito was upset he continued seeing her and taking her out even more than before. We were much happier since we felt Augusto was far too old, too much of a man being ten years her senior. One day Lyana arrived home as if in a trance and we, Jack and I, realized that she had had her first kiss and it was Coquito who had earned it. A week or so later when Lyana was really enthusiastic over Coquito she came back in tears. He had broken up with her! Lyana was devastated. Nothing I could say stopped her crying. Jack was in Trinidad on Company business so I phoned Basil who as usual immediately came to the rescue.

On his arrival Basil asked what had happened and then I showed him to Lyana's room. Since neither came out and I couldn't hear anything

I went to investigate. There was Lyana inside her bed, Basil on top of the bed, both crying their hearts out. "For Pete's sake, what the heck is going on?" I asked laughing. They really made quite a funny picture, then their sense of humour returned and they too joined me with laughter. Basil had received that day a letter from his estranged wife in England telling him that she had left him for good and gone to live with some other man! Afterwards we were told that before she left their UK house she had measured her new sitting-room and then gone back and cut off the required amount of thick rich carpet from Basil's house for her new one. We kidded him his tears were not for the wife but for the expensive carpet which now he would need to replace. If Coquito expected Lyana to go crying to him he was disappointed – his action was cold and calculated, instead she started going out with Augusto.

Poor Basil then received news of his immediate transfer to Trinidad. He was very sad as he enjoyed his bachelor life to the full in Lima. In fact all the time we were there he had enjoyed this style of living. Since the wife did not want to join him I did not see anything wrong with his gallivanting around and also I enjoyed the stories of his amorous encounters which he loved to relate to us. We would miss him although we too did not have much longer to remain in Peru.

My friend Betty arranged a lovely typical Peruvian party in her house for some very important businessmen from Barcelona, Spain. Jack and I were invited and it was really the first time that we had shared with them such an interesting event. All the food was prepared and cooked the way it was done upcountry. She had a black lady to do the typical fritters just as you would see them in their homes. On an open wood fire, there was a huge tin pan with boiling oil and these fritters were bubbling away and she moved them around with long wooden sticks. They had some potatoes in yellow sauce like we had seen the family of four eating on the train to Cuzco and these turned out to be quite delicious. She also served the 'anticucho' marinated meat in its special sauce and barbecued on skewers. I thought it was steak and found it very nice and tasty but once I discovered what the meat really was, heart, I could not eat any more!

We were enjoying a drink when some late comers arrived. As they approached I looked up and at the same time the man looked at me. Suddenly as our eyes met I felt myself trembling and I wanted to go and embrace him, he too was looking affected and came towards me. I turned to Jack and said "Don't, please don't leave me alone, I shall not be responsible for anything!" "For Pete's sake, Ly what is wrong?" I could not explain. It was not a sexual thing, it was as if we had known each other for a long time, everyone there noticed the strange happening. When I went home Jack told Lyana all about it, so when the following Sunday I saw him in church, I pointed him out to Lyana. Imagine our surprise and consternation when she too went all peculiar on seeing him. My friends, Olga, Betty and Agnes, kept on teasing me but it was not really anything to make fun of. Particularly when the next time we met, we never said a word but we did embrace. This happened several times. It was like meeting someone very dear from the past and yet I had never seen him before! I had to put up with a lot of fun making including from Jack!

Lyana graduated with honours and we were very proud of her. The graduating classes were organizing a trip to Northern Peru and Lyana wanted to go with her friends. We could not make any commitment since it was now September 1969 and we reckoned our return to England would be imminent. However we promised her that if we were still in Lima she could go. To our surprise our departure date was January 1970. Just as the witch woman had said, not as late as we were supposed to go, (our tour should have ended in June 1970), and not as soon as you think you are going! (October 1969).

We decided to go and visit Basil in Trinidad and then to visit Maria and Dick in Saint Lucia. Maria had had serious surgery and I felt I wanted to share time with her since she was not recuperating as well as she should. On our return to Lima the farewell parties started. Lyana and I were having a lunch in Ancon at the summer holiday house of a Peruvian friend when suddenly it seemed as if the sea was emptying and there was a dreadful silence. One moment we were sitting on the verandah and the next moment we were in our cars. Some of my friends with small children were already in tears and shouting "It is the end of the world". No sooner had we set forth back to Lima than the skies opened and rain fell in bucketfuls.

Pandemonium broke loose, since it never rained there the younger drivers started going very fast trying to splash as much as possible. There were no gutters and soon most places were flooded and cars were stranded in the water. When we finally arrived home we found Jack and Augusto bailing out water from inside the wardrobes since all the houses had openings in the roofs for ventilation. It was chaotic. Our cases were floating in the water and it seemed as if it would never stop raining. A few days later, there was quite a big earth tremor, everything was moving and for once we were terrified.

Our last Christmas there was a bit sad. We spent Christmas Eve quietly dining before going to Midnight Mass. On Christmas Day we entertained Katita and Gil, and Toni and her brother Vincent, who were alone as their parents had already left for the States. New Year's Eve dance we went once again with Edgar and Chela while Lyana went to the same Club with Augusto and his other group of friends.

My schoolchildren came to say their goodbyes, at the end we had all become good friends and now they were really losing both their teachers: Toni Marich who was returning to USA and I who was leaving for the U.K. Some pupils even promised they would come and see me 'one day.' The saddest of all were Edgar and Chela who had become really good friends and in fact Edgar sent his own carpenters to crate our heavy luggage. On a sunny Peruvian summer day we embarked on the Italian Line ship Donizetti for Guayaquil in Ecuador, Barranquitas on the Pacific coast of Colombia then through the Panama Canal to Cartagena on the Caribbean coast of Colombia, finally to disembark at LaGuaira (Caracas) in Venezuela. It was during this section of the trip that Lima's offices forwarded a note which Sir John McPherson had sent inquiring as to our welfare as he knew we were supposed to be leaving Peru and there had been yet another earth tremor, this one even bigger than the last one we had witnessed. In La Guaira we transferred from the Donizetti to the Oriana for our last lap home to Southampton and the grey cold winter days of England.

Part Six

New Horizons 1970 - 1980

Chapter 30

HOME POSTING

When we got home, our very own home, it was a great disappointment. The tenants, the Ministry of Defence, had left the place in a very poor state. Our beautiful garden which had been one of the main reasons we had decided to buy the house was an absolute shambles. All the paths with archways covered with climbing roses had been destroyed and the place was desolate. I looked around me and burst out crying.

Now in England we would not have help with servants as we did when abroad. Jack had been given more senior responsibility by this move which meant that although his basic salary would see an increase and improvement, with no other perks it was going to be very difficult. We had come down to earth with a great big thump! We decided to go Gibraltar for a short holiday before making the house ready and comfortable for our three year stay.

Although the frontier had been closed in 1969 it seemed that Gibraltar was booming with new business, boutiques exposing their wares in attractive array, restaurants and boites with exotic Arab girls performing their belly dances transporting one to the magical atmosphere of the Kasbah. The beaches were being transformed for the summer with boulevards, ramps in attractive engineering feats turning otherwise dowdy uncomfortable sea fronts into show pieces for the local and tourists arriving for good free-port shopping in the sterling area where they could speak the same English language and yet enjoy the continental style of living.

Where previously the Spaniards had served as domestic help, waiters, stewards, drivers and mainly unskilled workers, now Arabs and the beautiful Moorish girls took their place wearing unique costumes and make-up, giving more colour and flavour to a 'too British' town. The Gibraltarians this time when they lost the freedom to go to Spain had achieved so much and had turned the situation to their own good. The hard-earned money that had so freely flown into the neighbouring Spanish hinterland was now re-invested in Gibraltar. The new façade spelled prosperity to many. To my amazement the change had not only been physical but also social. People were being freed of their inhibitions, in certain cases to the point of shocking behaviour. Men who had previously hidden their homosexual tendencies now didn't hide them, while women exchanged partners in their new found freedom in a most blatant manner. Gibraltar was different, whereas at one time most executive jobs had been filled by expatriates, now these jobs were available to capable local persons and so their salaries increased, many menial workers found themselves in good official prosperous positions. The 'new rich' were able to buy their 'entrée' into society by lending money to influential people who had lost their fortunes gambling in the casino. It was amusing to see good old stuffed shirts, ex-snobbish people, having to socialize with people they would never have recognized in the past. It was fun to see the patronising air of the former underdogs over their social betters and sad too to find such fine families having to grin and bear it.

Many were now able to enjoy the comfort and amusements that were previously available only to a privileged few. Tradition and family names were no longer of any importance. The good old days were over, but if it brought prosperity and happiness to the majority – anything for progress! Fashion-wise the Gibraltarians had no reason to envy their English sisters. All were tastefully garbed in the most modern garments. The men too had changed as they allowed more freedom to their wives and sweethearts who were encouraged to wear the mini-skirt and allowed to walk in town in trouser suits. The men now actually tended to ignore the looks of admiration that were bestowed on their better halves!

At night all clubs and boites were crowded with ex-drab housewives beautifully dressed in their attractive exotically embroidered pyjama suits as they mingled with the tourists. At Eastern Beach the nightclub 'Panama' was a very in place where I was lucky enough to meet the English film star Richard Green, the BBC 1950's Robin Hood. It was all very exciting for the Rock. We naturally did miss being able to cross the frontier into Spain and we did in fact take the car ferry to Tangiers a couple of times to be able to drive distances to break the cooped up feelings we occasionally suffered. These feelings were one of the devastating things that the normal working class Gibraltarian had to put up with if they were not able to pay for trips to England or across to Morocco. The road to the top of the Rock would fill up with parked cars in order to enjoy the feeling of space away from the city centre. The children too suffered as they no longer knew what animals other than cats and dogs and maybe the odd horse looked like! But in reality everyone took the frontier closure in good measure and the assets gained outweighed any of the losses.

Parting time soon came but this time the thought that we would be staying in England softened the blow as my parents could come and visit as soon as we had settled into our house. So on a terrible stormy day Jack and I set sail towards Albion with the ship pitching and rolling. While normally I was a poor sailor, this time with the nervousness brought about by fear, I was hungry all the time much to the table steward's despair who on seeing me would say "Only a sandwich today!" At long last we arrived in England to be met by Clem and Bill.

Once in the house we had no idea where to start the interior re-decoration as this was a new venture for us. Jack had never pruned a tree in his life, so now I feared for him. The large fruit trees could only be done by a professional, while we did our best with the other chores. While Jack scraped all the doors to be ready for painting I decided to go out to the garden and try to put it into some semblance of what it had been. I had absolutely no idea about plants except that I loved flowers and big green leaves and cared enough to want the garden to look good once again. I worked hard pulling out weeds, cutting grass and shaping beds, all under the critical eyes of our neighbour, an old retired sea captain. He was obviously an excellent gardener judging by his glorious garden. After three days of back breaking work when everything looked a little bare, but clean and tidy, the captain approached my fence and said "Do you mind if I ask you a question, Mrs. Armstrong?" "Not at all, Captain, what is it?" "Well, why is it that you have taken out all your plants and left all the weeds?" he asked. Just as well he could not read my mind in those seconds. I just looked at him. The son of a bitch had let me go on doing what he knew was wrong and had not said anything until I had finished. This would certainly never have happened in Gibraltar or Spain or in any of the other countries where I had lived! However, I turned round and extremely sweetly I answered "Because I like them!" "Well, the plants were in any case going to seed" was his reply! Naturally I went as soon as I could to the garden centre and bought new plants that could grow easily and with a limited amount of attention. A beginner's garden!

There was a lot I did not understand about living in England. It was so cold and yet the housewives did daily shopping pulling along their shopping carts instead of using their cars. We were accustomed to go shopping once a week by car and only if we saw something extra that we fancied whilst walking in the High Street did we bother to buy it. I noticed too that to work in the front garden most neighbours dressed up with pearl necklaces and all! When I was doing any kind of work I dressed comfortably! I was always under the impression that neighbours kept to themselves yet those on both sides of our house, even the captain, were quite nice and helpful as was the one behind our house. I often gave them some of the beautiful Victoria plums as well as other fruit such as apples and cherries that grew in our garden. We felt the cold very much after so many years in warm countries and this gave cause for complaint as to our electricity bills!

Sometimes we complain about things not happening as we would wish or would like. Lyana had been extremely disappointed at missing the graduating class trip to Northern Peru where a number of her friends were going. In fact it was our leaving Lima before the scheduled time that saved her life. Almost all of her friends disappeared in May 1970 in the massive earth tremor and resulting landslide which took place in the Callejon de Huaylas where they had gone to celebrate. The main town was buried under the earth and only the church steeple could be seen!

Jack disliked having to catch the train daily from Hampton and then not only having this long trip, he had to get a bus to his final destination in London. We had had a very easy lifestyle and to start existing at this stage of our life we found it a little hard to adapt. Abroad either he drove his car to the office or the driver did and everything was near to where we lived!

Lyana returned from her holiday in Gibraltar accompanied by my parents who came to stay with us for a fortnight. Then they visited my sister Clem, now permanently living in Twickenham, for another fortnight. Meanwhile, Aunt Dora, Uncle George and Jack's Mum came for ten days which gave them all a chance to be with my parents. My good friend Eva had left Puerto Rico and now lived close by in Thames Ditton and another Brazilian friend, Teresinha, lived two roads away from us in Hampton itself so we did have some sort of social life.

Lyana went to the University of Surrey at Guildford to study Russian and we were alone once more. We decided to extend the house at the back so that we could have a separate dining-room, and also enlarge the kitchen to enjoy a breakfast room too. Once all the reformation work at home was accomplished our savings were naturally very depleted. When we started to build our extension we had a caller from the city council. He wanted to know if we had permission to do these alterations to the house. Apparently one of the neighbours had taken the trouble to notify the authorities. Since we always do things by the rule everything was fine but I wondered why anyone would do such a thing and decided that obviously there was very little of interest in their lives when they had to go checking on other people's affairs. This was again something that I had never encountered anywhere else. In fact, I had lived all over the world and always identified with the different cultures and customs. Here I was in England, a British subject having been taught by the Loreto Convent nuns in a private college, and yet I felt a real foreigner. The problem was, I suppose, that I had no desire to identify with them! Our way of living and standards were so very much superior!

I found that local people did not make things easy for outsiders to make themselves understood. When I went shopping to the greengrocers and asked for onions pronounced by me as it is written (onyons), the greengrocer would mimic me and repeat several times "onyons, onyons" like me. When asked why he did that he replied "Onions are pronounced uhnions!" I then said "If that is so why the hell don't you write it like that?" He just stared at me. Another time I had to make a trunk call to Reading and since I was not aware that it had a different pronunciation to the act of reading, the telephone operator made fun of me! While in London with an address in Leicester Square, I stopped the bus driver and very carefully pronouncing as clearly as I could each syllable Lei- ces- ter he shouted he had never heard of it and drove away! At the butcher's if I asked for three steaks he would always ask what weight. I neither knew nor cared, all I wanted was three nice steaks with whatever weight they made together. Accustomed to bargaining I found it very strange to pay the same amount of money for say three sweaters of the same kind but different colours all at exactly the same price per article as if I were buying only one! There was never a discount.

I decided to look for a job. I found a clerical job with Fourboys, a newsagent and general store in Hampton Hill that had many branches in the area. The job was not particularly stimulating after the positions I had held abroad but I did not wish to travel to London every day. I must confess I had no idea where all the towns were and I found it difficult to know the efficient distribution routes so I gave up after a few months. Then I went for another clerical job at Hampton and again I found it terribly depressing so I decided that if Saint Mary's College at

Strawberry Hill would accept me as a mature student I would return and take art. I enrolled and had a small allowance paid to me by the government. I was learning and in the company of young people with whom I seemed to have much more in common than with some of the neighbours. They accepted me as one of them and I was treated as such. It was rather fun when just because I kept a place for a young student in his late teens, or he kept it for me, right in the front row of the class that everybody else thought that we 'were going together!'

At St. Mary's the physical education teacher was none other than the father of Mick Jagger of 'Rolling Stones' fame. He often asked me to help introduce into his routines some of my dancing steps which I enjoyed. This was much more fun and certainly better than participating in the football games. Instead of chasing the ball on these occasions I would have to steer clear of not only the ball but the hefty muscular young men chasing it.

I loved beautiful things and when the teacher asked us to go out to the garden and pick up anything we fancied I discovered a gorgeous, most exotic looking root, when we returned to the class we were asked to paint what we had brought with us – the poor roots turned out to look more like a plate of spaghetti and not too appetising at that! Then the teacher said we were to create a metamorphosis by incorporating what we had just painted into another picture. I decided the plate of spaghetti could only be a shield so I painted a very peculiar Masai warrior with spear and shield, (my apologies to the elegant Masais). The worst thing was when the teacher in rapture, or was it kindness, said what a wonderful naive painting it was and to my shame and discomfort hung it in the class room! Eventually I turned out some good mosaics with all sorts of pulses and pastas and I think this helped me to get the grades. Every so often I would make a risotto and invite my class mates for lunch so I no longer complained to Jack that I had been like an encaged animal all day and was happy to stay in with him every evening. He was always too tired for anything else.

Lyana was given a lovely kitten, all fluffy and beautiful, by one of the male students at University. Its coat of many colours, white, beige, brown and almost pink, made it very attractive. As the kitten was female we named her Cachita (a little bundle) and we kept her at home in Cardinal's Walk until Lyana, feeling too lonely and out of place with her friend's blatant sexual behaviour at university, decided to return home and travel to Guildford daily.

At university she had gone to see a friend, knocked at the door, was asked to enter, she did, to find the girl copulating and continuing to do so as if Lyana had not been there. Although Lyana had been brought up quite differently from me and knew all about the birds and the bees, she also accepted that this act should be a culminating act of love and therefore to be treasured. Lyana applied for Saint Mary's and was accepted. It was rather fun since my sister Clementina was on her last year, and now Lyana had joined us both!

Cachita was such a lovely friendly cat that she soon became everyone's favourite. Ever since our first day there I had made a very nice friend. I was standing by the garage door when a little boy came to visit me carrying a posy of garden flowers which he had obviously picked himself "Hallo, my name is Robert" he said very solemnly. "What a lovely name you have. Do you live near by?" I asked. Pointing over to the other side of the road he said "Yes, there. What is your name?" Since I wasn't too sure what I should answer, if 'auntie' 'Mrs' or just my name, I hesitated saying "Eh, Lydia". He looked at me very intently and then said "I like that name, Elydia, tomorrow I shall come and visit you again!" From then on he always managed to pay me a visit and he subsequently became Cachita's best friend.

Cachita loved going for rides in the car, the problem was that it didn't matter whose car it was. If she saw a door or window open she would go in and hide until the car was driving off and quite often my neighbours had to bring her back, sometimes from as far as Richmond Bridge, five miles away. By far her favourite was the milkman's electric buggie. She would sit on top of the bottles and be extremely happy to ride at the slow pace. Somehow she never liked the postman. It was very funny to see him coming to the front of the house and desperately looking everywhere before entering the premises. Often Cachita would be hiding behind the large rhododendron bush and as he entered the front garden she would pounce on him. He would complain saying "Mrs Armstrong, I have never seen a cat so much like a dog in my life!" One day the milkman came and told me that he liked my moggy, that I had a very nice one. I didn't have a clue as to what he was saying as I didn't know what a moggy was. Was he being cheeky I wondered. I just smiled, thanked him and waited anxiously for Jack's return home when I could discover what it was I had nice! Jack laughed and said "It's another name for a pussy" and then had to explain further. My interpretation was not related to a cat.

She seemed to know exactly when Jack was arriving back from work long before he actually did. She would run to the front door and wait for him. Jack always knew if she had been told off by me. If she had done something wrong she would 'talk' to him as she brushed against his legs, if all was well she would greet him with very noisy purring. She was a good hunter who loved to bring her gifts to us to the back door and when she was outside in the garden no bird was safe! Like Ouiki, she came to us if she could not get clean herself and we were amazed when we discovered she actually loved going in for a bath!

Lyana longed to start playing the piano so I looked for a good second hand one as once we left the UK we would have to leave it behind . Shortly afterwards I met a lady who had a piano no one used as her husband, the pianist, had passed away. The piano was precious to the family and she would only sell it if it would be properly used. Lyana loved its sound and played for hours. On one occasion we returned home to find her crying at the front door and when asked what was wrong she said that while playing she saw a man standing by the piano listening to her and smiling. We nearly freaked out as at no time had I said how the piano had come on the market.

Although Lyana and I were quite happy with our lives Jack could not settle down to going into London every day and he found the mad rush too much for him. He kept on bothering Head Office for a transfer practically every day and it was not surprising that at the end, fed up with all his asking he was offered a posting to Manila, The Philippines!

We had been in the UK less than two years. I remember phoning my parents and telling them and my mother saying "For Pete's sake don't go, that is the land of prostitutes and killers, look at all the films, the bad ones are always Filipinos and the women like to knife their lovers in passionate frenzy!" When I heard this I told Jack that perhaps we shouldn't go but as far as he was concerned anything would be better than the life he had!

When we visited the Philippine Embassy the people were very nice and helpful so we all entered the new adventure with excitement and happiness. There were goodbyes and packing to do and once again we rented the house through an agency for the initial two year period we would be away as the posting was for two two-year periods. The agency had to make sure that Cachita stayed in the house and was looked after by the tenants who were deducted an appropriate amount from the rent for her upkeep.

The problem was that there was no ship going to the Philippines except for small cargo ships with limited passenger space and the journey took a very long time. The alternative was to travel by air but with all the problems I had had on and off with air travel we decided to go and see the cargo ship. The sleeping quarters were very ample and good but when I saw two doors, one on each side of the cabin, I enquired where they led, only to find that one was to the chief engineer's cabin and the other to the captain's. The Company insisted that Jack travel by air because of the long delay by sea so since Lyana and I were going to be the only two women on board I reckoned it would be safer not to sail. Instead I went to the doctor who put me under hypnosis treatment and Jack did his best to get the trip done in three stages. We eventually flew on SAS and stayed overnight in Copenhagen and Bangkok. We were supposed to also stay in Tashkent but this stopover was cancelled. The journey made in this way proved quite comfortable but I was extremely pleased when we finally made it to our new destination.

Chapter 31

SAMPAGUITAS

When we arrived at Manila International Airport there was a band waiting as apparently there were some dignitaries travelling with us. I was shocked to see a wire fence surrounding all the meeting and viewing places while lots of young girls in their national costumes met the descending tourists with lais (flower necklaces) of sweet smelling Sampaguita flowers. The heat, the noise and strong perfume gave me a tremendous headache and all I wished for was to get out of this dreadfully noisy place and go home.

We were met by Celedonio, an effusive Filipino, Jack's new deputy and who obviously knew his way around extremely well. I did not like the man, there was something quite repellent about him, perhaps it was his suave ways and the macho image he portrayed. There was a chauffeur driven car awaiting us. We were informed we would be taken to a 'holiday home' which was a home belonging to some other firm whose employees were away on a long holiday. We were to take it over for three months until they returned and keep their servants in our employ. After nearly two years in the UK doing everything by ourselves it was rather exciting to see the line of servants awaiting us. Cook, house girl number one, house girl number two, the driver and the gardener were all in line waiting to be introduced. At one side there was a young girl standing alone who had a lovely smile and who was ignored by the others. I walked towards her and asked "Who are you?"

Before she could reply the cook answered, "Oh, she is only the laundry girl!" I saw red, of them all it was she, Lucy, the one I liked best.

The house was beautiful and extremely big and tastefully decorated, I felt quite happy to be spending time here until we found our own house in Urdaneta village. These villages in Makati were compounds (or gated communities) where most foreigners and the Filipino elite lived. They were under surveillance twenty four hours a day and manned by security guards with guns. This at first shocked us a bit but eventually we became accustomed to them patrolling the streets. Some householders also engaged their own security guards.

The gardener Rudy and the driver Justin were employed by the Company while the others were employed by the tenants on holiday. Accustomed as I was to doing all my work in the UK and enjoying cooking as I did I would visit the kitchen regularly. Within a week cook decided she could not have me in her domain and said she would go and return only when her mistress returned. I asked Nora, the number one girl, if she would do the cooking but she refused saying she did not like this work. I had the same luck with the other inside maid. Lucy came to the kitchen and excitedly offered her service "Ma'am, I, Lucy cook, you teach me and I cook Filipino very good!" I had taken a liking to Lucy and accepted as long as they would share all the work amongst the three of them. Lucy spoke very little English but she was a very bright girl who wanted to improve her status.

For the first meal she cooked I asked her to make a Filipino dish. It turned out quite delicious. The cook had always served at table so this time Lucy did and as she approached us to serve she would say "Cus cus." Intrigued, I asked what she meant. "Ma'am, I don't know but cook said it all the time when serving." We had to laugh. "Lucy, the cook said excuse me. OK?" She gave us one of her beautiful big smiles and off she went. Nora came to tell me that her husband, a seaman, was arriving at the weekend for a few days and she would like to go to meet him. I told her to go for four or five days. However she did not return on the day she should have but the following day. Annoyed, I asked her why she had let me down "I missed the bus ma'am. Sorry!" I looked at her and said "I will not have you telling me lies, I don't like lies, if you wanted to stay a day longer you could have called me!" "Sorry ma'am, my husband only went back to the ship today." "Well, if you had asked I would have given you time off!" "Oh ma'am, I didn't ask because Filipino ladies never say yes!" "OK but remember I am not a Filipino lady!" The servants were not allowed to stay out overnight so when Lucy went out on her day off she was expected back in the evening but she did not appear. Next day she said that she too had missed her bus. I was furious and she also was annoyed so that for a few days she would not talk to me and even tried to avoid me. I cornered her and then laughingly she said "Ma'am is not angry with me anymore?" "No Lucy, but don't lie to me again!"

The custom was for the servants to receive as part payment rice by the sack and dried fish as well as other fish specialities. It really was not enough but Jack ordered that I should keep to what we had been told to do by the Company. One day I entered the kitchen and found the servants eating the leftovers from our plates and sharing one fried egg between the three of them. To hell with the custom I thought. I wasn't having anyone work for me and going hungry. I increased the amount of food cooked for us and then told them they could share. I hadn't broken the rules since the food was leftovers but not from our plates.

Amazingly enough I discovered that the Puerto Rican girl who had told me to clean my Baldrich house by hosing it down was also in Manila and although we had not seen much of her in Puerto Rico she became very friendly. Kim's two young boys were studying as boarders in the UK. Kim asked me to join her and a group of Spanish speaking girls at her club. The girls were talking about the party their husbands were attending that night. None of the wives had been invited as the men would be entertained by hostesses. Surprised I asked why and I was informed that all the various companies' parties were like this. Then they started saying how at some of these parties the hostesses stripped and took rolled dollar bills held in the men's hand with their sex organ. Amazed I asked how was this done and then in detail I was told how the men rolled the bill around their middle finger and this was 'sucked' in by the girl's vagina. Furthermore I was also informed that they would insert a peeled banana, cut it with their sex organ muscle, and throw it out in pieces. The piece-de-resistance however was that they smoked cigarettes with their vagina. At this I laughed. "Can you imagine girls, anyone for a smoke?" and then I opened my legs. Quiet and thinking about this I spoke up again "Perhaps girls, we should learn some of their tricks, think of what they can do to our husbands if any of them get the chance!" I didn't think I would like this place and I could see my mother was as usual right about what she had warned me.

I started going to meet Jack for lunch and then picking him up from the office so that he would not be led astray. I was getting too apprehensive and at the end I thought 'what the hell, if you cannot trust him, he is not worth it' but it still worried me.

The Company, as was the norm, gave a farewell/welcome party for the Company man who was leaving and for Jack who was replacing him. Everyone in the Company was asked. Several of the guests warned Jack and me that Jack's future secretary, Hattie, had tried with her two previous bosses without success to get them involved with her. She was nothing like the type to whom Jack had always been attracted. She had a flat ugly face, she was flat chested and had the disturbing habit of burping right into your face. Could she really be found attractive by any sane man? But one can never under estimate the power of persuasion and artificial sweetness. It was unfortunate that the girls were badly paid and were unable to travel even with their passports, therefore any European man regardless of age or appearance was like a prince charming to them. Once they could involve a man, get married and secure a foreign passport they were off leaving him behind. I am of course generalizing as there were good and decent girls too like everywhere else in the world, however the rotten ones seemed to predominate the society we had now come to share. Even the President and his wife were involved in sexual scandals from what I was told.

Time was going fast and it seemed we could not get a house in any of the villages. We had apparently arrived when the price of rentals was going up. It was a pity that the General Manager's wife did not have a profession of her own, other than being a manager's wife, and she felt she could also manage the wives. They lived in Forbes Park village and 'Matron' or 'Mother Superior' as she was referred to by the wives of the expatriate staff, did not want any of the other staff living in the same area. Since Forbes Park was one of the original and earliest villages I had found several houses at favourable rentals but they were always turned down. So was another house in a lesser village, this was because it had a swimming pool and the 'matron' didn't have one! The three months were up and we found ourselves without a house to go to. We were obliged to go into one of the Gilarmi transient apartments in Urdaneta which was not comfortable and in dire need of renovation. Nothing worked and I had to stop Jack from throwing the television from the 13th floor into the pool! Nerves were not at their best.

When time came for us to leave the holiday house, Lucy had said she wanted to come with us in a rather sweet way that touched me greatly "Ma'am, when you go, Lucy goes with you. Lucy likes you very much, as a matter of pact (most Filipinos pronounce the 'p' as an 'f' and vice versa) I love you". On hearing this I agreed to take her with me once the employer came home and she had served out a month's notice. Things did not work like this as the lady was furious, rang me up, insulted me for taking her maid and refused to give Lucy the permit that would allow her to take out her things from the village. I had to go and fetch Lucy in our car in order to get her things as Lucy refused point blank to remain in the house. So we had Lucy in the apartment too. At long last, after my saying that I would return to the UK with Lyana who was not too happy with the weather there, we were allowed to take a house in San Lorenzo Village which I fell in love with and felt it would be a 'happy house'.

We had just moved into this house when Jack came home looking very worried. "Remember the cargo boat you and Lyana were going to travel on from England to get here? Well, it has disappeared!" Shocked at this news I asked "What do you mean disappeared?" "Yes, gone, no trace of the ship or crew, you and Lyana would have gone too!" We were told later it had been lost with all hands during a severe typhoon.

Hattie hung around the house trying to befriend Lyana, who did not like her. She joined the Philippine British Society where Jack was one of the Directors and she became a pain in the neck. All the men in Manila were called 'Sir' so Jack became Sir Armstrong without a knighthood as did all the other men and how they enjoyed it too! Then the business parties started and since Jack was the General Sales Manager and this station a much more important one they would be many and frequent. I didn't care a bean what Celedonio said or did not say, but after Jack went a couple of times without me I was determined to cure this once and for all. The next time I was informed that Jack had to go to a party I turned to him and sarcastically but very sweetly said "Sir, I too have been invited to one in the Peninsular Hotel!" "But, you cannot go!" said Jack worriedly. "Why not, you said the girls invited were all very nice, decent girls. I have been invited, like the married girl who brought you home the other day, and I am going!" Jack did not believe me. The next day I went to the beauty salon, had a body massage, facial, sauna, and my hair done – I prepared like the Filipino ladies did. I arrived home and dressed to kill with high heel shoes, tight fitting black trousers, a very low cut black blouse with a huge red rose attached, I waited for Jack. When he returned from the office to change for his party he stared at me and said "Good Lord, where are you going like that?" "Don't you remember? I told you, Jack, I am going to the party near to where you are going" "But I need the car" he said. "OK Jack, you take the car, I shall call a taxi" I replied. His response was "Listen, why don't we meet and go for dinner? You keep the car. I'll call for a taxi." "Alright Jack, that will be nice!" "Eight o'clock then, will that be OK for you, Ly?" "Good Lord no, the party starts at 7.00pm and I won't have long enough there. Anyway you always stay until late, what will your friends say?" "Then we will make it for 8.30pm. You'll pick me up won't you?"

Arrangements finalized I got into the car and drove off. Where to go? I could not return to the house where the girls, (by now we had Lucy and Lita) were bound to say something and I hadn't been asked to any party. I went to visit a Brazilian friend Suely instead. I knocked at her door and when she saw me she exclaimed "Where are you going, dressed so beautifully?" "I have come to see you!" Naturally she didn't believe me and when I explained what I was aiming at she agreed that it was time that we wives should get together against the male chauvinistic treatment worked out by the Filipino males. She who neither smoked, nor allowed anyone to smoke in her house, asked me for a cigarette and nearly killed herself puffing smoke onto my clothes so that I would smell as if I had been to a party. A couple of drinks later, I left her house and drove to where Jack would be. It wasn't even eight but I saw Jack was already there waiting for me but as he hadn't seen me I let him wait for half an hour more. For the next party both Lyana and I got dressed to go with Jack and since I had phoned a couple of my friends who were also determined to go with their husbands we all arrived at the Company's get together. How we spoilt the fun for the males! From then onwards most of the expatriate wives were present at all the parties.

Lyana enrolled at an interior design and decoration course after leaving the university in Manila which she classified as a high school and had hated attending. We rented a piano for her and she loved playing all the time. The weather was however causing her some health problems and we wondered whether she would be able to stay for the whole tour there which in total would be for four years with a break after two.

I joined the Spanish speaking circle which was open to anyone who spoke Spanish and also the Latin American circle where I was accepted because of the length of time I had lived in South America. Practically all embassy wives were members and we soon enjoyed a fine selection of friends. When I told them I was going to start keep- fit classes at home they all wanted to join and I soon found myself working an hour daily doing what I enjoyed most. My classes became so popular that I ended up working three hours a day five days a week and with a long waiting list. When 'Matron' found out she came to see me and told me that I should not be working, that it was not right. I retorted that since what I was doing was not indecent and the people were all outstanding citizens in both foreign and local society I did not think I was doing anything wrong. "But, you should be coming over to my house to roll bandages for the Red Cross" she exclaimed. I figured that if she wanted to do this she had a perfect right to do so but not at the expense of the other wives' time. I had already involved myself with an orphanage where I drove out every so often delivering sacks of rice, toys and sweets for the children. I did this without asking anyone for help, so I told her this. I did however agree to go once a week to her morning coffees! What a sacrifice I made.

Although Lyana after a short time had made good friends she was really not too happy so we decided that the best thing was for her to return to the UK and resume her studies at university. Once she graduated from her course and her stint with Qantas Airways to learn about the trade as an unpaid student, Jack arranged for the two of us to return to England.

In England we stayed at the Exiles Club while we looked for an apartment for Lyana and found out about the universities. She was accepted by the University of London and we found suitable accommodation nearby. So we rented a car and went to see Granny Armstrong in the North of England before my return to Manila and she to her studies and work.

When I returned to Manila everything was different without Lyana to share experiences. I did not feel like accompanying Jack to outings arranged by the Philippine British Society and when I finally agreed to go I found that Hattie monopolized Jack all the time and always managed to get into any photographs taken of us. People too were noticing her behaviour. When I complained Jack said it was my imagination. One day when I was working at home he came to me, put his arms around me and said "Oh Ly, I do love you, you are such a good woman and yet I have been thinking of leaving you for the last couple of years!" I know I had walked out with Lyana several times during our married life but always returned, yet I had never ever considered leaving Jack, it was just impetuous reaction in anger or of being badly upset by him. Hearing Jack's words was like having a bucketful of iced water poured over me. I felt cut inside by razor blades. It hurt, how it hurt, and to think that I had never been aware of his feelings was even worse. I felt I did not want him to touch me, look at me or even see me. I couldn't stand the thought of sharing a bed and I became ill. I could not sleep, I could not eat, I would vomit even a cup of tea. I lost a lot of weight and at the end a friend (her husband was having an affair with his secretary so she was leaving him for good and returning home to the UK) took me to Dr. Augusto Camara who cared and looked after me. I had to remain in bed and it was Lucy who never left my side cooking nice things for me and keeping me company as during the night I was sedated and pep pills given me during the day. All the long summer school holidays I spent convalescing. Dr. Camara called Jack to his surgery and spoke to him. I never found out what he said to him. Jack would come home early every day and take me for short walks until finally I was physically well enough again to restart the keep fit classes once the holidays ended. In fact exercising made me forget and become normal again. Professionally I was doing amazingly well, doctors sent me post-natal patients, menopause women with problems and there was my own group of young women wanting to look good. The university sent me some of their teachers to find out about my method and I was interviewed for newspapers and magazines. My Sexometric Method of Exercise was becoming very popular and whenever any fashion models came to Manila I always had them coming to me. Juerg Tuescher, the husband of one of my star pupils, in Manila overseeing the building of the Manila Mandarin Hotel asked if I would consider setting up and running their health club once the hotel was completed. I was delighted and said I would consider the possibility.

Lyana was going to have her twenty-first birthday in March and was flying back to celebrate with us. She also told us that she had been seeing a lot of a young man we had both met while at St Mary's College and was fond of. Our baby was growing up. It was lovely having her back and hearing all the news. She did not like where she lived and she was giving up her studies to work for Qantas airline. She loved the tourist trade and this was what she eventually wanted to graduate in. I decided to return to England with her and try to get her into our Hampton house. I flew back and after visiting lawyers was able to get the tenants out of the house as it was needed for our daughter. She installed herself in the downstairs where she had her own shower and toilet, bedroom, lounge and dining room and had two Qantas girlfriends live upstairs each with their own bedroom, sharing the bathroom and a sitting room and the three of them sharing the kitchen. The girls' rental was almost sufficient to cover our mortgage so all was fine. I returned to Manila happy knowing that she was back at Cardinal's Walk, with her piano, which she never played when alone, and Cachita to keep her company.

Lucy was indeed a joy to have around me. Since my being sick she never left me alone. She was like 'Mary's little lamb' as she followed me everywhere and if I were alone writing she would come and sit next to me polishing metal, or doing some other work. If I was sewing she would sit and help me and if I stayed too long in the bathroom she would come, knock at the door and solicitously ask "Are you okay, Ma'am?" One day when I had taken to doing metal pictures by panel beating I started banging and making a lot of noise, the poor thing rushed to me asking "Are you alright Ma'am?" and on seeing what I was doing rather dramatically exclaimed "Oh, you artists!" I enjoyed my last hobby. I would draw a picture and then with chisel and hammer I would finish the work which I aged once it was ready. It had a terrific effect and the owner of the framing shop actually asked me to do a big supply for he could sell them for me at his gallery. I refused and told him I'd rather give them to my friends as presents. It gave me the greatest of satisfaction as every time I used the hammer I was beating away all the evil I had encountered.

I occasionally used bicarbonate of soda when I cleaned my teeth as I was told that it would keep them white and fresh. One day, however, I was recommended by a friend to use the bicarbonate of soda for my personal hygiene. I had filled up the bidet and noticing that I had run out of the product I called Lucy to bring me some. When she came to the bathroom and saw that I had the water in the bidet she looked startled and shocked "Oh ma'am, you poor thing, you have teeth down there?" she asked very concerned. I don't know how I kept my face straight as I asked her "Why, Lucy, have you any?" We both had a good laugh.

Another time she came to me and said "Ma'am, my breasts are too small, how can I make them bigger?" Jokingly I said "You get yourself a pail, put plenty of water and stand in it, you cross your arms in front of you and press your elbows. Here, like this and say I must, I must, I must increase my bust, all the time" teaching her the movements. I did not think any more of it until Lita came to me some days later and said "Ma'am I think there is something wrong with Lucy, every day she stands in a pail of water, makes movements and speaks!"

One Christmas at a party we gave at home for all Jack's employees Celedonio brought a ready cooked suckling pig. Taking it to the kitchen I told Lucy to place it on a silver tray where first she had to put some shredded lettuce leaves and decorate it with thin slices of tomatoes. Then as an afterthought I asked "Have we any apples in the fridge?" When shown one I instructed "Lucy, wash it well and then when you bring it to the dining room put an apple in the mouth!" Lucy nodded. A while later she came and called me to the side and whispered "Ma'am, must I put the apple in my mouth?" "Good Lord, Lucy no, in the pig's mouth!"

One day we heard desperate miaowing in the garden and we found that someone had thrown a plastic bag over the fence with a poor little kitten inside. I went mad, the kitten was terrified and a poor sight. When Jack came home we drove to the vet who after an examination said it would be fine given the right attention. We took the kitten home and carried out his advice. It was a female cat and we christened her Tiddles. The poor dear was anything but attractive, she had barely any tail, and her paws were not normal but she was extremely loving and friendly and we loved having her about. Lucy cooked Tiddles' food Filipino style with vinegar and always insisted on feeding her. One morning I heard quite a commotion and I discovered Lucy on the other side of the porch behind the wire mosquito netting passing the cats food in front of her nose but Tiddles couldn't, of course get to it. Lucy's face was rather a picture on being caught in the act. We reckoned Tiddles was a bit retarded and her body too was different from other cats as her bottom was held much higher than the rest of the body. Soon a tom-cat started hanging about but poor Tiddles did not know what it was all about. At first the tom-cat ignored her. Then there was a most extraordinary happening as Tiddles sensually gyrated in front of the male, slinking on the floor in a most inviting way and then when not producing any reaction she practically sat on the male's face. It was quite a seductive scene. Unable to stand any more of it he tried to mount her but was unsuccessful because of Tiddles defect and left her in a pitiful state. As soon as we could we took her back to the vet so that she could be doctored and thus avoid her any more frustrations.

A good thing we all liked cats for soon afterwards another cat turned up at the house. We could see it was male and was very hurt but he would not let us go near him. I ordered that food be left for him and we noticed that every day he came, ate and went away. I would ask Lita or Lucy "Has Charlie Boy eaten today?" and so he was given that name. Eventually he allowed me to get near and stroke him and as soon as he became docile enough to trust me I put him in the cat's basket and with Jack took him to the vet. The vet's secretary, a new one, asked "What is his name?" "Charlie Boy" I said. She opened the box and probably expecting to see a pedigree cat said "It is only a native cat!" in a rather derogatory way. I looked sweetly at her and asked "What are you, aren't you also a native Filipina?" If looks could kill I would have been dead by now! On seeing the cat the vet marvelled at his being alive. Apparently he had been pierced through his stomach by an iron garden fence. We were warned that there was nothing to be done but to make his last days happy and comfortable. One day, poor Charlie Boy disappeared just as he had come and we reckoned he had found a place to die.

The Filipino women were causing havoc to the Company's expatriate wives. A French lady, who was young and pretty, with two young children, but tired of her husband's misbehaviour, tried to knife him. Another, poor Kim, phoned me early one morning and said "Ana Lydia, please come, please come quickly, the cherubim are coming to take me away!" I got dressed and went to her house in the same village. She was in a pitiful way and I had to take her to the hospital with a nervous breakdown. Her husband in the company of those fast women would ring her up from the dirty clubs and say "Honey, listen, they are playing our song!" So many marriages were broken. We were really living in a den of iniquity! These Filipino girls definitely knew how to play their games to embroil men and steal husbands away from the poor wives.

Lyana wrote to remind us that soon it would be our silver wedding anniversary and that we had promised her that we would remarry and she would be our bridesmaid. With the way I was feeling with all that had happened only a few months back I was not too enthusiastic about this. I mentioned what Lyana had written about to some of my Filipino friends and they became very enthusiastic about my celebrating the event. As some of them had married during the war and were not able to have a big wedding in those turbulent days they had gone overboard celebrating their twenty-fifth, but I had had a lovely wedding! Before I knew it I was being organized. Rosita a pupil and friend, the owner of a dress designing atelier was determined to make my dress, off white with silver threads and she was also going to be my matron of honour. Jorge, an Argentinean was the best man, Lyana the bridesmaid and Jess, Jack's new assistant was Lyana's companion, (Celedonio was now a political prisoner having voiced his opposition to martial law which was then in force). We always had three musicians come to play at the parties we gave at home but unfortunately they had a previous engagement which they could not cancel. Jack seemed quite happy about it all and we became the main topic of conversation amongst all our friends and business contacts. Some argued that having been together for twenty five years why did we now bother to get married. The Papal Nuncio was keen to see us married since we had a daughter so it would be good to legalize our union and have the church's blessings! No matter how often we insisted we were legally married many still disbelieved!

Before our anniversary day the Company had held a big celebration party and when after much persuasion Jack got up to dance with me and we were both enjoying the dancing, Jack suggested asking the orchestra as perhaps they or some of them could come to our house where we would be entertaining one hundred guests. We stopped dancing and I walked to the leader. I hadn't taken more than a minute for he was unable to accept a contract. I turned round and lo and behold Jack was not waiting for me but instead he was dancing with Hattie and her partner was waiting to dance with me! By the time I returned to the table I was ready to murder her and Jack too. It had taken me a lot of cajoling for him to get up and dance but he was not able to refuse Hattie. When I said "If she comes near here again I shall forget I am a lady and in front of everyone I will throw a dish with food over her". All Jack said was "Let's go home!"

From this event onwards I had no feelings about our celebration. What did I have to celebrate? I felt like a cheat going to church when I had so much hate in my heart, it was being pure hypocrisy and nothing else. Caught as I felt I was, I decided that this time I would plan what I was going to do, and diligently went about arranging it.

Fefa, a very dear friend and wife of a South American Ambassador was a few years older than me and caught me by surprise one day. She arrived home and said "Well. Lydia, what have you been doing that I haven't heard from you at all. What is wrong? I know you and I know that you are up to something!" "Fefa, I have been busy with all the arrangements for the celebration and Lyana will be arriving in a couple of day's time too, so I've had lots to do." "You think I'm a fool? Out with it." she replied. I started to cry and told her that I could not stay in Manila any more, that I could not stand Hattie and the way Jack did not bother to send her to hell, he kept on swearing that there was nothing between them but all was so terribly confusing and hurtful and I had had enough. "As soon as Lyana returns to England I shall leave as well" I told her. "You are going to England?" "No, Fefa, I am organizing everything to go to the USA. I have two job opportunities and somewhere to live until settled." "My dear girl, you are crazy, what are you thinking of? Here you have a lovely home, servants, people that care and Jack, Yes Lydia, Jack loves you. You only have to see the way he looks at you. If you go to the States you will be alone, working hard, and if you need a man, young as you are, you'll have to look for one. Here you have Jack. You have a flourishing business and the prospect of a great job with the Mandarin Hotel. Why do you want to destroy yourself and lose all you have? Think, woman, think, don't be such a bloody fool!"

Suddenly, I grew up. What Fefa was saying made a lot of sense. Jack and I were two individuals with no blood connection. We had a daughter together. Jack did not belong to me nor I to Jack, we were together so far because we wanted to be and had had a great love for each other. Nothing really belonged to any of us. We have things and people with us temporarily, the children have their own lives and just like I had made my own decision to leave home it had not stopped me from loving my parents. From now on I would invest more time on myself and all that I enjoyed and what would be would be. I would go to church and thank God for what I had and for the new beginning that I was going to make seeing marriage in a different way. I would cease to use the word 'my' so strongly and meaningfully. Having taken this decision, I went to my room and cried until I cleansed myself. It is being made to look a fool that hurts the most!

On November 17th 1974 we had the church and house celebration and what an affair it was. What I had not had the first time I was married I did have this time. A beautician and hairdresser came to make me 'look good' as they said. I hadn't made any arrangements, they just appeared. The photographer came home just to photograph my wedding dress and accessories, it was really comical. Rosita came home to dress me and arrange a pink veil with a cabbage rose on my head and this I hated. Jack and I were so nervous we went into church through the wrong door. Worst of all were the guests, they were all so emotional and some were crying because 'we looked so young and yet had shared so many years together'.

Funnily enough Jack arranged for a friend of his to offer Hattie a job with Cathay Pacific Airways (and several months later when next I met her by chance she was still single and still looking for someone else's husband.) It had happened too late when I no longer let it bother me. I was enjoying my life going out as much as possible with my girl friends and getting involved in many things.

Another Company's man had now taken his mistress to his house and the wife, not knowing what to do or where to go had put up with it but at the same time she was having affairs with various Company local employees who were only too delighted to boast about their conquest. All this was to spite her husband but she was also belittling herself.

Chapter 32

MABUHAY

Soon it was time for our mid- term get away back to the UK. It seemed incredible that so much had happened in the relatively short time of two years. Both Lucy and Lita remained in our house in Manila as we were to return there. It was lovely being back in the UK and seeing our friends. Lyana and Al got engaged. We met his parents who we liked very much and then Jack and I went to Gibraltar where we spent some of our holiday. It was lovely catching up with all the family and meeting young nephews and nieces. My brother Winston had married Vickie and already had a boy Dominic and a girl Velda. Winston worked with Dad while Vickie stayed at home (looking after the children). Lottie was still teaching and now had a boy James and a girl Carla. Her husband Jaime was in the same Company as Jack but as a local employee. Lina was now Head of the Physiotherapy Department in St Bernard's Hospital and Jon was Editor of the Gibraltar Chronicle. Their daughter was called Marisa and the son had been christened Dominique. After the short stay in Gibraltar we went to visit Jack's Mum in Durham and then my parents came from Gibraltar to visit us in Hampton and later my sister Clementina and her family. She was teaching in Twickenham and now had three children, Vandra, Martin and Gavin. The 'family' was certainly on the increase. The vacation away from all the depravity had done us all good and we were happy together and a close family again.

Back in Manila Lucy and Lita were delighted to have us there again and I looked forward to starting my classes and other activities once more. During one of Lyana's visits we had participated in a big Filipino show called Daupang-Palad organized by the Philippine Normal College Faculty Association with Madame Imelda Marcos the First Lady and Acting Secretary of Foreign Affairs Manuel Collantes as patrons. Eleven embassies and six cultural societies participated. Lyana, I and three of my pupils took part representing Brazil by dancing a Samba and Italy by a lively Tarantella.

The two girls who had shared our house in England had left and after having had us at home Lyana now felt very lonely so I asked Lucy if she wanted to go with me to England and stay in our house with Senorita. Without thinking about it twice she accepted not even asking what terms she would have. She was such a trusting and wonderful girl and still looked in her teens even though she was in her late twenties. Although it was difficult to get her a working permit we found that if we took her as part of our family she would be allowed to travel so with some delays this was arranged.

As time got nearer I took Lucy shopping for as heavy a coat as I could find in the shops in Manila and also had one of my real winter ones altered to fit her. "Oh Ma'am, it's too hot for Lucy" she said. "Lucy, it is very cold in England and you will definitely need warm clothes". "What is cold, Ma'am?" She asked mystified. "Cold is like the iced water inside the fridge, or like being inside the fridge" both Jack and I replied. She nodded her head and walked away. Suddenly Jack and I looked at each other, got up, and ran to the kitchen. We had had the same thought. Lucy would not be so silly as to get inside the fridge, would she? No, Lucy was pouring iced water over her arm! We then had to teach Lucy how to use the cutlery since her normal habit was to use her fingers and occasionally a spoon. She was very bright and intelligent and was soon even drinking tea with her little finger held out like she had seen in a film!

I was invited by Swiss Air to an inaugural flight from Zurich to Strasburg and so I travelled from Manila first class, courtesy of the airline. Lucy sat just behind the first class section. It was snowing on arrival at Zurich and Lucy's face and reaction was absolutely priceless. "Oh Ma'am, look, snow like on the Christmas tree, it's wet Ma'am". Everything was a novelty to her and I felt enriched to be sharing her new experiences. Unfortunately she had to travel alone from Zurich to England and before takeoff we both had a really bad time as she held on to me and cried like a baby. The airline people were very kind and they promised to 'look after my little girl'. Lyana was at the airport in London to meet her.

By the time I joined her in the UK she had settled down quite well and to my surprise she enjoyed best of all the foggy weather! She had to learn not to call everyone ma'am, I became Mum, and the other ladies would be Mrs. Men were not called 'Sir' any more but only 'Mr' when appropriate. She listened to all attentively and was soon in command of herself and those who tried to be too personal. I returned to Manila leaving both Lyana and Lucy very happy and sharing Cachita's attention and love.

Back in Manila, Lita was now our chief maid and cook and a new girl, Gliseria. was employed to share the housework and do the laundry. Poor Tiddles had missed Lucy for her vinegary food and missed me for her care. She soon realized that Lucy wasn't coming and finally began to eat well again.

It seemed I had only arrived back when Lyana wrote saying she and Al wanted to get married. We managed to phone her to see what she wanted. Was it to be a Filipino wedding in Manila or was it to be in England? To our surprise she said that if she was to marry in church she would only do so at St Joseph's in Gibraltar where her grandparents and her parents had married otherwise it would only be a civil wedding. I returned briefly to Gibraltar to make arrangements and left my sister Lina to take care of things in my absence. In July 1975 Lyana and Al were married. We took the opportunity of Jack having business to see to in Europe so he was able to be at his daughter's wedding beforehand. Lyana and Al were married at St Joseph's and wore typical Filipino clothes which caused quite a sensation. Gibraltar's Chief Minister, Sir

Joshua Hassan, in a short speech remarked with tongue in cheek that had he known that the family would all be wearing open necked shirts he would not have worn his suit. He was referring of course to the men's 'barong tagalog', the Philippine national dress. Their wedding was celebrated in the Garrison Library Gardens and was the first time for a long period that these premises were used for such an event. I travelled with Jack to Madrid and Rome but then preferred to return to Hampton for the extra time Jack had to do business in a couple of other European countries and waited for him to join me to return to Manila.

I busied myself in all sorts of activities even modelling national dresses for the Italian Embassy. I also performed in the Manila Theatre Guild production of Garcia Lorca's 'House of Bernarda Alba' where I played the part of Prudencia. This was my first straight acting appearance and I enjoyed the new experience. Although I was invited to take the main part in their next production 'Butterflies are Free' I did not accept. I realized that I enjoyed my dancing best of all and I found the responsibility of remembering all my lines and giving correct cues too distressing.

Not long after our return I went to the doctors and what I had thought was the 'change of life' turned out to be another pregnancy. On hearing the news I cried "I am too old for this. Jack only has seven more years left with the Company, how can I be pregnant?" The doctor calmly said "If you are not too old to conceive you are not too old to have your child". "Can you guarantee I will not miscarry again, that the baby will be well, that I shall be alright?" "I cannot guarantee anything" was the reply. In a way I was thrilled to be expecting again, as was Jack, but we were both worried and scared of the possible consequences. When I spoke to Fefa of our worries she arranged for me to go and visit her own gynaecologist, a professor in whom she had a lot of faith. The gynaecologist upon hearing my clinical history and loss of eight babies said he would give me an injection if I so desired. It would not do me or the baby any harm if all was in order but if anything was not quite right, I would miscarry. I lost the baby that same day.

Jack and I were closer than we had been for a long time and we were able to laugh and share much time together. I had started a painting collection and loved the work of Mabini Street artist Paco Garospe and we often went downtown together in search of his works. One day as I was getting into our car a young woman accosted Jack. I saw him laugh and she went away. "What did she want?" I asked him. "She offered me a 'quicky' and when I told her you were my wife she told me to get rid of the 'old bag' and return to her." Just as well I had not heard for she would have felt my bag on her! But we had a good laugh. Filipino men did not have much facial or body hair and Jack with a moustache and beard was reckoned to be a real sex prodigy! If a local man had a hair or two on his chin he would cultivate them as precious gold.

Kim was out of the hospital but lonely as her husband never changed. She was amazed when visiting her doctor she was told that if she needed a man there was a club where only top local professional men would only be too happy to meet with her or any of her friends and arrange a sexual weekend any time! All expenses incurred by the man! They seemed to think of everything!

By now Dr Camara and his wife, who had become very good friends, arranged for a personal assistant to help me with all the work I had with my classes and other commitments. Connie was a lovely, charming and competent girl just out of secretarial college and her engagement offered me a more comfortable time at a slower tempo. I hated the secretarial work which was in addition to my physical work so life was made much easier.

Time had passed rather rapidly and happily this second half of our term in Manila. We had gone to visit several beauty spots and had by now a number of good friends in both local and expatriate communities. Juerg Tuescher renewed his offer for me to set up the Mandarin Health Club. I accepted and signed the contract. This time although we were expecting to return to the Philippines for another period we had to pack up and leave our heavy luggage in storage in accordance with the Company rules. We told Lita and Gliseria that we would keep in touch and when we returned we would have them back once again if they should desire and we found Tiddles a new home. Since Connie had proved to be such a conscientious worker Jack was pleased to recommend her for employment in the Company. In June 1976 we left for England.

Lucy who by now had become quite good in English and had made good friends at the sewing circle where I had enrolled her was delighted to see us. She had kept the house and garden in perfect shape and life with her in the house was quite a luxury. Jack and I decided to go overland to Gibraltar. It had been a long time since we had visited Spain and we were delighted to see the many improvements. We had a shock when on stopping to buy fruit we found the price had soared up beyond belief. I remember explaining to the vendor "For this price I could buy a whole case of peaches!" His laughing reply was "One can see you've been away for a long time!" People were freer and women liberated. When we arrived home and told my parents how we enjoyed this new up and coming prosperous Spain Dad in disbelief said "It's all propaganda Chamaca, it's what they want you to see." "Dad, we weren't curtailed as to our movements. We were free to go wherever we wanted." Dad would not accept that Spain could improve so much while the frontier with Gibraltar remained closed.

Chapter 33

NEW ARRANGEMENTS

Then came the news. We were not returning to Manila, instead Jack was promoted and transferred to Hong Kong as Commercial Manager, the senior overseas marketing appointment. Towards the end of 1976 we arrived in Hong Kong. I could not break my contract with the Manila Mandarin Hotel so both Jack and I knew we would have to separate until the health club opened and was well established. We still had a few months to go before this happened so we enjoyed our stay at the Excelsior Hotel and waited to be allocated a house. Jack's seniority entitled us to a detached house in the area where other senior staff members lived but we opted to take an apartment in the Mid-levels area where we would have a more private life and was a more convenient location for his work.

The apartment in Magazine Gap was beautiful and we enjoyed a most marvellous view overlooking the harbour and Kowloon. It was very big and bright and I fell in love with it as soon as I saw it. While living in the hotel I was asked if I wanted light or dark coloured furniture and I was given the opportunity to choose curtains and other furnishings. It was all very civilized. The day before we had to move, since we had already been given the keys we decided to go and see the apartment. On walking in we noticed all the furniture was of light wood. I wondered why, if they had given me the choice and I had stated my preference for the dark colour, they had then given me the wrong colour. Frustrated and remembering my psychiatrist cousin's words of advice I kicked whatever I found in my way and returned relaxed to the hotel. The trick apparently had worked! During the night my foot throbbed and I was unable to sleep. By morning it was swollen and extremely painful. Jack took me to the Company doctor. When asked how I had done this, the toe was fractured, Jack told him that I had stumbled against a rock. As we were leaving the Doctor said "My wife stumbled against that same rock when we arrived!" We had to laugh. The worst part, which also taught me a lesson, was that when we did move into our apartment next day all the furniture had been changed to dark wood just as I had requested! I didn't kick anything this time! I couldn't complain either, we had gone to look a day too early.

We asked Lita if she wanted to come and work for us in Hong Kong and since she agreed only too eagerly we arranged her papers for her. At the beginning of 1977 I was required to transfer to Manila leaving Jack behind. It was the very first time I was to be on my own. I had mixed feelings, excited at being able to prove myself and worried in case I would not be capable of carrying out my job. I had a beautiful suite given me and I was free to use any of the restaurants and choose whatever I wanted. My laundry was taken care of and the only expense I would have would be for drinks. I had executive medical aid and a limousine at my disposal. It really made me feel good and the excitement of it all made my being alone less frightening. Jack arranged to visit me at least one weekend a month and could stay with me at no expense paying only sixty percent of the food bill. I also had an expatriate salary which made me feel rather rich! I must admit it was very difficult at first to be taking important decisions without having anyone I could discuss them with but eventually as the club, my baby, was taking shape, staff engaged and trained, things became much easier.

As soon as the club was ready I needed a secretary/receptionist and I asked Connie if she would return to work for me at the hotel. It was great having her with me as I knew I could trust her. With her I had three masseuses and a masseur who was called Dr. Agbuya and who gave the most fantastic shiatsu massages. A male instructor and two female instructors all taught my Sexometric method to be used exclusively in our club.

Up to now health clubs in the Philippines were of dubious repute, so we had to be extra careful that we did not give any wrong impression. I made a rule that none of the employees could make dates with house guests and I would never meet with any single male. This caused quite an unpleasant experience for one of my Gibraltarian friends, Sol, who had recently been sent to the Philippines as the Ambassador for Israel. On discovering I was at the hotel he came to visit me. He was obliged to go home, and then with his daughter to return and only then would the hotel receptionist call me! All my ex- pupils joined the club which also offered swimming pool facility and we were, in fact, the one department that actually started making money from the inception of the hotel.

Each morning I would meet with Juerg Tuescher who would inform all of us in managerial positions who would be arriving and where they were from. The Japanese all loved using the Clubs' facilities and in particular the saunas and massages. They were the most uninhibited of all the club guests. If the men's section was too full they never thought anything about walking stark naked into the ladies' section. I had to be on the alert all the time. The Arabs enjoyed saunas too but they had a peculiar way of enjoying them. They all sat on their haunches as naked as when they were born - it was quite a sight, I must say I never had a dull moment. The Health Club did not provide room service and we would get the 'meek' British guest politely asking for this service and when refused would come down to the club in person to enquire further. We all dressed with white coats unless exercising and they would hesitate as to asking what they really wanted to know. One such guest, a middle aged very well spoken man came to enquire and rather nicely asked Connie if the massages we gave were 'happy massages'. Connie politely asked him to wait saying that she would call the manager. On asking him if I could help he asked once again "Are your massages happy ones?" I smiled and answered him very gently "Our massages are excellent ones but we do not sing!" His face was a picture and how fast he walked away.

You get tired of eating always in restaurants no matter how excellent the food. I had Sol and Frances and Fefa's homes to go to eat those lacy fried eggs and crispy bacon or Gibraltarian food I could not get at the Hotel. It was lovely having such good friends and I spent many wonderful hours en famille with Sol's wife Frances, her mother-in-law and their daughter Susan.

Whenever Jack needed me to entertain any visiting dignitary I flew to Hong Kong from Manila to act as hostess. After one such visit, when I returned to Manila I felt happy to be back alone once again. Scared as to my feelings and always honest I phoned Jack to tell him how I felt. It was good to be able to do whatever I wanted without having someone telling me "Don't eat that, it's too late, you'll have indigestion. Turn off the air conditioning." And so on. If I had indigestion it was not because of what I had eaten but because of the aggro at not being able to do what I felt like. When I told Jack he replied "Don't worry, I feel the same way!" "What are we going to do?" I asked. "Please yourself, it's up to you!" Since it did not seem to worry Jack I continued with the work I did so enjoy. Perhaps Jack thought that I would tire and come to terms as I had done all the other times but for once I felt I was really having success with my professional career.

Then I received a telephone call from Lita "Ma'am, I think you better come home." On hearing this I asked "What is it Lita, what has happened?" "I don't know, Ma'am, but Sir goes to the office, comes back for lunch, returns to the office and back home early, he doesn't go out and has photographs of you all over the house!" "Okay Lita, don't say anything to him. I shall arrange matters here and leave as soon as I can." When I returned to Hong Kong without letting Jack know it was really weird to see   photographs all over the place as if I had died. I then decided to propose a new deal to Juerg. I would go for one week every month to Manila since the Club was doing extremely well and everyone knew how to behave. I loved the work but I also realized I loved Jack more and did not want to lose him or have him ill.

One evening the phone rang and when I answered it was Lyana "Mum, I want you to know that Al and I are going to have a baby!" "A baby? But how, Lyana?" "Well Mum, the same way you had me!" She replied with a laugh. I shouted for Jack "Lyana is having a baby, we are going to be grandparents." Jack rushed out still wet from the shower. "Lyana honey, when is this happening?" We were all so very happy and delighted with the good news. Imagine I would have had a baby only a year older than our grandchild had I not miscarried in Manila!

It was while I was working under the new arrangement that my parents came to visit us in Hong Kong and then to the Philippines for a short stay with me. I was there waiting for them but Sol in his capacity as Ambassador was waiting for my parents by the plane. How happy and proud they were to be received with such honours. When my parents returned to Hong Kong with me, I found the three weeks there without being able to work rather boring so I handed in my resignation at the club and decided to remain full time with Jack.

Jack had to go to England on business a few weeks after my parents had to return home which was also a little after the baby was due. It was decided that I accompany my parents to the UK and be there with Lyana for a while before our grandchild was expected. It would be the last chance to have Lyana all to myself. As we arrived at Cardinal's Walk Lucy opened the door and said "Oh mum, Senorita is in the hospital and she is not having the baby!" I asked the taxi-driver to wait and as soon as the luggage was taken into the house I was driven to the hospital. On arrival I found my sister Clem sitting outside looking rather forlorn and I thought the worst. "It's okay Ly, Lyana is in labour but she hasn't had the baby yet. She is early with the birth!" Feeling only slightly more relaxed I entered the hospital. The receptionist on being told that I was there to see my daughter, looked at me and said "Sorry, only her husband or boyfriend can go in." She must have seen the look on my face when I answered "I am her mother and I have just arrived from Hong Kong and I want to see her." "One moment please, I shall see what I can do!" She replied. I was allowed in and Lyana on seeing me said "Oh Mummy" put out her arms and started to cry. "Lyana, darling, don't cry, Mummy is here, nothing will happen, but don't cry or these people will send me away!" Shortly after a baby boy was born. It was September 26th 1977.

Lyana was taken to her room and the baby put next to her. I always loved babies and found them lovely but our new baby looked more like a cat than a child. Lyana stared at him, sleeping with huge hands crossed on top of his chest, and then softly asked "Mummy, will he get any better?" Fascinated by him, I replied "Well darling, he can't get any worse". The sister who was in the room came running to the baby's side and said "Shame on you both, he is a lovely baby" This caused Lyana some embarrassment for the social services visited her at home several times unannounced, perhaps thinking that as we had thought the baby was ugly we would not love him but he became the king of the house and was soon a gorgeous little boy. Apparently he had looked like this because Lyana had had a dry birth and the poor child was severely dehydrated.

When Jack arrived our grandson was christened Anthony John Domingo and a lovely reception was given in his honour by us at the Exiles Club. Lucy was delighted with her baby and was only too pleased to baby sit for Lyana as often as could be. We, Jack and I, returned to Hong Kong.

Alberto, our Gibraltarian friend whom we had met in Nairobi was now living in Hong Kong as was Suely, my Brazilian friend from Manila. Suely had been talking about my classes and I had several ladies waiting for me to start them. Jack suggested we turned our main bedroom which was exceedingly big and bright with an ensuite bathroom into my exercise studio so we had mirrors installed and classes began. RTV television heard about me and invited me to visit them to do a programme for them. I had been on Gibraltar TV every time I visited so I had some idea of what was expected of me. The first series of my programme "Keep Fit with Ana Lydia" successfully started in February 1978. This programme was also dubbed into Chinese for the local viewers. Although I loved being on television I was finding it difficult being a celebrity and I found it rather ridiculous for people to run after me and wave excitedly. I never knew how to react, wave like the Queen or try to ignore them. Right after the first series finished Jack and I returned to England for our mid-tour holiday leaving Lita in Hong Kong to take care of the home.

On our return my second series started in September 1978. I went to a shop with Jack and suddenly the shop owner came out saying "Is it possible, can it be, but it is you Ana Lydia!" I really felt stupid and awkward. My reaction on seeing admirers was to run and it was doing this that I fell and actually ended up being taken to the hospital by the male admirers from whom I was running away! I was hospitalized for ten days and after I returned to finish my contract I decided it was time to say goodbye to the limelight! I did return but only briefly in another programme on my fiftieth birthday to perform a Spanish dance to illustrate that even at that age you could be active and enjoy life. My studio however thrived and I felt much better without being in the limelight. In Gibraltar people seemed to take things lightly and everywhere else I had been I had never felt so restricted in my private life.

At this time we were happy to see that Phillip and Betty from our Kenya days were appointed to Hong Kong in a senior civil service position. Unfortunately we did not get the chance to meet with them. The Hong Kong Mandarin Hotel asked me if I would consider taking over their health club but employed as local staff for the time needed to recover control of all their other health clubs in Asia. Then they would reconsider my contract and I would be in charge of all the clubs having to do a lot of travelling. Jack only had a few months left to serve in Hong Kong and although the plan was for him to return there, after what had happened when I went to Manila, I declined the hotel's offer as I did not want to take any chances of leaving him alone again. He still had another tour to do before retirement. Jack had not been too well while on our mid tour vacation and he was checked by a Harley Street heart specialist who discovered he had suffered three heart attacks and had therefore to take care of himself and take things easy. Hong Kong was taking its toll on him.

We were therefore very happy that our term in Hong Kong was nearly over and that although we had been notified of a return there for Jack's last tour before retiring, we would be having several months vacation, which we would make the best of, particularly now that we had our little grandson to look forward to.

All packed we made our way to the Kai Tak airport and since we had a long wait there we went to the VIP lounge where we knew we could rest and refresh ourselves before the long flight. We had just sat down when three Chinese men entered and sat down near us. The very old gentleman of the trio kept on looking at us with great interest so much so that feeling rather uncomfortable I asked Jack to change places with me. We were just about to move when the youngest one approached us.

In perfect English he excused himself and explained that his granddad was making his last trip to England and was very interested in the yin and yang Chinese philosophy horoscopes and astrology and wondered whether we would mind having our fortune told to us as he found us very intriguing and interesting.

We laughed and since I enjoy these things and now knew why he had been staring we agreed to join them. The venerable old gentleman spoke no English so the grandson translated. Turning to me he said "You are wood, a strong, big, straight tree and your husband is water, my grandfather has studied your faces and wants to know the year of your birth". If it made the old man happy, we were game! When we gave our birthday dates and years the old gentleman shook his head and said rather fast to his grandson, the young man smiled at what was being said. We looked, waiting for an explanation. "My grandfather wants to know if you are newly married." Jack and I smiled and more or less together we replied "Over thirty years ago!" the old man shook his head and seemed rather distressed, or was it amazement! Then he spoke once again. "My grandfather says that you are a snake and your husband a tiger, how can you be together for so many years?" Jack and I laughed as the young man continued "From yin and yang studies the water destroys the wood, they do not go well together. With the snake and the tiger in the Chinese horoscope the snake crushes the tiger, or the tiger kills the snake, they also do not go well together. In the European horoscope you are Taurus, the bull who wants security and loves the home, your husband is Aquarius, the water carrier and water goes whichever way it wants and never in a straight line. All wrong, my grandfather says only a great love and understanding could have kept you two together!"

Once in London Jack decided to ask for early retirement and take life easier and enjoy his grandson. Anthony was growing up into a lively sturdy little boy and with Lyana's permission we decided to take him and Lucy with us to Gibraltar for a holiday. Since we found England remarkably cold and did not envisage staying there permanently we also looked for a place to buy in Gibraltar. There was hardly anything available and the ones we found and visited were small and excessively expensive for what was offered. As the frontier with Spain was still closed we decided to go by ferry to Tangiers and Algeciras to stay in Marbella where we had a beach front studio apartment we had bought while in Hong Kong. Anthony loved all the attention given him particularly by my Dad who thought him to be a real Latin 'macho' boy in every way! We had only been back in the UK for a few months when we heard that Jack's replacement had had a nervous breakdown and had taken early retirement as well.

In England I enjoyed being with Eva and all my Brazilian friends and as soon as I could I started giving my classes again but this time at the local church hall. Our neighbour's son Robert had grown up quite a bit but he still called me Ehlydia. He was no longer the baby of the family as a new sister had been born. Loveday came from Rhodesia to visit relatives and we got together for a few days. Agnes and Johnny also came to see us before settling in South Africa as they found life in Rhodesia no longer bearable and they were getting out before it was too late. My school friends had all married and had established families. Funnily enough Rosina had married Tony, the boy who had whistled at me long before in Madeira. Muriel married an army officer Peter and was now living in Kent and life went on.

We were delighted to receive an invitation from Sol and Frances to the wedding in London of their eldest daughter Donna. It was a lovely wedding and celebrated in great style. We were seated at a table with Frances' family and a young man in his twenties from Gibraltar who reminded me of someone. It was amazing to discover that this young man George was the son of a boy I had had a crush on when a school girl in Madeira. A couple of years older than me George Senior. did not know I existed. Now we found his son enjoyed our company and little did we imagine that a great and lasting friendship would develop between us.

Lucy wanted a salary increase and now with Jack on a pension we could not really afford it. So we arranged her papers so that she could work elsewhere but we still kept in touch and she visited us regularly as Anthony had become like a son to her. In 1982 we had had enough of the cold weather and English style of living and we packed up sending our most treasured furniture that we had picked up throughout our time abroad and put in storage and decided to go to Marbella.

Retirement promised to be good!

Ana Lydia - guest speaker at Makati-Paranaque Medical Society, Manila

Our Silver wedding anniversary in Manila in 1974

Ana Lydia at home with some of her own creations

Lyana and Ainslie's wedding, Philippine style, in Gibraltar

The family at Lyana's wdding reception

PHILIPPINE NORMAL COLLEGE FACULTY ASSOCIATION

in association with the International Embassies of
BRAZIL, CHINA, FRANCE, GREAT BRITAIN, INDIA, INDONESIA, ITALY, JAPAN, SPAIN, THAILAND and the UNITED STATES

DAUPANG-PALAD

BRAZIL

Os 'Pintinhos No Terreiro' (Choro)

Samba is the most typical and best kno___ originating in Brazil. It has a gre___ fluence as can be noted throug___ made by both female and ___

First introduc___ 20, it was only in 1945___ ne appearance of the r___ Miranda, it became popul___ __d.

OS PINTINHOS NO TERREIRO — Choro
Contributed by the Brazilian Embassy

— *Mrs. Ana Lydia Armstrong*
Lyana Patricia Armstrong
Dennis Faustino

___ done in a 2 by 4 tempo and ___ is similar to that of the Rhumba a___ ___velier.

In the early sixties the so-called classical samba became popular and ceased to be of an essentially picturesque nature to slowly tend towards the social message.

an international cultural show

ITALY

The **Tarantella** is a popular dance of Southern Italy that has become a characteristic of the Neapolitan people by tradition. The origin of ___ name is not certain, but according to the et___ of the word, some believe that it coul___ from the name of one of the most ___ Italy, Taranto. Others belie___ hand, that it is derived f___ ___a, whose bite produces ___ feeling stimulating th___ ___ovements. These movem___ ___d the rhythm of this w___ ___e which was also used ___ ___e regions of Italy to c___ ___ bite of the tarantula.

TARANTELLA
Contributed by the Philippine-Italian
Association in cooperation with the
Italian Embassy

— *Mrs. Ana Armstrong*
Mrs. Sofia Raimondi
Mrs. Margarita Tomasini
Mrs. Brenda Histet

___ ___a" is a folkdance in rapid 6/8 ___ n couples and characterized by light, ___ps and tapping foot movements. It has ___ famous since the XIV Century. The artistic quality of the dance has been the source of inspiration for many well-known composers, to mention a few, Liszt, Chopin, Bazzini, Mendelssohn, etc.

ANA LYDIA ARMSTRONG

Ana Lydia who comes from Gibraltar is a qualified slimnastics instructor and a professional dancer. She started dancing at the age of eight and has danced professionally in Rhodesia, Kenya, Brazil and Puerto Rico. In Puerto Rico, she appeared on T.V. and runs a physical-fitness programme. This is her first straight acting part and she brings to it all the expertise of the true professional.

The House of

Bernarda Alba

Housemaid	Louise Villarosa
Prudencia	Ana Lydia Armstrong
Beggar-woman	Xerlita Martin

Federico Garcia Lorca

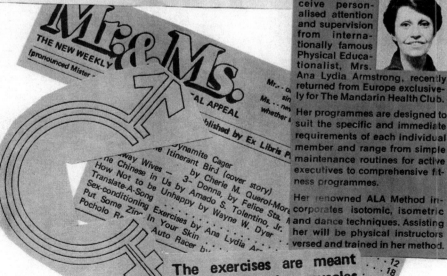

Mr.&Ms.

THE NEW WEEKLY
(pronounced Mister ...

...AL APPEAL

...blished by Ex Libris P...

Mr... o...
Ms. ... sin...
... ne...
whether ...

...e Dynamite Cager
Itinerant Bird (cover story)
...way Wives — by Cherie M. Querol-More...
...e Chinese in Us by 3- Donna, by Felice Sta. ...
How Not to be Unhappy by Amado S. Tolentino, Jr.
Translate-A-Song by Wayne W. Dyer ...
Sex-conditioning Exercises by Ana Lydia Ar...
Put Some Zinc In Your Skin
Pocholo R... Auto Racer b...

The exercises are meant to train the muscles used in the sex act

... 12
... 18
... 20
.. 23
. 24
. 3...

The Manila Mandarin

Makati Avenue – Paseo de Roxas, Makati Tel. 85-78-11

This is your invitation to join one of the most exclusive health clubs in this part of the world. The Manila Mandarin Health Club. Features highly sophisticated physical fitness programmes for ladies and gentlemen conducted in luxurious environment.

Members will receive personalised attention and supervision from internationally famous Physical Educationalist, Mrs. Ana Lydia Armstrong, recently returned from Europe exclusively for The Mandarin Health Club.

Her programmes are designed to suit the specific and immediate requirements of each individual member and range from simple maintenance routines for active executives to comprehensive fitness programmes.

Her renowned ALA Method incorporates isotomic, isometric and dance techniques. Assisting her will be physical instructors versed and trained in her method.

Hongkong Standard

RTV2-English

4.00 PM KUM KUM (new animation series): Set in the Stone Age. The adventures of Kum Kum, an irresistible five-year-old boy, his family, friends and pets.
4.30 KEEP FIT WITH ANA LYDIA (new series): The proper exercise techniques of staying fit and happy.
5.00 FIVE O'CLOCK CLUB (for children):

KEEP FIT PROGRAMME

ANOTHER between the children's programme during week days on RTV2 is one aimed again at women. This is the Keep Fit With Ana Lydia series, a new half-hour programme starting on Wednesday, February 22 at 4.30 pm.

The series is part of the films first introduced to Gibraltar television audiences and which were produced during the host's periodic visits to the rock island where she was born.

The much-travelled Ana Lydia Armstrong started out

as a flamenco dancer then phased out as physical and beauty culturist, the art of which she has been imparting to audiences from Gibraltar itself to Africa, South America and recently in the Philippines.

In Manila where she has a private studio which popularises her keeping fit method, Ana Lydia also gave seminars on physical education at professional level. There, she wrote a book, at pre... manual...

Eve

MORE THAN JUST A PRETTY FACE

Special Focus: Travel

The Flight Stewardess

Causes of Divorce in HK

Women Men Don't Marry

Sex-ercise and Be Happy

Ghosts: Fact or Fiction?

VOL 1 NUMBER 2 AUGUST 1979

MIRROR
10 Hair: How to Make It Behave Beautifully
39 Eve's Shape: Sex-ercise and be Happy *Ana Lydia Armstrong*
42 Eve's Make-up: Face: How to Take It With You

Publisher: M. Mohindar **Editor:** Blanche D. Gallardo **Design Consultant:** Bert Gallardo **Assistant Editor:** Mabel Auyeung **Beauty/Health Consultant:** Ana Lydia Armstrong **London Photographer:** Sam Sawdon **Production Manager:** Timothy Wong **Assistant Production Manager:** Albert Wong **Circulation Manager:** C. W. Charles **Financial Controller:** Brian Liu **Group Advertising Manager:** Lina Ross **Advertising Executives:** Judy Lam, Jennifer Lau **Assistant to Publisher:** Rashpal Dillon **Subscription Clerk:** Vivian Hau **UK Representative:** B. C. Gothard, Robin Turner (Trade Press) Ltd., Nassau House, 122 Shaftesbury Avenue, London, W1V. 8HA. ENGLAND. 01-734-3052 Telex: 261140 **USA Representative:** Grant H. Webb, Grant Webb International Inc., Keene, York 12942, U.S.A. Tel: 212-688-7550.

INTERVIEW

A grimace a day keeps the wrinkles away, says Ana Lydia

by Zelda Cawthorne

SOME people really shouldn't be in the body beautiful business. Ana Lydia Armstrong is a definite exception. She stirs not guilt, but hope, makes it all sound perfectly feasible, not some calculated torture.

Partly it's the lady herself. Not one of those impossibly svelte models of physical perfection, but a mature, attractively-proportioned woman who proudly admi' she's a grandmother and i' ashamed of the lines a fu' uberant life has etched that she disregards ther

"Recently I came b' a gruelling business er in Manila and lool haggard. For a wh' considered a then decided a my facia' worke' it

Simple way to a beautiful body

ANA Lydia's sex organ exercises are an all important aspect of the Ala method which is based on the principle of making exercises as simple as possible and involving as many muscles as possible. The ultimate ai' of which is to make one more aware of the functions of one's body.

Regular viewers of the highly-rated programme and Ana Lydia's private pupils are well aware that these exercises are not related to the more intimate side of life, as far as the manner they are even tually put to work, though Ana Lydia will admit, "My sex life has improved...

her well-being.

"Fortunately, I wasn't doing my facial exercises," she said, my face in a jaw exercise, "or else they would certainly hav' thought that I was havi' epileptic fit."

Laughter Lydia's m' cise. t' passic vivacity

Sex—ercises

"WHY call these exercises — Sexercises? Very simple. When you exercise the correct way — the Ala way — you bring into use all the muscles of your body ... of these muscles, a very important pair are in the Sex Organ Region..."

Famous last words, indeed! For when Ana Lydia Armstrong mentioned the 'unmentionable' on her "Keep Fit With Ana Lydia" programme (RTV-2), there were prompt orders 'from above' that she should substitute the "SOR" with another term.

"They suggested that I say 'groin' instead, said Ana Lydia, her animated face curling in mock distaste, "Or 'inner thigh,' but that is not even the same thing."

With due vehemence, but with that perpetual twinkle in her eye, Ana added, "There is nothing naughty at all in my reference."

Live it up with Ana Lydia Armstrong

● ANA Lydia Armstrong... if I was not going to have a beautiful face, I was going to have a beautiful body

Lightning Source UK Ltd.
Milton Keynes UK
07 December 2009

147155UK00001B/46/P